the Queen
of Peace
Visits
Medugorje

The Augustinians of the Assumption
(ASSUMPTIONISTS)
who sponsor publication of this book
work all over the world for the coming of
the Kingdom of God

First edition: July 1985, 43,000 copies
Second edition: December 1986, 43,000 copies
Third edition: September 1987, 30,000 copies
Fourth edition: October 1988

the Queen of Peace Visits Medugorje

Joseph A. Pelletier, A.A.

Assumption Publications
50 Old English Road
Worcester, MA 01609

Acknowledgments

I wish to express my gratitude to Stan and Margie Karminski for the tremendous assistance they provided in gathering accurate information; to William F. Kuhn for his generous editorial help; to O. Warren Creelman of Creelman Advertising, Inc., for the cover design and mechanical preparation of the book; and to many other people — too numerous to name — for the aid they provided in proofreading, in sharing information and photos, and in other ways.

I likewise wish to thank the following for granting permission to use extracts from their publications and talks.

Franciscan Herald Press, Chicago, Illinois (The Apparitions of Our Lady at Medugorje, by Svetozar Kraljevic O.F.M.).

Servant Books, Ann Arbor, Michigan (What Time Is It?, by Ralph Martin).

John Bertolucci (Talk: The Grace of Pentecost, March 26, 1983) and John Finkbiner Studio, 23 Old Farm Road South, Pleasantville, N.Y. 10570, for use of the tape recording.

Declaration of the Author

The events at Medugorje are presently under investigation. The author wishes to affirm his readiness to accept the final judgment of the Church.

Table of Contents

Table of Contents

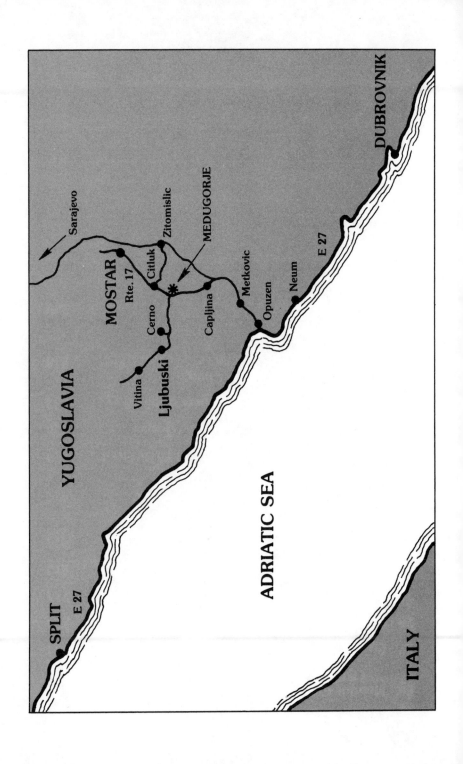

Chapter 1

Do Not Fear, I Am Sending You My Mother

When Father Tomislav Vlasic, O.F.M., left the rectory of St. Francis of Assisi in Capljina, Yugoslavia, on a spring day in 1981, he undoubtedly did so with mixed feelings of sadness and joyful expectation. He was going, as one of the delegates from Croatia, to attend the International Leaders' Conference of the Catholic Charismatic Renewal that was to take place in Rome from May 4 to May 9. He knew that meetings like this were the occasion of outpourings of God's Spirit, and he needed to be buoyed up. He had recently resigned from his own Franciscan council in Herzegovina, saying, "No one can do anything about the problems of the Church. All we can do is pray."

It is not surprising, therefore, that at the conference he asked to be prayed over for the healing of the Church. His prayer was answered, but certainly not in any way that he could have anticipated. The reply came in the form of a prophetic vision, or mental picture, and a prophetic word.

One of the persons praying over the Croatian priest was Briege McKenna, a Sister of Saint Clare from Tampa, Florida, well-known for her healing and evangelistic ministry as well as for her special ministry with priests. While praying, she had a vision of Father Tomislav seated in a chair and surrounded by a great crowd; beneath his seat great streams of water gushed forth. Another person praying over him was Father Emilien Tardif, a French-Canadian member of the

Missionaries of the Sacred Heart stationed in the Dominican Republic. He received this prophetic word: "Do not fear. I am sending you my Mother."

It was not long before Father Tomislav was given the meaning of the message imparted through this vision and this prophetic word. On Wednesday, June 24, two weeks after he had returned to Capljina from Rome, came the fulfillment of the prophetic word, "I am sending you my Mother." In the late afternoon of that day, which was the Feast of the Birth of Saint John the Baptizer, Our Lady appeared to several young people. This took place on the lower part of a small mountain called Mount Podbrdo, which is located close to the hamlet of Bijakovici, one of five hamlets that make up the township of Medugorje. The parish of Medugorje is under the patronage of Saint James. In addition to the main church of Saint James, there are three other satellite churches which are necessary because the town's population of 2,500 is spread out over a considerable area.

What was the religious status of this parish which grouped people of Croatian extraction? According to Father Tomislav it was pretty much a run-of-the-mill parish, not particularly fervent, but "more or less like every other parish in western Herzegovina, rather Catholic with a strong traditional emphasis." The people there did go to church "more than in other regions of Yugoslavia, but they were already on the road of a declining faith."

The specific conditions Father Vlasic describes are not too different from those that prevail in many areas of the United States. The prayer life, the touchstone of Christian vitality, was at a low ebb. "Many young people did not pray, did not go to church often. The families did not pray. Few prayed . . . Many young people did not know what the rosary was."[1]

Chapter 2

On A Rocky Mountain Side

The First Day, Wednesday, June 24, 1981

The first day our Lady came to Medugorje, she appeared twice in the late afternoon.

It all started around four o'clock, when two close friends, sixteen-year-old Mirjana Dragicevic and fifteen-year-old Ivanka Ivankovic, left the latter's house in the hamlet of Bijakovici for a walk. At a sheep pasture on the way back, Ivanka happened to look up on Mount Podbrdo and saw a shining figure hovering above the ground at a distance of two or three hundred yards. As she looked more intently, she was able to discern the form or figure of a young lady. Though perplexed and unsure, she exclaimed, "Mirjana, look! There is *Gospa* (Our Lady)!" Mockingly, and without bothering to look, Mirjana replied, "Come on! Would Our Lady appear to us?" The two then continued on their way to Bijakovici. Such was the first encounter with Our Lady.

The second encounter was as unexpected as the first. Mirjana and Ivanka left the village again with Milka Pavlovic, who had asked them to help her round up some sheep. These three girls saw Our Lady on Mount Podbrdo at the same place where she had been seen before.

Seventeen-year-old Vicka Ivankovic, who was a close friend of Mirjana and Ivanka, on waking from a nap received word where these friends would be. She soon joined them. On her knees, praying, Mirjana said to Vicka, "Look up there!

Our Lady!" Greatly frightened, the latter did not take the time to look, but kicked off her slippers and ran away.

Along the road, Vicka saw sixteen-year-old Ivan Dragicevic and Ivan Ivankovic, who were picking apples. She told them what was happening on Mount Podbrdo and ended up returning with them to rejoin the three girls she had deserted.

After rejoining the three girls, Vicka turned to speak to Ivan Dragicevic and saw him running off. The other lad, however, stayed with Vicka. The two of them knelt down and prayed with the three girls.

Ivanka has said that Our Lady was holding the Infant Jesus and was passing her hand over his head. Vicka did not distinguish things that clearly. She has affirmed that Our Lady had something in her left hand and kept covering and uncovering it, as though she was showing something.[1]

As the five young people looked at the distant Vision, she beckoned them to come up the mountain side to her. They stood there, rooted to the spot and afraid, although the two girls who had seen her before were less fearful than they had been the first time. Notwithstanding their fear, they experienced a deep peace and happiness. Our lady remained about forty-five minutes.

Vicka was the first to go home. The others followed her five or six minutes later. It was after six-thirty and getting dark. It was also raining a little.

The Second Day, Thursday, June 25, 1981

The next day, the young people went to work in the tobacco fields, as was their custom. Ivanka, Mirjana, Vicka, and Ivan felt drawn to return to Mount Podbrdo where they had seen the Vision, and decided to go when they had finished their work in the fields. Ivanka suggested that they take a walk in that direction, adding that if they saw the Vision it would be "good," and if they didn't, they wouldn't say anything about the affair so that people would stop laughing at them.

Before leaving, they decided that if the Vision returned they would come back to Bijakovici and tell Marija Pavlovic and ten-year-old Jakov Colo. It was nearly six p.m. when they left.

Ivanka walked ahead of Mirjana and Vicka, who followed, talking to each other. Some other children and two adults also went along.

As on the previous day, Ivanka was the first to see the Vision. She turned to her two friends and said, "Look! Our Lady!" Although the three girls were on the road at the base of Mount Podbrdo and the Vision was considerably higher up the mountain than on the previous day, Vicka could see "her face, eyes, hair, and dress" very clearly. Remembering the decision they had made, she ran off to get Marija and Jakov who came immediately.

From her high spot way up on Mount Podbrdo, the Vision summoned the young people to come up to her. They answered the call and were utterly amazed at the ease and speed with which they advanced up the steep and treacherous slope full of sharp-edged stones and prickly briers. Vicka described it thus: "We ran quickly up the hill. It was not like walking on the ground. Nor did we look for the path. We simply ran toward her. In five minutes we were up the hill — as if something had pulled us through the air. I was afraid. I was also barefoot, but no thorns had scratched me." Those who watched were greatly surprised at the speed of their ascent and were unable to follow them up to the top of the hill.

Astonishing things continued to happen. "When we were about two meters (six feet) away from the Madonna, we felt as if we were thrown to our knees. Jakov was thrown kneeling into a thorny bush and I thought he would be injured. But he came out of it without a scratch."[2]

Vicka asked Marija if she could see Our Lady. She replied that she could see something white that was getting clearer and clearer. Eventually she was able to see her as clearly as the others did.

Jakov exclaimed, "I see Our Lady!"

The six young people feasted their eyes on the Vision. She appeared young, nineteen or twenty. She was strikingly beautiful, with a beauty beyond anything of this world. Her eyes were particularly beautiful and expressive. They were light blue and so tender and kind. They were simply wonderful.[3]

Ivanka was the first to speak. Her mother had died suddenly about two months before. She had been a good wife and mother but was not known to have been a particularly devout Catholic. Ivanka inquired about her. Our Lady said that she was well and with her and that she shouldn't worry about her. When people heard about this, they were reassured to learn that one did not have to do extraordinary things to get into heaven.

Mirjana now addressed Our Lady. What she said gives us an inkling of how some of the people in the village had reacted to the events of the previous afternoon and how the young people had been affected by these reactions. She said to her that, should they return home and tell people what had happened, they would say that the young people were crazy. If Mirjana had hoped that the gracious Visitor would promise a sign to convince people, she must have been disappointed for her only answer was a smile. However, the humanly unexplainable flight of the group up the mountain side and the lack of any injury to the barefooted Vicka and to Jakov who knelt in a thorny bush, these were signs that must have impressed people who heard of them with an open mind.

Vicka asked Mirjana what time it was. She replied that it was three-fifteen.

Surprised at this answer, Vicka asked her what she meant by three-fifteen, remarking that she must have set her watch wrong. In fact, the number 12 had changed into a 9.[4] This was the first event which the seers took to be miraculous. It appears that Mirjana still has this watch in her possession.

The young people who had seen Our Lady on the previous afternoon had experienced considerable fear. Those who saw her on this day likewise experienced fear, but less than before. They cried a little and they prayed a little.

Mirjana's grandmother had told her to say seven Our Fathers, Hail Marys, and Glory Be's when in the presence of the Vision. This was a traditional prayer in honor of the Seven Sorrows of Our Lady that was said in the region. They now said these prayers and Our Lady joined in with them, although she did not say the Hail Marys. She told them that these prayers pleased her and to continue to pray them. She also asked them to join a Creed to the prayers, because many people have forgotten the Creed.

The apparition lasted ten or fifteen minutes. As Our Lady was leaving, she bade the young people farewell with these words, "Go in the peace of God." She rose in the air and the young people watched her as she departed.

In his book, Father Ljudevit Rupcic mentions "another phenomenon which took place on the second day." Before Our Lady appeared, a bright light "something like lightning" was seen by those who were on Mount Podbrdo and also by people in the village who happened to look toward Mount Podbrdo. People reported seeing the same kind of light on the third day.

The six young people who saw Our Lady on June 25, the second day of the apparitions, namely, Ivanka Ivankovic, Mirjana Dragicevic, Marija Pavlovic, Vicka Ivankovic, Ivan Dragicevic and Jakov Colo, have continued to see Our Lady each day. Ivan Ivankovic and Milka Pavlovic, Marija's sister, who had seen Our Lady on the preceding day, have not seen her since.

The six seers have all asserted that Our Lady came each day preceded by three flashes of light. The people who saw the flashes on June 25 and 26 understood them as signs that something important was taking place on Mount Podbrdo. These will not be the only signs given the people, as will be seen.

As the seers were coming down the mountain, a neighbor of theirs, Marinko Ivankovic, was just arriving at Mount Podbrdo. That morning he had taken Marija and Vicka to Citluk, where he worked as a mechanic. They had gone there for some classes. Marija told him about the apparitions. He became interested and wanted to learn more. That afternoon he spoke with Ivan Dragicevic who had seen Our Lady the previous day and decided to go to the place of the apparitions. He got there late, thinking the apparition would occur at seven-fifteen.

Marinko noticed Ivanka coming down the hill. She went to her grandmother who was waiting for her on the road and embraced her. Ivanka was crying as she told her grandmother that she had asked Our Lady about her deceased mother and had been told that she was well and in heaven. Marinko is a good and compassionate man and he tried to console Ivanka, but she kept crying. He then decided to go to the rectory and tell the priests what was happening, for he felt that it was a spiritual matter which concerned them and which they should know about.

Marinko would have liked to speak with the pastor, Father Jozo Zovko, but he was in Zagreb. Since Father Zrinko Cuvalo was there, Marinko told him about the young people and what they claimed to have seen over the past two days. He added that they had been crying this evening and were in need of help. He suggested that the priest go and talk with them to console them and to find out if what they were saying were true. Father Zrinko was noncommittal in his reply, but his behavior in days to come will reveal that he was prudently open to what was happening.

That night the village hummed with the news of these unusual events.

From that day on, Marinko became an important part of the early days of the apparitions. He very actively befriended the young people who he felt were badly in need of support. Four of the youngsters were experiencing a lack of family support. Ivanka had recently lost her mother, and her father was away working in Germany. Vicka's father was also away for the same reason. Jakov rarely saw his father who worked in Bosnia. Mirjana was spending the summer in Medugorje with her grandmother, while her parents remained in Sarajevo where the family was living at the time. Marinko's dedication and sincerity won the confidence of the seers who came to lean heavily on him. He has faithfully kept a record of the events at Medugorje,[5] and this makes him a particularly valuable witness of the apparitions. His value as a witness is heightened by the fact that the record of the early days kept by the priests of the parish was confiscated by the police on August 17, 1981.

Chapter 3

Higher Up On The Mountain Side

The Third Day, Friday, June 26, 1981

On this day Marinko and the seers agreed to go together to the base of Mount Podbrdo where Our Lady had first appeared. They saw a brilliant light that illumined not only the village but the entire area three times and that was seen by many people as well as by the seers. The latter looked intently and cried out, "There she is!"

According to Marinko, Our Lady was higher up Mount Podbrdo than she had been on the two previous days. The seers immediately started up the mountain side toward her. Ivan and Jakov were ahead of Marinko and the four girls. Marinko, who knew the area very well, had to help the girls who were having trouble with the protruding sharp-edged stones that blanket the mountain side. Eventually the seers all came together and knelt in front of a stone. Marinko asked them whether Our Lady was there, and they replied that she was. She stood on a cloud. Vicka took some holy water and sprinkled it on the Vision saying, "If you are Our Lady, stay with us. If you are not, go away." Her only answer was a beautiful smile.

Mirjana had lost her grandfather a year before, and she inquired about him. Our Lady answered, "He is well."

Ivanka questioned Our Lady again about her mother who had died in the hospital without any member of the family present. She wanted to know whether the mother had left any message for her children. Our Lady replied, "Obey your grandmother and be good to her for she is old and cannot work."

Ivanka asked a question that had been given her by Marinko, "Why have you come here and what is it you want?" Our Lady scanned the large crowd that had gathered. It was as if her eyes rested on each individual. Then she said, "I have come because there are many believers here. I want to be with you to convert and reconcile everyone."

The day was intensely hot. The heat and the crush of the crowd were more than Ivanka, Mirjana, and Vicka could bear. They fainted and had to be removed from the crowd and revived. The apparition lasted approximately thirty minutes. When it had been going on for ten minutes, Our Lady had the seers get up from their knees and stand, undoubtedly because of the stifling heat.

Finally the seers asked Our Lady if she would come again. She said she would, and then took her leave, repeating the farewell she had used on the previous day and would always use in the future, "Go in the peace of God."

The three girls who had fainted were helped down the mountain. Marija went down with some women. When she was about halfway to the village, she ran from the women and went to her left. Falling to her knees, she exclaimed, "Our Lady is here!" She saw a cross with the colors of a rainbow; just a plain cross without the body of Christ portrayed on it. Our Lady was standing in front of the cross, crying. As tears streamed down her cheeks, she asked where the other girls were, and then said, "Peace, peace, peace. Reconcile yourselves." Her last words were, "Go in the peace of God."

On this third day, when Our Lady was asked by Ivanka what she wanted, she gave a summary of the message that would be expanded upon in the days ahead. Her message was peace, the peace that can come only from conversion or reconciliation with God and with one's neighbor.

Marinko has estimated that, by the end of the apparition, there were two or three thousand people on the mountain side. This was the first time that he was present during an apparition, and he has affirmed that he "firmly believed that something was happening."

In the Hail Holy Queen, Mary is invoked as a "mother of mercy." At Medugorje she will continually reveal herself as having come to her children of the earth on a mission of mercy. She will do it both by her actions and by her words, as she did on June 26. She tells the seers that she has come to bring to her children the deep peace and happiness that come to them when they have been reconciled with God and their fellow men and women. She precedes this message with a compassionate glance over the entire gathering; thus emphasizing her desire that no one be excluded from this peace and happiness. She also manifests her compassionate love for the seers by having them stand up on this debilitating day, long before the apparition has ended.

Chapter 4

Government Authorities Step In

The Fourth Day, Saturday, June 27, 1981

June 27 was for the seers a most unusual and extremely busy day. The pastor of Saint James, Father Jozo Zovko, had returned from Zagreb, and in the morning he went to the hospital at Mostar to visit his mother. He was with another Franciscan, Father Viktor Kosir. In front of the hospital they met Dragica, the wife of Marinko Ivankovic. She had hurt her hand and her leg while working and had come for treatment. She urged Father Jozo to go to Medugorje because the Blessed Virgin had appeared there. This was the first indication that either priest had received concerning the apparitions.

When they arrived in Medugorje, Father Zrinko told them what he had learned. He gave them tape recordings that he had made when the seers had come to the rectory to see the pastor and tell him what was happening to them. In the absence of the pastor, Father Zrinko had listened to them and questioned them about the apparitions. The priests played the tapes. Since they were inconclusive, Father Jozo sent for the young people and questioned them. He simply listened to their answers without any comment. He told the children to pray. Father Viktor also questioned them but was not able to come to any definite judgment on the matter.

News of what was happening on Mount Podbrdo had reached the local government authorities at nearby Citluk who were responsible for Medugorje. They summoned the six seers on the afternoon of June 27 and interrogated them at police headquarters. Nothing that took place there could induce the children to deny that the Blessed Virgin had appeared to them. The seers were then sent to Dr. Ante Vujevic, a general practitioner. He spent more than an hour examining Ivan Dragicevic; then he began to examine Vicka. As the time of the apparitions was approaching, the seers wanted to leave; so the doctor let her go after a brief examination. The seers took a taxi and went to Mount Podbrdo, except Ivan who went home a little later with one of his relatives.

The doctor found nothing wrong with the seers. Not wanting to become involved in an investigation which he knew would be unpopular with the people, he said it was not of his competence to pass a final judgment on the seers. He declared that his own private conviction would remain secret.

What took place after the seers arrived at Mount Podbrdo is quite complex. The reason is that Marinko Ivankovic and Mate Pavlovic, another man from the neighborhood, wanted to submit the seers to a test concerning the apparitions. The plan was to split the seers into two groups of three. One group was to be made up of Ivanka, Mirjana, and Vicka; the other, of Marija, Jakov, and Ivan. Because Ivan did not come with the other seers, the second group had only Marija and Jakov in it. Each group was to go to a different site where Our Lady had previously appeared. The group of Marija and Jakov was to go to the bottom of Mount Podbrdo and wait there for Our Lady. The other group was to go up on the mountain and wait there.

Marija and Jakov went to the place at the bottom of Mount Podbrdo where Our Lady had appeared. With them, as observers, were Mate Pavlovic and Father Zrinko Cuvalo, the associate pastor of the parish. Marija and Jakov saw the light which preceded Our Lady and then Our Lady herself. She invited them to come to her. Marija departed on a dead run. Her speed was tremendous. Father Zrinko and Mate tried to follow her but were unable to stay up with her. Those who watched her were utterly amazed. Later Marija explained that all she saw in front of her was Our Lady. She was not aware of the people who swarmed all over the area. She felt that Our Lady was leading her and carrying her up the mountain.

It took Jakov and Mate several minutes to reach Marija. They found her about twenty yards higher up than the place where Our Lady had appeared before. Marija was standing alone, her hands clasped. She appeared perplexed and said to Mate, "I don't know, Mate. Our Lady brought me here and then disappeared."

Because the place was thick with people, it was impossible to see any distance. So Mate went to the place where Our Lady had previously appeared on the mountain and where Ivanka, Mirjana, and Vicka had been told to go. He told them what had happened to Marija. They came to her and started singing and praying, and the people who were there joined in with them.

The seers had a strong feeling that Our Lady would re-appear and indeed she did. Suddenly, the five young people went down on their knees. Our Lady had come. Her coming was preceded by a light which the people saw. They did not see Our Lady, but they felt sure that she was there and surged toward the seers. As they closed in on the seers, something unusual happened. The latter clearly saw the people treading on the veil which Our Lady wore and which went from her head to the ground. With tears in their eyes, they asked the people to move away from the place where she was standing. When their repeated pleas went unheeded, Our Lady disappeared.

After Our Lady appeared a second time, the pressing of the crowd was so great that a boy stepped on her veil; again she disappeared. When she reappeared a third time, Marinko and Mate organized a protective cordon around the seers and the place where Our Lady was standing and she remained.

The seers put a series of questions to Our Lady. Vicka asked her to prove to the people who were present that she was indeed there. Her reply was that those who do not see should believe as though they were seeing.

Mirjana was very much concerned with what some people were saying about the seers and particularly about herself, namely, that they were drug addicts and epileptics. She unburdened herself to the Blessed Virgin who told her that there had always been injustice in the world, that there always would be, and that she should pay no attention to what was being said. Ivanka asked the heavenly visitor who she was. She answered, "I am the Blessed Virgin Mary."

Although Marinko had befriended the seers, he was well aware that it was the priests of the parish, and especially the pastor, who were responsible for the apparitions. Earlier that day, he had asked Father Jozo whether he had a message for Our Lady. The pastor had said that he did not but that he would like to know whether Our Lady had a message for the parish and for the Friars, as the priests are referred to in the area. Her reply was, "The Friars should believe firmly."

When Our Lady disappeared for the third time, she did not say, "Go in the peace of God," as she had done on the past two days. This surprised the seers and led them to believe that she might return; so they stayed where they were for a long time, praying and hoping she would return. The people stayed also. When Our Lady did not return, they finally left the mountain top and the people followed them. Marinko and several others held and supported the seers as they walked down the mountain side.

When they were halfway to the village, the seers suddenly pulled away from those holding them, exclaiming, "There she is!" Once again, Marinko and others formed a protective cordon around them. Our Lady greeted the children in a touching and tender way: "My angels! You are my dear angels." She told them she would return the next day at the same time and at the same place. Her last words were, "Go in the peace of God."

The reason that Ivan did not go to Mount Podbrdo with the other seers was that his parents had asked him not to. They did this out of concern for him. The attention of the vast crowds of all kinds of people coming to Medugorje worried them. Ivan also had stomach cramps that day.

He was, however, not to be left out of the picture. While Our Lady was appearing to the other seers she also appeared to Ivan as he was taking a walk a short distance outside the village. She greeted him, told him to be at peace and to take courage, and then smiled as she left him.

The message of an apparition is not confined to its verbal

content, to the words spoken by the heavenly messenger. Messages, sometimes important messages, can come through events, actions, the time and place where events occur, and through still other ways. At times, the messages conveyed by such things are quite obvious; at other times, quite subtle.

There are a number of messages transmitted through the events of this fourth day and the most important one is that of Mary's tender, motherly love. It is on this day when the seers went through the ordeal of their first encounter with the police that Our Lady chose to call them her dear angels for the first time.

Marinko was very much concerned with establishing whether the apparitions were authentic or not. So much was at stake in this. Father Zrinko shared this concern and for the same reasons. Several signs were given on this day that could help them in their discernment.

The first sign was the way in which Our Lady appeared on this fourth day. It was completely different from the manner in which the apparitions had occurred previously. It was so complicated and involved that it would seem to surpass the capacity of the young people to have thought it up by themselves. Marija broke away from Jakov and raced up the mountain alone. Our Lady appeared to her alone at a different place than before and then mysteriously disappeared. When Our Lady appeared to all five seers together, the people saw the light which immediately preceded her coming. During this apparition, she disappeared twice when people stepped on her veil, only to reappear later. She appeared again to the five as they returned home and, finally, she appeared to Ivan alone — her sixth appearance in that single day. Many people felt that the pattern of what happened proved the apparitions were not under the control of the seers. In this regard, the apparition to the five seers on their way home was particularly impressive. Together, they all pulled away from the people who were supporting them and together they suddenly saw Our Lady.

The most obvious sign given on this day was the speed with which Marija raced up the mountain side before the first apparition. This ecstatic flight was something that surely surpassed the natural capacity of this young girl.

A most unusual facet of this apparition was Our Lady's departure in two separate instances when people stepped on her veil. A thing like this had never happened during any other Marian apparition. It will be repeated in subsequent apparitions.[1] It can be said then that on this fourth day there was heavenly confirmation of the authenticity of what the young people claimed was happening on the side of Mount Podbrdo.

Chapter 5

Believing Without Seeing

The Fifth Day, Sunday, June 28, 1981

June 28 was a beautiful sunny day, and about fifteen thousand people swarmed into the Bijakovici section of Medugorje. They came from the whole area and among them were Fathers Viktor Kosir and Zrinko Cuvalo.

Shortly after six, the seers left for Mount Podbrdo. Marija and Jakov went with Fathers Viktor and Zrinko who had accompanied them to Mount Podbrdo on the previous day. Suddenly Marija cried out, "Look, look, look!" According to Father Zrinko, she and Jakov " ran ahead at what seemed incredible speed." Since Marija wore a red skirt and white blouse, he could easily keep her in sight as she ran far ahead of him, "almost seeming to fly."[1]

It was exactly 6:30 p.m. when Our Lady came. The seers requested that the people kneel. They asked Our Lady a series of questions. Eventually some local person had the seers repeat the questions and answers and these were recorded on tape:

> The seers — What do you want of us?
> Our Lady — Faith and respect for me.
> The seers — Dear Blessed Virgin, what do you want of our priests?
> Our Lady — That they believe firmly.
> The seers — Dear Blessed Virgin, why don't you appear in the church so that everybody can see you?
> Our Lady — Blessed are they who have not seen and who

believe.

The seers — Dear Blessed Virgin, will you come again?

The seers — She will, she will come to the same place. She will come. *(They had seen her acquiesce by nodding her head.)*

The seers — Dear Blessed Virgin, do you prefer that we pray to you or sing to you?

Our Lady — Do both, sing and pray.

The seers — Dear Blessed Virgin, what do you want of these people gathered here?

Our Lady *(She is looking at the people and smiling.)* — That they believe without seeing.

The seers — She is disappearing. She is gone!

Vicka — Let us pray some more. She did not say anything to us. *(What Vicka meant was that Our Lady had not pronounced the usual farewell: "Go in God's peace." So the seers began to pray again. They recited two Our Fathers, two Hail Marys, two Glory Be's.)*

The seers — There she is again! Let us sing a song! *(Marija started to sing: "Marija, Marija, O kako lijepa si — Mary, Mary, how beautiful you are.")*

Our Lady — My angels, my dear angels.

The seers — Dear Blessed Virgin, what do you want of these people?

Our Lady — That those here who do not see me, believe like the six of you who see me.

The seers — Dear Blessed Virgin, will you leave us some sign here on earth that will convince these people that we are not liars and that we are not playing games.

Our Lady — Go in the peace of God.

The seers — She went away! A light follows in her wake. She is gone! *(The seers began to sing well-known Croatian hymns.* [2]*)*

As soon as the apparition was over, Father Zrinko Cuvalo questioned the seers, trying to determine if the apparitions were authentic or not. Nothing negative came out of his interrogation. Eventually he became a firm believer in the apparitions.

On the third day Our Lady appeared, she was asked, "Why have you come here and what is it you want?" She had replied, "I have come because there are many believers here. I want to be with you to convert and reconcile everyone." On the fourth day, when asked to prove she was appearing, Our Lady had said that those who do not see should believe as though they were seeing. Also, when asked if she had a message for the parish and the Friars, she had replied that "they should believe firmly." On this fifth day, Our Lady re-emphasized the message of faith, saying that this was what she wanted of the priests, the seers themselves, and the people gathered on the mountain side, adding that the priests must believe "firmly" and that the people must believe without seeing, "like the six of you who see me."

It is not surprising that Our Lady said the priests should believe "firmly," since it is their role to lead their flock in faith. But, looking back now at the major role the priests of Medugorje have been called upon to play with the seers and the people, it becomes clearer why she said this. The kind of deep involvement that has developed between the parish staff of priests and sisters and the seers and the people is something unique in the annals of Marian apparitions.

Chapter ⑥

More Questioning And Examining

The Sixth Day, Monday, June 29, 1981

Monday would be a long, trying day for the seers. Once again they were called in by the authorities in Citluk who sent them to a hospital in Mostar for psychiatric testing. After a thorough examination, they were declared physically and mentally healthy by Dr. Mulija Dzudza. They returned home late that afternoon.

The seers went to the mountain side where they began praying and singing hymns at 6:19 p.m. The people assembled there, more numerous than ever, joined in with them. Father Viktor Kosir was present and not more than ten feet from the seers. Another Franciscan, Father Tomislav Vlasic, was also there. This was his first visit to the place of the apparitions.

Our Lady came at precisely 6:26. Once again the seers engaged in conversation with her. When Our Lady had departed, the seers cried, "There! She has gone! Look! The light!"

Marinko had come with a stone on which was painted a cross. He asked the seers where Our Lady had stood and they guided him to the exact spot.

Grgo Kozina, one of the local people, taped the conversation between the seers and Our Lady as it was related to the people immediately after the apparition. There are some important items to be gleaned from this taped conversation.

Our Lady said it was "firm faith and confidence" that she desired from those who were there. Faith was the basic message of this day.

Because the seers had already begun to feel the anguish of persecution, they asked Our Lady if they would be able to endure it. To encourage and comfort them her reply was expressed in endearing terms, "You will endure it, my angels."

A woman, Dr. Glaumuzina, was sent by the authorities at Citluk to observe what was taking place at the site of the apparitions. The seers asked Our Lady if it was permissible for the doctor to touch her. Our Lady's answer was, "There have always been unfaithful Judases. Let her come." When the doctor touched her, Our Lady disappeared. She reappeared after the people and the seers began to sing a hymn.

Following Our Lady's return, the seers pleaded for the healing of Daniel, a boy who was paralyzed and could not talk. Here is the report of this pleading as recorded by Grgo Kozina:

> The seers — Dear Madonna, will this little boy, Daniel, ever be able to speak? Please make a miracle so that everyone will believe us. These people love you very much. Dear Madonna, make one miracle. She is looking at him. Dear Madonna, say something.
>
> Grgo Kozina — Is she still looking at the boy?
>
> The seers — She is looking at the boy, who is mute. Dear Madonna, say something, we ask you. Say something, we ask you. Say something, dear Madonna!
>
> Our Lady — Let them *(Daniel's parents)* believe firmly that he will be healed. Go in God's peace. [1]

It was after this that Our Lady took her final leave.

Daniel started to speak later that afternoon. His healing has been a gradual process which will be discussed again later.

Something further needs to be said about people touching Our Lady. It is one of the more intriguing facets of the Medugorje apparitions.

Among the questions which Father Ljudevit Rupcic asked the seers was, "Did you touch Our Lady?" Ivanka said,

"Yes." Jakov and Ivan answered, "I touched her dress." Marija replied, "Yes, I touched her dress. Every time I touched it, it was with my whole palm. Many people touched it also."

Mirjana's answer speaks powerfully of the warm, motherly relationship that the Blessed Virgin had with the seers. She said, "I can touch her. In the beginning, I considered her as inaccessible, but now, when she is with me, I look upon her as a mother, as my best friend who helps me."

Vicka gave an answer which is important from the point of view of the authenticity of the apparitions. She said, "Yes, I touched her dress. But it resists like metal."[2] An apparition is a mystical experience. What the seer sees appears similar to what the seer knows and has experienced on the human level. But the object, in this case the person seen, is not present to the seer in a human body, as one human being is to another. Likewise with the dress. It appears to be a dress made of material similar to that of dresses women wear, but it is not. Vicka's answer, which might appear disconcerting, is in reality completely in harmony with what would be expected from someone undergoing a true mystical experience.

When Father Tomislav Vlasic came to Medugorje on June 29, he was associate pastor in the town of Capljina, eighteen miles away. He spoke with Mirjana after her return from Citluk and before her departure for Mount Podbrdo. What she told him is instructive about what the seers went through in Citluk. Father Tomislav says that she was still "agitated" from the frightening experience of her interrogation. She had been taken to a "morgue" and had been with some "lunatics." When asked if she would go to the mountain side again, she said that she "doubted" that she would, adding that she "probably" would not "because if they take me two more times to the morgue, I will have a nervous breakdown."

Actually Mirjana did go to the place of the apparitions and Father Tomislav questioned her about this later, asking why she had gone after what she had told him before the apparition. She replied that when the time had come to go to Mount Podbrdo "no one would have been able to stop me. There was simply no question of shall I go or not go."

There was a similar incident at Fatima in 1917. After the June 13 apparition, the pastor of the parish told Lucy that what was happening at the Cova da Iria might be a deception on the part of the devil. This was followed by a frightful dream involving the evil one. The result of all this was that Lucy resolved that she would not go to the Cova da Iria any more and told this to her cousins, Jacinta and Francisco. However, as the time for the next rendezvous approached on the morning of July 13, she "suddenly felt she had to go, impelled by a strange force that she could hardly resist."[3]

After the apparitions were over on this day, the seers were taken to the rectory for questioning.

Later that night, the seers went to Marinko's house. There, they stood on the terrace and talked to the people about the apparition. They repeated all that the Blessed Virgin had told them. The people were hungry for her words and the seers were very happy. It was about eleven o'clock when everyone finally departed.

Chapter 7

Apparition At Cerno

The Seventh Day, Tuesday, June 30, 1981

June 30 is important in the history of the apparitions at Medugorje for it saw these happenings move away for the first time from the immediate area of Mount Podbrdo.

At about two in the afternoon, two assistant social workers from Citluk came to Bijakovici to get the seers. They were Ljubica Vasilj and Mirjana Ivankovic. Apparently the government felt that it could put an end to the apparitions by keeping the young people away from the site where everything had happened up to that time. The women told the seers that they wanted to see if Our Lady would appear to them at some other site than Mount Podbrdo. They said that they wanted to take them in their car for that purpose.

Some of the seers were eating when the two women arrived. They hurried and five of them finally got into the car and drove off. The one missing from the group was Ivan.

The women had a simple plan. They would drive the seers around the area until the time for the apparitions at Mount Podbrdo had passed. So the seers were taken to Citluk, Pocitelj, Capljina, the waterfalls of Kravica, and Cerno. They arrived at Cerno at the time the apparitions had been taking place at Mount Podbrdo. Thousands of people were on the mountain side waiting for the children and Our Lady.

When they came to a certain place along the road at Cerno, the seers felt compelled to ask the women to stop the car. At first they refused, but finally yielded. The place where they were at that time was but a few miles from Mount Podbrdo which they could see. They were out in the open countryside and there were no houses in the immediate area. They got out of the car and the seers began their usual prayer. Then they saw a light on Mount Podbrdo illuminating the place where the people were waiting and the light began moving toward them.

Ivanka asked the two women if they saw the light. They said they did. The seers knelt and sang hymns and Our Lady appeared to them.

Mirjana apparently felt some uneasiness about having accepted the assistant social workers' plan of seeing if Our Lady would appear to them at some place other than Mount Podbrdo, for she asked whether Our Lady minded that they had not gone to the mountain side but had come to this other place. She replied that she did not mind.

No doubt because of the problems stemming from the place, the seers asked if she would mind if they did not go to the mountain side any more but went to the church. With some hesitation she answered, "I will not, my angels." [1]

Then she just looked at the seers for a long time.

The seers asked if she would leave them some sign. She did not answer, but began to depart slowly and said, "Go in the peace of God."

Once more the seers saw the light on Mount Podbrdo at the place where the people were.

When the young people arrived at Medugorje, it was some time between six and seven. They met immediately with Father Jozo who taped the conversation he had with them. As he had given them some questions he wanted them to ask Our Lady, he inquired if they had done so. Mirjana replied that in their haste to leave with the two assistant social workers they had forgotten to take the questions along.

After the report of what had happened that afternoon, a discussion began at the rectory concerning the advisability of the seers going to Mount Podbrdo where the people were still waiting and telling them what had happened at Cerno. Mirjana said she felt drawn to go and let the people know that Our Lady had appeared there and tell them what she had said.

After talking the matter over, the seers decided not to go. One thing that the discussion brought out was the seers' shared feeling that Our Lady would appear henceforth in the church if they went there. But no decision was taken to make that move yet.

The seers' day ended on a sad note. When they arrived at Bijakovici at about ten o'clock, they were told that their good friend Marinko Ivankovic had been taken to the police station for questioning. Despite the late hour, the seers decided to go and assure the police that Marinko had not initiated the apparitions and that he was not guilty of anything. That night was a painful one for the seers and their families.

Chapter 8

Extraordinary Answer To The Pastor's Prayer

The Eighth Day, Tuesday, July 1, 1981

July 1 saw a number of important new developments in the Medugorje event. The first had to do with the pastor, Father Jozo. His was the main responsibility for what was happening and he did not take this responsibility lightly. Though he deliberately kept away from the site of the apparitions, he was in close contact with the seers. He spoke with them, questioned them, and gave them advice, but he could not bring himself to accept the apparitions as authentic, even though he prayed much about this. On July 1, God answered his prayers in such an unexpected way that he still vividly remembers the details of how it happened.

The government was having no success in its efforts to bring the events of Medugorje to a halt. The two assistant social workers who had been sent on June 30 to stop the apparitions had not only been unsuccessful in their attempt but had handed in their resignations, so affected were they by their experience at Cerno.

It was at this point that the police intervened directly. Toward noon they came to Medugorje to try to stop the seers from going to the mountain side. Learning of the arrival of the police, the seers fled Bijakovici and ran through the vineyards toward the church, the police in pursuit.

In the meantime, Father Jozo was praying in the church, in the third pew on the left side. The breviary and the Bible were in front of him. He was alone in the church. "Then," he told

Father Svetozar Kraljevic, "something happened that for me was important and decisive. . .a turning point and a moment of revelation. While I was praying, I heard a voice say, 'Come out and protect the children.'"

He got up immediately, leaving the breviary and the Bible where they were, and went out the center door of the church, which faces north. As he stepped out, the seers ran toward him from the left side of the church and cried out, "The police are chasing us. Hide us!" They crowded around him and began to cry. With the seers was Vicka's sister, Ana. He embraced the children and went to the rectory with them. There he placed them in a room that was not occupied and locked the door.

Soon the police arrived on the run and asked Fr. Jozo if he had seen the children. He told them that he had and they raced off toward Bijakovici in pursuit of them. Then Fr. Jozo returned to the children and talked with them, telling them it would be safer for them to stay in the rectory. This they did. Our Lady appeared to them in that room. It was the first time that Our Lady appeared inside of a building. In the days ahead, there would be seven other apparitions in that same room, and a number of apparitions in other houses also.

During the course of the afternoon, word was sent to the people who were gathering on the mountain side that there would be a service in the church. At about five o'clock, Father Jozo asked the associate pastor, Father Zrinko Cuvalo, to lead the people in the rosary. It was the first time that the rosary was prayed with the people. At six o'clock, Father Jozo celebrated the Eucharist. The church was jammed right up to the altar with people. Speaking about this first Mass, Father Jozo said, "In the homily, I asked the people to pray and to fast, begging God to help us to understand the events in our parish. This mass of people responded to my request with a great exclamation, full of faith, 'We will.'"[1]

Father Jozo was able to bring to an end the questioning of the seers by the police by invoking an existing law which prohibits them from questioning minors without the consent of their parents. When the police were advised by the parents that they were opposed to the interrogation of their children, they stopped.

In addition to the voice which Father Jozo heard in the church on July 1, another very significant thing happened to him on a summer night in 1981. At six-thirty p.m., "during the daily ceremony," the seers had a silent apparition that Father Jozo was privileged to share in. "He saw and was stupefied." People noticed a change in him afterward, a change which affected his preaching and other dimensions of his life.

This episode, including the flight of the young people from the police, the voice heard by Father Jozo, and his rushing to their defense, is extremely important in terms of the authenticity of the Medugorje event. Had the young people been inventing and simulating the apparitions, is it likely they would have continued their duplicity after this incident? To spare themselves further grief they could have said that Our Lady was no longer appearing to them. On the contrary, within hours of their close escape from the police, they claimed that Our Lady had visited them again in the rectory.

Equally important is the part played in this incident by the voice heard by Father Jozo and his response to it. This is all the more significant for it was well-known that Father Jozo was extremely cool to what the young people were claiming before he heard that voice.

Chapter 9

Who Are These Young People?

It is interesting to note how God uses children as His heralds when He wants to communicate messages of great importance to His Church. At LaSalette in 1846, He spoke through two children, Melanie and Maximin. At Lourdes in 1858, there was but one child, Bernadette, whereas at Fatima in 1917, there were three, Jacinta, Francisco, and Lucia. If we were to gauge the importance of an apparition by the number of young people involved, we would have to rank Medugorje very high for there are six of them at this place.

There are a number of rather evident reasons why God chooses youngsters as His heralds. They are very open to His action in them. Their minds and hearts are not cluttered and blocked with the false notions and prejudices that people acquire as they progress in age. They are more likely than adults to transmit without alteration the messages they receive. Finally, their limited knowledge and the limited development of their minds are relative guarantees that they are not inventing everything. The younger the children, the more the above reasons apply.

The number of young people that God uses also has much to do with the acceptance of the message by the people. The greater the number, the more difficult deception becomes. This is particularly true when the apparitions are very numerous as they are at Medugorje. When several children never disagree in what they relate day after day over a long period of time it can be presumed that they are telling the truth.

The range in the ages of the six young people at Medugorje is noteworthy. When the apparitions began, one was only ten years old, another was fifteen, three were sixteen and one was seventeen. In view of what was said above, the presence of a ten- year- old boy is particularly important. It so happens that he is one of those who live in Medugorje itself and therefore is one of the three who see Our Lady each day in the village church. Because of the protection for truth that comes with numbers, one would have to say that this trio is especially important. The other two who live in Medugorje and are members of this little group were fifteen and sixteen when the apparitions started in 1981.

Who are these young people to whom Our Lady has appeared at Medugorje? They are all very normal, but different from each other, and have quite distinctive personalities. With one exception, all of them are of very average intelligence. The exception, Mirjana, is considerably above the others in mental capacity. Although two of the group are not living now in Bijakovici, all six of them were born there.

Vicka Ivankovic, the oldest of the group, was born July 3, 1964. Her father, Peter, works in West Germany. Her mother's name is Zlata. Her grandmother, Vicka, is in her late eighties and in good health. There are eight children in the family. Her oldest sister, who has a degree in pharmacy, is now married, as is the next oldest sister. The latter graduated from a commercial high school. The younger children are still in grammar school. Vicka is learning the textile industry in a professional school at Mostar. The unmarried older children cultivate the family land on which grapes and tobacco are raised.

Vicka is of medium height and thin. She has strong features and her face is very expressive. She has dancing eyes and a delightful smile. She is the charmer of the group, although there is nothing artifical or put-on about her. She is fascinating to watch during the apparitions. She simply radiates delight. Her rather large lips move rapidly. She frequently nods her head in approval. Her almost constant smile occasionally expands into what could be termed mild laughter.

Though her health is not good, she is filled with energy and is strong-willed. She is not afraid to assume responsibility. This manifested itself in the fall of 1981, when Our lady indicated that it would not be good for all the older seers to go away to school and leave little Jakov alone in Medugorje. Vicka immediately volunteered to stop going to school in Mostar, and did. She now works in the tobacco fields but plans to enter the convent eventually. Her family, particularly her father, is devoutly religious.

Mirjana Dragicevic is the second oldest of the seers. She was born on March 18, 1965. Her father, Jozo, is an x-ray technician in a hospital and her mother, Milena, works in a shop. She has one brother who is at school. Very intelligent, Mirjana is an undergraduate at the University of Sarajevo, where the family now lives.

Mirjana's grandmother is still living and resides in Bijakovici. Mirjana spends her summer vacations with her and that is how she happened to be in Medugorje when the apparitions began.

Of medium height, she has blond hair, a fact that distinguishes her from the other three girls.

Marija Pavlovic is the third oldest member of the group. She was born on April 1, 1965. Her father, Philip, works in agriculture. Her mother's name is Iva. She has three brothers who work in West Germany, and she has two sisters. The older is married and the younger is in grammar school at Bijakovici. She has been studying in Mostar where she is completing her apprenticeship as a hairdresser. Mostar is only eighteen miles away and Marija travels back and forth by bus and gets home in time for the daily evening apparition.

She is of average height and thin. Like all the other girls, she wears dresses — never slacks nor dungarees — when she comes for the apparitions. The dresses worn by the teen-agers of the area are very much like those worn by American girls of the same age.

Marija is the most serene and deeply spiritual of the seers. She is a retiring and unobtrusive person. Those who know her describe her as "just beautiful" because of her deep spirituality, prayerfulness, and humility. Several times, Our Lady has called her to pray more and she has responded with a growing commitment to prayer. She is planning to become a nun.

Ivan Dragicevic, the older of the two boys who see Our Lady, was born on May 25, 1965. He, his father Stanko, and his mother Zlata, cultivate the family holdings. There are three other younger children in the family. Although Ivan and Mirjana have the same family name, they are not related.

The tallest of the group, he is also the most timid and retiring. His thick dark hair covers half of his ears and forehead. A nice-looking lad, he never seems to smile and usually has a serious, pensive look on his face. His simple, dark clothes reflect his rather somber personality.

Ivan entered the minor seminary in Dubrovnik at the end of August 1981, but had to leave because he was not adequately prepared for the studies there by his previous education in Medugorje. He has not, however, abandoned the hope of becoming a priest. He wants to become a Franciscan and is presently studying on his own through a correspondence course. His family is very religious.

Ivanka Ivankovic, the youngest of the four girls, was born on April 21, 1966. Her father, Ivan, works in West Germany. Her mother, Jagoda, died in May 1981. Though born in Bijakovici, Ivanka now lives with her family in Mostar. She has one brother and one sister. All three of them attend high school in Mostar. Her grandmother, Iva, who is quite old, takes care of the house since the death of the mother. Ivanka helps her considerably.

The prettiest of the girls, Ivanka appears to be somewhat more typical of today's teen-ager than the other three girls, but she also seems to be well-balanced and firmly religious. She is the only seer who is clearly considering marriage.

Although the family lives in Mostar, it has kept the old homestead in Bijakovici where it spends its vacations and cultivates the land. During the school year, Ivanka comes there on Saturdays and Sundays.

Jakov Colo, the youngest of the seers, was born on June 3, 1971. His father, Ante, works in Sarajevo. His mother, Jaca, died on September 5, 1983. Her death affected Jakov all the more deeply since his father rarely comes home. Jakov now lives with his uncle, Philip Pavlovic, and his family.

Short for his age, Jakov makes up in energy what he is lacking in height. The youngster is like a jack-in-the-box. It is very hard for him to stand still in any one place for any length of time.

The presence of this young, fidgety lad among the group of seers is of special value in terms of the authenticity of the apparitions. It is highly improbable that he would come to church for two and three hours of prayer every single day, in winter as in summer, in bad weather as in good weather, and for well over three years, simply to make believe that he is seeing the Blessed Virgin.

Jakov is quick-witted, as the following incident illustrates. The Bishop of Mostar, who has personally interviewed all of the seers, questioned Jakov about the secrets Our Lady has confided to them. The youngster replied that he was not permitted by the Blessed Virgin to talk about them. Then the Bishop said, "Well, you could write the secrets on a piece of paper, put them in an envelope, and leave the envelope here." Jakov replied, "Yes, but I could also write the secrets down, put them in an envelope, and leave the envelope at home."

Although there is a considerable gap in age and in character development between Jakov and the other five young people, the latter all accept him fully and relate to him very easily.

All of the seers get along together very nicely, notwithstanding their distinctive personalities. They manifest great respect for each other and there is no rivalry nor visible jealousy among them. Even though Vicka is the most active, neither she nor any other member of the group can be called its real leader.

The seers are typical of the area of the world from which they come and indeed of the times in which they live. The clothes they wear are quite like those of our own country. During the day, the girls can be seen in jeans and a sweater or a flannel skirt and a sweater, and the boys in jeans, a sweat shirt, and sneakers. Vicka had lunch one day with our group. She wore a red sweat shirt with NEW YORK in large black letters across the front.

The seers do not isolate themselves from others of their age. The girls sing in a choir at Sunday Mass and Jakov is an altar boy.

Father Tomislav Vlasic has affirmed that the seers are "ready to die for Mary and the apparition."

Chapter 10

The Important Role Of The Parish Staff

Each authentic Marian apparition is a unique event with characteristics of its own. One of the unique features of the Medugorje event is the very close association of the parish pastoral staff of priests and sisters with the visionaries. These Franciscan religious are like secondary supporting personages. It would seem that God was telling the world that this is the way it was going to be by the way it all started in Rome when Father Tomislav Vlasic was being prayed over for the healing of the Church.

This close association between the official spiritual leaders of the parish and the young people to whom Our Lady has appeared has been knit in a variety of ways, as will be seen as this account unfolds. An indirect but very powerful and effective one is the way in which they have been called to participate in the message of penance and reparation which our heavenly mother has given to the world at Medugorje.

All of the Franciscan priests and sisters who have been assigned to Saint James parish at Medugorje have suffered to some degree. Three categories of demands have been made upon them, those of the parishioners, the seers, and the pilgrims who have been coming to Medugorje in ever growing numbers. The demands of the seers and of the pilgrims have been heavier on certain members of the parish staff than on others.

The one who suffered most is the man who was pastor when the apparitions began, Father Jozo Zovko. He was in the most difficult situation as the person mainly responsible for the spiritual welfare of the parish. Part of his problem was that he had come to Medugorje on November 11, 1980, and did not really know the parishioners nor the seers when the apparitions began.

In the first days, he deliberately avoided going to the site of the apparitions and adopted a standoffish attitude that confused many. His refusal, however, to become openly associated with the seers did not mean that he was not concerned with what was happening. Not only did he interview the seers in the very early days of the event, but he spent much time in prayer, seeking discernment. As was seen, it was in response to this fervent prayer that heaven intervened to guide him.

In the middle of August, Father Jozo told the associate pastor, Father Zrinko Cuvalo, "Be prepared to take over my job." The reason for this mysterious statement was soon discovered.

On August 17 the police came, arrested Father Jozo, and raided the rectory. The sisters were locked up in one room for the entire day without food. All the money, records, and documents were confiscated; the reports of the early apparitions were among the things taken. This explains why there is not full agreement among the members of the parish staff about the events of the first days.

Father Jozo was tried on October 21 and 22 and condemned for fostering sedition. He was sentenced to three-and-a-half years in prison. Signs were seen by many people on Mount Krizevac on both days of his trial. The cross became a column of light and assumed the form of a T. Then it changed into a luminous lady who could only be seen indistinctly. This lasted half-an-hour. It was later seen again a number of times when it was less intense and of shorter duration.

Strong pressure was brought to bear on the government and Father Jozo's sentence was shortened. He returned to Medugorje on February 17, 1983. He had been in jail eighteen months.

Father Jozo benefited spiritually by his painful experience. "Every good priest," he said, "should see the inside of a jail and suffer for the faith. I discovered in prison what the Catholic faith is and the strength and dignity of a life being offered." He did not remain in the parish very long after his return from prison.

When Father Jozo first came to Medugorje, Father Zrinko Cuvalo was the associate pastor and had preceded him in the parish only by a couple of months. After Father Jozo was imprisoned, Father Zrinko took charge of the parish but was not immediately named pastor. Father Jozo continued to be considered pastor for a while, but eventually Father Zrinko was named to that position which he fulfilled until August 28, 1982. Initially, he does not seem to have believed in the apparitions. At least his remarks in the early days were far from manifesting any such belief. The priests of Saint James parish can certainly not be accused of having instigated the apparitions. This is so true that Ivanka complained to Father Jozo in the very early days of the apparitions, "The only ones who do not believe us are the priests and the police!"

Father Tomislav Pervan, a scripture scholar, took over as pastor when Father Zrinko left the parish.

Father Tomislav Vlasic, who was present at the June 29 apparition, was transferred from Saint Francis of Assisi parish in Capljina[1] to Saint James of Medugorje on August 18, 1981. For three years he fulfilled the major roles of spiritual director and of unofficial mouthpiece of the seers and was deeply involved in the evening services of the parish. He was transferred to nearby Vitina in the latter part of 1984.

A third priest, Father Slavko Barbaric, has also been serving in the parish for some time.

The parish staff is rounded out by three Franciscan sisters. When their convent was completely gutted, they were not granted permission to restore it and they now live crowded into a small room attached to the modest rectory. In order to accommodate visitors, the sisters have to give up their beds and use sleeping bags given to them by pilgrims.

One of the sisters, Janja Boras, who arrived in the parish in 1982, has become very close to the girl members of the group of six seers.

There is a marvelous spirit that reigns between the priests and the sisters of the pastoral staff and between that staff and the parishioners and visitors. The demands of visitors on the busy parish staff are very great. This is particularly true during the summer vacation months and on weekends when the number of visitors goes up into the thousands. For a considerable time, the evening service in the church always ended with individual praying for healing. But this became a crushing burden, going on at times until midnight, and so the individual praying for healing has been greatly reduced and is no longer a nightly affair.

There can be no doubt that much of the conversion and spiritual renewal of the Medugorje parish and region is due to the prudence and zeal of the parish priests and also to the strong support given them by the sisters who work with them. They have successfully tied in the messages of the apparitions with the traditional liturgical and sacramental life of the church.

The key factors in this marriage of the messages with the liturgy and sacraments are the daily six o'clock Mass instituted by Father Jozo Zovko and the monthly triduum that culminates in the feast of reconciliation.

The triduum of reconciliation was an ingenious way of implementing Our Lady's request for conversion and monthly confession. It will be considered in a subsequent chapter.

Although much sacrifice is asked of the members of the parish staff, the rewards have not been lacking, as witnessed by this statement made by Father Tomislav Vlasic:

> It is very interesting to be living all of this, to literally be living by faith. I would need a month just to write down all that is happening personally inside me. Even my recitation of the psalms *(which constitute the major part of the daily breviary prayers said by the priests)* has changed, psalms I never even understood before. This personal change is something very important to me.[2]

Chapter 11

Diversity In The Apparitions

All of the apparitions of the first six days had taken place at or in the vicinity of Mount Podbrdo. When on the seventh day Our Lady appeared at Cerno, this marked the beginning of a new phase in the Medugorje event, the appearance of Our Lady at a number of different sites.

Although the apparitions continued on a daily basis, there is no information available concerning the precise sites of many of the appearances after Our Lady visited the seers in the rectory on the eighth day. The principal reason for this is the loss of the records which were confiscated by the police when they raided the rectory.

The seven other apparitions that took place in the room of the rectory, after the first one on July 1, occurred apparently on the following seven days, from July 2 to July 8. Sometime prior to August 12, 1981, when the apparitions completely ceased taking place on Mount Podbrdo, Our Lady stopped appearing to the six seers for a period of five days. At the next apparition, they asked her why she had done this. She replied that it had been to test them; to see if they would continue to come to pray even if she did not come.

In addition to the government's attempt to stop the apparitions through the children, various measures had been taken to try and stop the people from reaching the site of the apparitions. The government viewed the ever-growing number of those coming to Medugorje with considerable apprehension. It was feared that this might end in an uprising of the Croation people against the government, because a desire for independence was known to exist among them.

Because all the various attempts of the government to stop the apparitions had failed, a more drastic measure was taken. On August 12, the police issued an order forbidding anyone to go to the place of the apparitions on Mount Podbrdo. A law was invoked which stated that the church is the only place where religious services are permitted legally.

Because of this, Our Lady began appearing at various sites in the area of Bijakovici. She appeared in the fields, in the woods, in the homes of the seers, and in most of the other homes, especially in one of them that had a large room. Secrecy was maintained when the apparitions were in the homes, because of the danger of police reprisals. The apparitions in the fields and the woods occurred while the weather was still mild.

Our Lady generally came when the seers were praying together. In the course of these apparitions, she talked with them and gave them messages. She also prayed and sang with them. All during the period when Our Lady was appearing in these various locations, the evening rosary and Mass were maintained in the parish church and the people came to them.

The next major change in the site of the apparitions came on January 12, 1982, when Our Lady began appearing in a little room off the sanctuary in the parish church of Saint James. With this change, the apparitions would have found a home for a couple of years, only to be forced to move again.

When Ivan did not go to Mount Podbrdo with the other seers on June 27 because his mother asked him not to go, Our Lady appeared to him alone, at the same time that she visited the other seers on the mountain side. This is a pattern she will follow in the future. When one of the seers has a legitimate reason for not being with the others at the usual time of the apparitions, she will appear to that person wherever he or she is, as long as he or she is in prayer at that time. Three times, when Vicka went to Zagreb, Our Lady came to her there while she was appearing to the other seers in Medugorje.

At the end of August 1981, when Ivan went away to the minor seminary in Dubrovnic, Our Lady told him she would not appear to him until he got acquainted with his new way of life. Because he found it difficult to adapt himself to that way of life, Ivan did not see her for seven days. She also said that after the adjustment period she would appear to him at two o'clock because he could not be in prayer at the time of the apparitions in Saint James church. Truly an accommodating mother!

Ever since Our Lady began appearing in the church, almost all the apparitions have taken place in the late afternoon or early evening, from approximately five-fifteen to six-thirty, depending on the season of the year.

Some apparitions have taken place at other times. How many is not known. Marinko Ivankovic speaks of one of these that took place "about twenty days" after the start of the Medugorje event. This would place it at about the middle of July 1981, while the regular site of the apparitions was still the mountain side. He related the event to Father Svetozar Kraljevic approximately as stated in the next paragraphs.

One evening, Our Lady told the seers to come to the place of the apparitions on Mount Podbrdo at about eleven p.m. They invited Marinko and some thirty to forty other "believers" from the village. When they had gathered on the mountain side, they began praying. At a certain moment, Marinko looked up and saw the sky apparently opening up some nine to twelve feet and a great, intense light coming toward him and the other people present. Everyone exclaimed together, "Look! The light!"

The spot where Our Lady had appeared was marked by a hole and an old wooden cross. The hole had been dug by people as they removed earth and stones. Marinko and the others were standing in a circle around the hole. Then something unusual happened that Marinko said he could not explain, nor could the others he talked to about it.

It seemed to them that a globe of light came out of the cross and burst in their midst into thousands of bright stars. Some of the children became panicky and started to scream.

Immediately Marija cried out, "Calm down, Our Lady is

with us." Everyone knelt and for forty minutes prayed and cried together. Marinko describes the prayer as one that a person "could rarely experience" and where it felt as if "Jesus and Our Lady were with us."

At the end of the forty minutes, everyone stood up with the seers who said, "Our Lady is looking at all of you and telling you that those who would like to touch her may do so." Everyone ran to the place where Our Lady was and the seers began leading people to Our Lady so they could touch her. But her veil was stepped on and the seers cried out, "She has left." Those who had touched her said that they felt like a numbing of their hands.

In the meantime, people from the nearby neighborhood called Cilici saw the place where Our lady was appearing circled with light. They went there and arrived when the people were touching Our Lady. When she left, everyone departed.

There are some interesting features about this apparition. There is the unusual hour at which it occurred and there is the fact that the seers were told in advance of the apparition by Our Lady. This has happened quite frequently at Medugorje.

However, the most significant facets of this appearance have to do with the tender, motherly love manifested by Our Lady when she invited the people to touch her, and her sudden departure when someone trod upon her veil.

In addition to the characteristics of this apparition, the signs which accompanied it are worth noting. There is the light which came out of an opening in the sky. There is the globe of light that came forth from the cross and exploded into a myriad of bright stars. There is also the light that was visible at Cilici and attracted people from that hamlet to the scene of the apparition.

The same sort of light manifested itself to the seers every time Our Lady appeared to them. It was witnessed on June 30 at Cerno by the two assistant social workers who saw the light illuminate Mount Podbrdo and then move toward them and the five seers they had taken for a ride. Lights in the sky were seen by many other people, sometimes in forms similar to those just described and sometimes quite different. They will be treated in greater detail in later chapters.

The departure of Our Lady when someone walked on her veil recalls what happened on June 27: because her veil was stepped on twice, she departed twice. These are the only two instances when this reaction of Our Lady was noted at Medugorje; indeed such a reaction has been unheard of at any other Marian apparition. This is a good sign. Three other well-known apparitions, La Salette, Lourdes, and Fatima, all possess particular characteristics that one doesn't find at the others. Medugorje has some traits that distinguish it from the three.

The statement by the seers that Our Lady was looking at "all" of the spectators and saying that those who would like to could touch her, speaks powerfully of Mary's motherly love, the love of a true mother who excludes none of her children.

Another apparition that manifests Mary's motherly love for her children of the earth is one that Marinko described to Father Svetozar in the same conversation in which he related the preceding apparition. It occurred in the fall of 1981 when Marinko was making brandy from the local grape harvest, as many of the local people do. He pinpoints it by saying that it took place "exactly two days before Father Jozo's trial."

One interesting feature of this vision is that it took place at Vicka's house, in her room. Jakov and Vicka were to have an apparition there and they invited Marinko. He went with his son, Davor, and another child, Matan Sego. When they arrived, they found children there, singing religious hymns in front of the house.

Jakov and Vicka entered the house alone. Suddenly Jakov called out, "Marinko, Our Lady is here." Marinko ran up the steps to the little landing in front of the door and knelt there, without going in. His son and Matan knelt behind him. He raised his hand and exclaimed, "Dear Blessed Virgin, prove now or never to the unbelievers that our Jozo is not guilty." Then the seers said, "Marinko, the Blessed Virgin is smiling at you. She is coming to you." Apparently following Our Lady as she went toward Marinko, the seers turned to him and continued, "There she is. She is kissing you, embracing you, and blessing you." Marinko was excited and "felt as though his heart was going to break and come out of him." The seers went on, "Marinko, Our Lady is telling you, 'Marinko, do not give up your faith. Keep your faith.'" His reply was, "I am not afraid to give my life for Jesus, but let him show me the path I should follow."

Jakov and Vicka then turned back to where Our Lady had been at the start of the apparition and once again spoke out, repeating Our Lady's words, "Look at those children who are glorifying me." She was alluding to the children who were with Marinko in front of the house, singing religious hymns. The seers continued, "Our Lady is asking that all those children be brought here that she might bless them." The children came to the door, as did Marinko's mother and sister-in-law. Apparently following Our Lady, Jakov and Vicka again turned and said, "Our Lady is above you. She is blessing you." With this the apparition ended.

No comment needs to be made on Mary's tender, motherly love that radiates from this apparition. It is a case where actions speak louder than words.

Marinko is responsible for the account of another very interesting apparition which has several features that make it worth relating. One of these features is the fact that it took place in an open field. It is the only detailed account presently available of such an apparition.

Marinko reports that the field or lawn in question is located between Bijakovici and Cilici. People from both neighborhoods began meeting there to sing and pray. As this became known, other people joined them. On the evening of the Feast of Our Lady of the Angels, people were gathered at this field. About ten o'clock, after the Mass and prayers over the sick at the church, the seers joined the people at the field. As they were all praying the Creed and the seven Our Fathers, Hail Marys, and Glory Be's, Our Lady appeared.

At one point, the seers announced, "Our Lady allows those who so desire to come and touch her." As the people responded to the invitation and came forward one by one, the seers indicated to them, "You are touching her veil . . . her head . . . her dress." This went on for about ten or fifteen minutes. When Our Lady departed, Marija cried out, "Oh, Marinko! Our Lady left us completely blackened." When Marinko asked Marija why that happened, she told him, "There were sinners here who were touching her and as they did her dress got dark and black." Marija then asked all those present to go to confession as soon as possible.

After the apparition was over, Marinko stayed on for a while, talking with Marija. He learned about another apparition that had taken place shortly before the preceding one and that almost seems to be a preparation for it.

Marija told him that, after the church service that evening, she had gone home to change her clothes before coming to the field. While alone in her room, Our Lady appeared to her and said, "The devil is trying to infiltrate himself here in order to get something. My Son wants to win over all the souls, but the devil is exerting himself to get something. He is making every effort and wants at any price to infiltrate among you." Marija added that Our Lady told her something else which Marinko reports in this fashion: "I don't know if Marija understood Our Lady correctly or not. Supposedly, she said that she does not know how it will turn out, if the devil will succeed or not, or how much he will succeed."[1] (Father Svetozar adds the editorial comment that this has to do with "the events at Medugorje.")

The episode in the field in which Our Lady allowed people to touch her contains some powerful teaching. Since the invitation to touch her came from Our Lady, it speaks eloquently of her love for her children on earth. It is her manifest wish that she enjoy a close and intimate relationship with all of her children without exception. This needs to be heeded. Too many people tend to be excessively formal and distant in their dealings with our heavenly mother, whereas she expects a more simple and childlike approach.

This same episode ended with another powerful teaching on the evil of sin. There were several related parts to this teaching: the blackening of Our Lady's dress, her departure because of being touched by sinners, and Marija's request that everyone go to confession as soon as possible. In Marinko's account of this event, he does not say whether this request was made by Our Lady and simply transmitted to the people by Marija, or whether Marija made it on her own. In any event it follows logically from the blackening of Our Lady's dress and her departure after being touched by sinners. It also ties in perfectly with the message she gave a number of times at Medugorje, namely, repentance and reconciliation with God through confession. It was a concrete way of expressing this message, one that could be readily understood by everyone.

The message about the devil that Marija was given in her room would seem to be advance warning to prepare her for the trials and tribulations that always accompany such events as were being experienced at Medugorje. The evil one always attacks and tries to destroy anything that has great potential for good. The greater the potential for good, the more power-fully he opposes it. Rarely does he begin by an open, frontal attack. He is the great deceiver and usually starts by working under cover, infiltrating, and often using good and well-intentioned people.

The Church's traditional teaching on the devil and hell has been challenged and even repudiated by some Catholics. Contrarily, it is interesting to note that at Medugorje Our Lady began early to speak about both. She has mentioned the devil a number of times in her messages and has even given the seers a vision of hell.

The latest hour at which an apparition has occurred — according to available information — is two a.m. This happened on August 7, 1981. Our Lady called the seers to Mount Podbrdo and asked them to pray there that people would do penance for sinners. She promised them that she would give a special sign so that the world would believe. During the month of September she gave additional information about this sign. On September 4 she apparently said that the sign would be given at the end of the apparitions. Then, at the end of September, she told all the seers except Marija the precise time of the sign and held them to secrecy about it.

The very hour, two a.m., contained a message about penance. It was a concrete way of showing the seers what she meant by penance for sinners. Our Lady will not be afraid to ask these young people to be generous in their practice of penance and they will respond generously. Their generosity has been an example not only for the people of the area but also for the parish staff of priests and sisters, as they themselves have admitted.

There has been considerable diversity in the duration of the apparitions, particularly of the early apparitions before they began occurring in the church. When queried by Father Rupcic about the length of those apparitions, the seers gave the following times: 5, 6, 10, 15, 20, 30 minutes.[2] Most of the apparitions in the church have been quite short, lasting from three to five minutes, although there have been exceptions. In the middle of July 1983, one apparition lasted thirty minutes and the next day another lasted forty-two or forty-three. These were attended by some Americans. During the five days that the author spent in Medugorje in mid-October 1983, they lasted only three or four minutes. The following summer many, if not most of the apparitions, were lasting one minute and even less.

There has been diversity in the persons appearing at Medugorje. Our Lady has not been the only one who appeared to the seers. The Sorrowful Christ, crowned with thorns and covered with blood, has been seen by them. Of Him Our Lady said, "This is my Son. See how He suffered for mankind."[3]

This vision is very important in view of the stress on penance and reparation in the Medugorje message. It complements the visions of hell and of purgatory that some of the seers have had and serves the same purpose of inspiring them to detest sin and to be generous in making atonement for it.

In regard to Jesus, Our Lady has appeared with the Infant Jesus in her arms on certain feast days such as Christmas; He has not spoken on those occasions.

In his interrogation of the seers, Father Rupcic asked them what else they had seen in addition to Jesus and Mary. Here are the answers he received:

> Marija — We saw heaven, hell, and purgatory. Our Lady showed us that also. She showed it once at Vicka's house and once at my house and a third time, but I don't remember where. I saw people in heaven who were so happy. The beauty of heaven is indescribable. It is positively visible that God's

love is present there. Hell is a place of pain and suffering. It is horrible.

Jakov — I saw angels in Vicka's house.

Vicka — When Father Jozo was in prison, Our Lady showed him to us once. It was like in a film. We saw heaven and hell. There is a large space. Here and there are many people. When you enter, on the left, there is a man. I didn't ask who he is or what he does. He opens the door . . . There are groups of people . . . smiling, talking. Angels circle above them. And hell. There is a great fire that has no embers but only flames. There are people, who go along, one by one, crying. This one has horns, that one tails, and another has four feet. God help us!

Ivanka — *(The 1983 Croation edition of Father Rupcic's book has a blank here. However, in the French version of his book, Ivanka is quoted as having given the answer that follows:* "I also saw two angels, my mother, hell and heaven."[4])

Mirjana — Yes, I saw the devil. I was waiting for Our Lady and just as I was about to make the sign of the cross, he appeared instead of her. I was frightened. He promised me the nicest things. I said: "No!" Then all at once he disappeared, and Our Lady came. She told me that he always tries to turn the true believer from the right path.

Our Lady showed me heaven. It is a wonderful place, where there is happiness and contentment. Happiness. Happiness and contentment can be seen on all faces. The trees are completely different than they are here. The sun is also much stronger.

Ivan — Jesus.[5]

It is interesting to note that heaven, hell, and people in hell have been represented to the seers in traditional images familiar to Catholics. Besides heaven and hell one of the seers mentioned purgatory in her reply to Father Rupcic. The fact is that all six of them have seen heaven, five have seen purgatory, and four have seen hell. The two who have not been shown hell indicated that, when they were offered the opportunity to see it, they declined because they were too fearful of such an experience.

A most unusual incident occurred concerning these visions. One day Vicka and Jakov, who are close friends, disappeared from the face of the earth. They were gone for twenty minutes.

This happened at Jakov's house. His mother had seen him in the house just prior to his disappearing. She called him, thinking he had left the house to go into the village. As this brought no response, she went in and out of the house, fearful that something had happened to him, but nowhere was there a sign of either one. When they finally returned, they said they had seen heaven and hell and had passed through purgatory. They affirmed that when Our Lady took them through purgatory she stated, "These people are waiting for your prayers and sacrifices." It is not difficult to imagine how quickly news of this event must have spread throughout the region and beyond.

A unique feature of the Medugorje apparitions is the way the seers have been asked to prepare for certain special feasts, such as the Immaculate Conception, with days of prayer and fasting.

The diversity in the apparitions at Medugorje manifests itself in still another way that is unique and has to do with Our Lady's outward appearance. She usually comes wearing a bright, pellucid grey dress that the seers find hard to describe. She has a brilliant white veil and on her head is a glowing crown of stars. Usually also, she appears smiling and holds her hands out from her side and lifted upward.

However, on important feast days of the Church, Our Lady smiles more joyfully and her dress appears different, "golden," "brilliant." This has happened on the Feast of the Assumption, which absolutely stands out in the minds of the seers, the Nativity or Birthday of Our Lady, the Immaculate Conception, Christmas, Easter[6], and a few others, such as June 25, which is the anniversary of the day on which Mary first spoke with the seers and which is also the day she wants the Church to designate as the Feast of Our Lady, Queen of Peace.

Our Lady told the seers that she would impart ten secrets to all of them. These have been received on an individual basis. The first to receive ten was Mirjana. She received the tenth secret on December 25, 1982. On that day Our Lady told Mirjana that she would not appear to her any more on a regular basis, but only on her birthday *(March 18)* and when she was experiencing some special difficulty in her life. She told her she would have to live by faith henceforth, as other people do.

The other seers have all received nine secrets, except Vicka who has received only eight.

The early months of the apparitions were characterized by considerable diversity. This diversity manifested itself not only in the apparitions themselves, but also in the signs that were immediately associated with them. In addition to those signs, there were others linked less closely in time with the apparitions. These will be examined in the next chapter.

The diversity in the apparitions is a reassuring factor in terms of the authenticity of these happenings. It is indeed highly improbable that six young people varying in age from ten to seventeen would have invented and agreed upon the strange and complicated scenario that has unfolded since June 24, 1981. This is particularly true of the first eight days. It is much more likely that their stories would have been simpler and much less intricate.

Chapter 12

From The Fields And Homes Into The Church

It was on June 30, 1981, that the seers asked Our Lady if she would mind appearing in the church and were told that she wouldn't mind. Nevertheless, it was not until the early months of 1982 that the apparitions moved from the fields, woods, and homes into the church.

This was a tremendously important move, the full consequences of which it is impossible to weigh. Much of what has happened at Medugorje must be attributed to this. It brought about a fusion of the apparitions and their messages with the sacramental life of the Church.[1] The result has been a marvel — a special transformation of a people and of an area never before witnessed in the annals of Marian apparitions, even at such places as Lourdes and Fatima. Some of this started as soon as Father Jozo introduced the evening rosary and Mass on the first of July, but it was intensified when the apparitions began taking place regularly in the church.

When the apparitions moved into the church, a program was worked out which integrated the apparitions with the evening service that had been initiated July 1, 1981. It was possible to do this since the apparitions took place at approximately the same time each evening. The program includes the Sacrament of Reconciliation, the rosary, the apparitions, the Eucharist, and a healing service or some other religious activity. In the summer the program starts an hour later than it does in the winter. The program has included those elements in the above order for some time, except that what takes place after the Eucharist has undergone some changes.

Here is what can be called a typical evening in the church. The rosary starts the program at about five-thirty. People start arriving at the church considerably in advance of that time. On some days the church is filled by five o'clock. As the crowd assembles, priests come and begin to hear confessions in various parts of the church. If there is an overflow crowd outside, priests will hear confessions there. The Franciscans have a number of parishes in the region and a large monastery in the nearby village of Humac. Priests from these parishes and particularly from the Humac monastery help with these confessions. There are always several priests so engaged. Their number varies according to the crowd that is anticipated. On Sunday there is an early morning Mass for children, then a late morning Mass at eleven, and an early evening one at six-fifteen. Some twenty priests will hear confessions on an average Sunday from four-thirty to approximately eight or eight-thirty. On a major feast day and on some Sundays there may be thirty or more priests available for confessions.

On November 27 and 28, 1982, Bobbie Cavnar of Dallas, Texas, a leader in the Catholic charismatic renewal, visited Medugorje. In the report he wrote in December after his return to the United States, he imparts interesting information about the large crowds of people he saw walking long distances to the church and about the impressive sight of people going to confession in the open air.

When he and his group arrived by automobile at Medugorje on Saturday, November 27, the evening Mass was over. It was dark and they were still over two miles from the church. "The road," he says, "was absolutely jammed with people walking home. Many of them walk as much as twenty miles once or twice a week to attend the rosary and Mass."

On Sunday they were in the village for both the late morning and the evening Mass. "Parishioners," he states, "began to arrive for the eleven a.m. Mass about ten a.m. By ten-thirty, the church was almost full with 25 or 30 people standing . . . Many priests from the surrounding area arrived during the afternoon and were hearing confessions everywhere. It seemed like there were priests under every tree with a line of people waiting to receive the Sacrament of Reconciliation. I have never seen anything like that before anywhere in the world."

When the rosary starts at five-thirty, the church is frequently filled to overflowing. Often every square inch of the large edifice is occupied, the aisles completely blocked, the choir loft filled, and even the sanctuary invaded. (The author witnessed such a throng on Saturday, October 15, 1983; a friend had had the same experience on a weekday in March 1983.)

For a long time, those seers who were in the village led the five-thirty recitation of the rosary which includes the Fatima invocation between the decades. They knelt on the floor in the sanctuary behind the altar, facing the people as the priest does when celebrating the Eucharist.

If a priest is available, he will announce the mysteries and give a meditation on them. When the rosary is over and the seers depart for the room of the apparitions, he will lead the people in the recitation of the litany of the saints.

It is after the rosary that Our Lady appears. Those of the seers who are in Medugorje on a given day enter a small room in the front of the church to the right of the main altar. This room, which had been used as a storage area, is directly across the sanctuary from the sacristy. The room is open in the morning and early afternoon for those who want to pray there. If many people are expected, the door may be locked in the course of the afternoon to avoid overcrowding since the room is small, about fifteen by fifteen feet. The appointments are very simple. Along the wall immediately to the left of the doorway, is a plain wooden table covered with an altar cloth. Its principal purpose is to hold the various objects that people place there before the apparitions: rosaries and other religious articles, bottles of water filled at the well near the rectory, and slips of paper carrying requests for divine favors and blessings. Occasionally visiting priests may use this table as an altar of celebration as the author himself did.

In the corner, to the left of this table or improvised altar, is a large statue of Our Lady of Lourdes, a hold-over from the previous church. On the wall opposite the door is a large window. Benches, stools, and chairs line the open spaces along the various walls of the room. Along the wall with the door is an electric organ and a piece of furniture with drawers. Since October 1983, the table and the crucifix above it have been shifted to the wall opposite their previous location.

During the five evening services at which the author was present, this is the way things took place. On Thursday, October 13, Vicka and Jakov came into the room before the rosary began but later left it. The rosary in the church, led by a priest, began at about five o'clock. At 5:25, Ivanka, Jakov, and Vicka entered the room of the apparitions and lined up before the table. They could be heard making the sign of the cross and beginning the Our Father. After the first few words, several things happened in quick succession: their voices died away, they went down to their knees together, and their heads tilted back, as they raised their eyes to the cross on the wall several feet above the table. Our Lady had come. The voices of the priest and the people reciting the litany in the church could be heard.

The apparition lasted three or four minutes. When it was over, the three seers went out into the sanctuary and knelt behind the altar, facing the people. They led the people in the recitation of the seven Our Fathers, Hail Marys, and Glory Be's and the Creed. Jakov held a microphone during these prayers and the two girls prayed out loud with him.

This was followed by the Mass with a fifteen to twenty minute homily. Afterward, the Blessed Sacrament was exposed for an hour. Worship was led by Father Tomislav Vlasic and was attended by all those who had been present at the Mass. With his gaze always fixed on the Blessed Sacrament, Father Tomislav prayed out loud for several minutes. Then there was a time of silence followed by hymn-singing. This went on for about an hour. The last part of the hour was devoted to praying for healing. The entire evening session from the start of the rosary to the end of the hour of adoration lasted about three hours. The message Our Lady imparted to the seers that evening was tape-recorded in the sacristy.

Friday was a repetition of Thursday: the same three seers witnessed the apparition and Father Tomislav led the people in an hour of prayer in honor of the Passion of Our Lord. He spoke for several minutes. There was a pause for silent prayer followed by singing on the part of the congregation. The service continued on in this way for the whole hour. These Friday devotions after the Mass were introduced as part of the celebration of the Holy Year of the Redemption.

Saturday differed somewhat from the two previous days. Five seers participated in the apparition. Mirjana, the girl from Sarajevo, was not present. Also, the recitation of the seven Our Fathers, Hail Marys, and Glory Be's took place in the church after the Mass. It was led by the seers and was followed by prayer for healing. A priest and the five seers prayed individually for healing. This did not last very long and ended the evening service.

Sunday evening was basically the same as Saturday. The only difference was the way in which the healing service was conducted. Standing behind the altar and facing the people, Father Tomislav Vlasic prayed over the congregation in Croatian and Father Tomislav Pervan, the pastor, in German. Father Pervan invited those visiting priests who were in the sanctuary to join him as he extended his hands and prayed silently. There was no praying over people individually. The general prayer by the parish priests was of relatively short duration and marked the end of the evening service. The church was full. Many were standing but they were not so tightly packed as on Saturday, because visitors from distant places had apparently left for home.

On Monday, things were back to a weekday routine, similar to that of Thursday and Friday except that the service ended with the Eucharist. There were no special devotions after the Mass. There was, however, a meeting of some thirty young people (late teens and early twenties) that took place in the church proper quite some time after the conclusion of the Mass. The church has no halls or meeting rooms.

On these five evenings there were minor differences in the time at which the apparitions began. The largest difference may have been fifteen or twenty minutes and this was caused by the time of the seers' entrance into the room. They did not come into the room at exactly the same time each evening. However, once they had all entered the room, had lined up before the table, and had started to pray, Our Lady came almost immediately.

As the seers fall to their knees, their gaze is immediately directed upward toward the crucifix on the wall directly behind the table. Little Jakov, who usually is in the center of the group, has his head tilted backward quite sharply but his eyes stare at the same place on the wall of the low-ceilinged room as the other seers. The faces of all are intent and serene. Vicka's face is the most expressive and reflects the greatest joy.

On four of the five days the author was in the room of the apparitions, he was very close to the seers and positioned in front of them so that he could watch their faces. Vicka was engaged in conversation with Our Lady during almost the entire time of all four apparitions and her face reflected joy and happiness in various degrees. The lips of her large mouth were moving most of the time. Occasionally she nodded her head vigorously, evidently in approval of something Our Lady said, and at times she broke out into a big smile that bordered on laughter. There was little change in the expression on the faces of the other seers. Sometimes their lips moved ever so slightly but they never seemed to be in real dialogue with Our Lady.

For some time the seers could transmit questions to Our Lady that they had received from people. She would often answer them, but not always. Occasionally after a number of questions had been asked, she would say, "That is enough questions."

When the seers ask Our Lady to pray for certain intentions that people have referred to them, she will say, "Let us pray for them," and she will lead them in prayer. When the seers respond, they can be heard by the people in the room. Our Lady will never lead the seers in the recitation of the Hail Mary.

The seers look fixedly at the same spot during the entire apparition. Their eyes blink occasionally but do not seem to react to light; they do not flicker when flash bulbs go off right in front of them and close to their faces, nor do they manifest any detectable reaction.

The seers have been submitted to some tests during the apparitions. On Christmas day 1983, one of the Franciscan priests put some pressure on Vicka's arm. She manifested no awareness of this and continued talking with Our Lady and smiling as though nothing had happened. Then he lifted little Jakov. He appeared heavy but there was no evident reaction on his part and he continued his contemplation of Our Lady. When the apparition had ended, the priest questioned the two seers, who indicated that they had felt nothing while the tests were going on.[2]

On another occasion Ivan's brain activity during an apparition was measured. The encephalogram indicated normal brain activity. There was no sign of dreaming or hallucination. Once, a member of the Bishop's Commission of Investigation stuck a needle in Vicka's back, shoulder, and arm. Though blood was visibly drawn, she manifested no sign of pain.

If the seers are unresponsive to and oblivious of what is done to them and around them, at times they are even unaware of what is happening to each other. This occurs during Our Lady's admonition to one of them, or during the correction of a fault. Only that one being corrected hears her — like a good mother she avoids humiliating her child in the eyes of others.

So far, we have seen what could be called the externals of the apparitions. What about them from the seers' point of view? What do they see? At the beginning of the first apparitions, the seers used to see three brilliant lights or flashes of light, and then Our Lady. After a few days, Our Lady was preceded by only one brilliant light. Our Lady appeared coming out of this light. She stood on a cloud that grew wider the longer she stayed.

She is of medium height and appears to be nineteen or twenty years old. She wears a dress of bright, translucent grey, which the young people find hard to describe. It is not held in at the waist by a sash; it also completely covers her feet. She has a brilliant white veil and a bit of black curly hair can be seen on the left side of her face. On her head is a crown of glowing stars. She has rosy cheeks. Her eyes are light blue and expressive; they speak of kindness and tenderness. Her countenance is indescribably beautiful and generally she appears to smile. Her open hands and her forearms extend outward toward the seers.

Our Lady is the one who always speaks first, and in "pure" Croatian. Her first words are significantly, "Praised be Jesus!" Her farewell, like her greeting, is always the same, "Go in the peace of God."

She departs as she comes, in a great light. When she does, the seers exclaim, *"Ode* — She's gone!" They blink their eyes, stand up, and smile.

Every effort is made by the parish staff to get in touch with the seers as soon as possible after the apparition and get a report on it. In the author's presence a priest announced that during the apparition that evening Our Lady had said, "People must take seriously what I say." There is a sense of urgency about the messages of Our Lady which will be examined later.

What strikes visitors are the attention, reverence, and participation of the congregation during the entire lengthy evening service, and also the relatively large number of children, young people, and men who come each day. Before the apparitions, if the Eucharist lasted more than forty-five minutes, the people would complain!

There is always considerable singing and it seems that just about everyone takes part in it. A Franciscan priest plays an electric organ located at the front of the church and a small choir stands next to him.

Visiting priests who concelebrate with the local clergy are often asked to help give Communion at stations throughout the church. They are deeply touched by the faith in the divine presence that is so evident on the faces of some of the middle-aged peasant women and some of the young people. An American priest of Croatian extraction who heard confessions in the open air once for four-and-a-half hours said that the quality of the confessions of people of all ages, children, young people, and older ones, was the thing that impressed him most on his visit to Medugorje. Their confessions were not just the routine recitation of a shopping list of sins.

A great blessing that has flowed from moving the apparitions into the church and out of sight of the people is that the parishioners and visitors do not come to witness a spectacle, to look at the seers in ecstasy. They come to the church out of a deep spiritual conviction. There is no emotionalism or sensationalism at Medugorje. Everything is on a very high spiritual level.

Chapter 13

Signs And Wonders

Signs visible to the people began manifesting themselves very early at Medugorje. Since a large number of these have to do with the large cross that stands on the summit of Mount Krizevac, a word must be said of its origin. The cross gives a clue as to why Our Lady chose this village and region for this particular manifestation of her love and concern for her children of the earth. Overlooking the church of Saint James and visible for miles and miles around the vast valley below, this cross speaks powerfully of the strong message of penance and atonement Our Lady came to bring to the world. It does so, not only by reminding everyone of the suffering of Christ for the redemption of mankind, but also, in a very special way, through the story of its erection.

The fifteen-ton concrete cross was put up by the people of the area in 1933 to commemorate the nineteenth centenary of the Redemption. Their spirit of penance and their under-standing of its importance were manifested by the fact that all the material which went into the construction of the cross was carried up the 1770-foot mountain by hand. The cross was so meaningful to the people that they changed the mountain's name from Sipovac to Krizevac. *Kriz* is the Croatian word for cross. It became the custom, even prior to the apparitions, to celebrate Mass there each year on the Feast of the Exaltation of the Holy Cross *(September 14)*.

It is difficult to give precise dates for many of the signs that have been seen at Medugorje. This is not surprising, given their great number and the long period of time over which they have been witnessed. Also, when the police confiscated the parish records on August 17, 1981, some of the early dates were lost.

Signs were particularly numerous, as one might expect, in the first months of the apparitions. They were witnessed by many people and especially by those of the hamlet of Bijakovici in which all the seers were born. They were an important factor in drawing local people to the place of the apparitions and they undoubtedly account for the enormous crowds that thronged there in a matter of days after they began.

The very first signs were given as early as the second day of the apparitions, June 25, 1981. That was the first day on which the seers ran up the steep slopes of Mount Podbrdo with amazing speed and ease, notwithstanding the fact that the surface of the mountain side is covered with sharp-edged stones and prickly thickets. Vicka, who was barefooted, commented, "And yet no thorn pricked me," and she added, "When we came to about six feet of Our Lady, we felt as though we were being seized and pushed to our knees. Jakov knelt in a kind of thorny bush. I thought he would get hurt, but he came out of it without anything happening to him."

These initial signs were quickly followed by manifestations of light that would assume many forms and become the most frequent signs witnessed at Medugorje. The first of these was seen on the third day Our Lady appeared. On that day, her coming was preceded by a brilliant light that illumined not only the village but the entire area and was seen by everyone. On the fourth day, the people gathered on Mount Podbrdo saw the light which immediately preceded Our Lady's coming to the five seers who were there.

On the seventh day, June 30, the seers were taken for a ride by the two assistant social workers from Citluk. When they stopped the car at Cerno at the time the apparitions had been occurring on Mount Podbrdo, the young people saw a light that illuminated the mountain side of the apparitions and then moved toward them. The two assistant social workers said that they saw the light too.

All of these first signs were basically of the same nature and were witnessed by people before an apparition began or just as it was starting.

After June 30 there was no other definitely-dated light phenomenon until August 2. The sign observed on that day was a very impressive one that recalls the dance of the sun that took place at Fatima on October 13, 1917, [1] and which was the miracle Our Lady had promised the three little shepherds she would perform on that day so that people would believe. The Medugorje dance of the sun has been seen a number of times since August 2.

The dance of the sun witnessed on August 2 had considerably more facets to it than the October 13, 1917, phenomenon at Fatima. There seem to be some constant elements that were witnessed by all of the approximately 150 people who saw it while they were on the mountain side of the apparitions. Here are the constant elements. It took place late in the afternoon when the sun was about to set. The sun was seen to spin around on its own axis. The people could look at it without hurting their eyes. It seemed to come toward those who were watching it and then to recede from them. As it came closer, great darkness appeared behind it. The reaction of the people was varied. Some prayed, some cried, some were afraid, and some ran away. At the end, a white cloud was seen coming down over the mountain side of the apparitions. It moved toward the sun which continued to spin briefly but then set in its normal fashion. The entire phenomenon lasted about fifteen minutes.

In addition to these common elements seen by everyone, a large number of people saw numerous globes of different colors moving around the sun, while others claimed they saw Our Lady, the Sacred Heart, and a great number of angels with trumpets coming out of the sun. It is to be noted that August 2 is the Feast of Our Lady, Queen of Angels. Some people saw the sun spinning as though in a large heart and later a large heart with six small hearts beneath it. What did the large and small hearts represent? Our Lady and the six seers?

Somewhat similar phenomena were witnessed on August 3

and 4. Father Umberto Loncar, a Franciscan priest, gives witness to what he saw on these two days, but in doing so he also mentions the events of August 2. At the time he was living in Gradnice which is some distance from Medugorje.

Father Loncar says that on August 2 and 3 many pilgrims observed that the sun had become pale and that it had bright rings around it. These rings were casting reddish rays on the parish church of Medugorje. A little later, they saw bright globes of different colors rotating around the sun. All this was seen while Our Lady was appearing to the seers from 6:20 to 6:40 p.m. Father Loncar says that he had not looked at the sun or the sky on August 2, nor had he observed any of the phenomena, and he candidly admits that he did not believe in them.

On August 3, Father Loncar looked at the sun and observed the same things the pilgrims had seen the previous day and at the same time of day they had seen them. He still did not believe in them. He thought they could be explained by purely natural causes.

August 4, however, was a different matter. He deliberately stayed home and his observation was made at the rectory. At six p.m. he came out of the rectory and cast a quick glance at the sun through the fingers of his hand. He wanted to avoid being dazzled by the sun and becoming the victim of visual impressions. The sun had already started to pale and a mild, very pleasant breeze had come up.

He looked toward Medugorje. At exactly 6:20 p.m., he was surprised to see a most unusual, reddish-violet cloud coming from Cerno. It traveled with considerable speed, much faster than clouds usually do. It arrived over the huge cross on Mount Krizevac, stayed there a minute or two, and then started to move eastward and down toward the earth. At this point, Father Loncar lost sight of the sun because of the trees and hills in front of him. He had seen all this from the upper part of the parish house.

From there the priest went through the house to the terrace which lies between the rectory and the church where something even more unusual greeted his eyes, something that left him awe-stricken. He saw a magnificent, reddish-violet figure of a wonderful lady rising from Mount Crnica (Podbrdo).[2] It rose majestically in the sky and, slowly losing its delightful reddish-violet color, it disappeared.

The last thing Father Loncar saw was a white veil. It was unusually white under the lady's feet and fluttered elegantly in the air under them for about half-a-minute.

Father Loncar remarked that what he saw occurred on a day that Our Lady appeared to the young people at Bijakovici and at the very same time. A noteworthy facet of this sign is that Father Loncar was not in the immediate area of the apparitions when he witnessed it. He has expressed the opinion that it was a miraculous sign, bearing witness that the events at Medugorje are from God.[3]

An eye-witness report of sky phenomena which occurred on December 9, 1983, and which involved the sun and the huge concrete cross, was written by a person travelling with a group of pilgrims. The following is drawn from this report on the events of December 8 and 9:

> Medugorje was a deep experience for everyone in our group. It shook us all! Marija received the ninth secret before our eyes in the apparition chapel. She wept profusely. *(We know from Mirjana who has received all ten secrets that the ninth and tenth ones are "grave matters . . . a chastisement for the sins of the world . . .")*
>
> The day after the eighth we had a sun miracle at 1 p.m . . . We had just walked behind the church in order to look up to the cross mountain when a storm commenced. It almost threw us over and the church seemed to shake. Clouds, as dark as night, were driven across the sky by this brief storm . . .
>
> Suddenly, the sun broke through with spectacular rays and then some saw the sun spin. Our leader, the "doubting Thomas," and two women of our group saw it especially clear.
>
> But all the people assembled got on their knees because we all saw the darting and fiery rays breaking through the dark clouds in various directions.
>
> As the clouds disappeared, the sky became rose-red and the sun paled. In the sun was the Andrew cross, and as it disappeared, a huge cross began to be raised above the sun, peaked by a crown. All this was light and around it the darkness grew again, as though the judgment of God was at hand.

All the while, the cross on the cross mountain was invisible. The land below and the sky around grew in darkness. Only the spectacular rose colors twirling around the illumined cross raised above the sun grew brighter and brighter.

Then, it all vanished and the dreary winter day took its normal course.

In the evening, Father Slavko told us that he had gone out after the evening Mass to look up at the cross mountain, where such a spectacular sight had deeply touched us all.

The sky behind the mountain was being colored by a far-off sundown — blood red!

Thus Mary on her high feast *(the Immaculate Conception)* had given us two signs. Father Slavko was evidently moved by it all.

A most important sign was the word *Mir*(Peace) that was written one evening in large bright letters in the sky above the cross on Mount Krizevac. This occurred in the early days of the apparitions and was seen by the pastor and many people from the village. It has been witnessed a number of times. As will be shown later, peace is at the very heart of the message Our Lady brought to the world at Medugorje. This was a dramatic way of manifesting it.

The most frequently observed phenomena have involved the cross on Mount Krizevac and have been quite varied. People have seen the cross change into a column of light that stood on top of the mountain between the earth and the sky. Father Svetozar Kraljevic affirms that he himself witnessed this and that it had also been oberved by many others. [4] The horizontal bar of the cross and its lower part have turned bright white, forming a T or tau cross. The cross has also changed into the bright or luminous form of a young lady "which fits the description of the Blessed Virgin Mary given by the seers without being as clear." [5] This phenomenon has apparently been observed many times, at different times of the day, when the sky was clear and when it was covered, and has lasted from a few minutes to half-an-hour. [6] It was more intense and lasted for half-an-hour on October 21 and 22, 1981, during the trial of the pastor, Father Jozo Zovko. [7]

It is significant that the luminous figure of a lady has been seen by many people and from such places as Miletina, Citluk and Gradina. It has also been observed a number of times by pilgrims who have come to Medugorje.

Because of the major importance of the heavenly signs, especially of those involving the figure or silhouette of a lady, an event that took place at Medugorje on October 22, 1981, is related in the following pages. Several Franciscan priests were among the considerable number of people who witnessed it and three of them have written detailed reports about what they saw.

On October 22, 1981, Father Luka Vlasic went to Medugorje from the Franciscan monastery at Humac, where he was stationed. Three other Franciscans from the same monastery went along with him. They were Janko Bubalo, Vinko Dragicevic and Stanko Vasilj. These four priests went each day to the parish church of Saint James, where they helped with confessions.

As usual, the four priests arrived at the church shortly after four p.m. The pastor of the parish, Father Zrinko Cuvalo, asked him to wait in his office because he wanted to talk to him. While waiting there, he just happened to look out the window toward Mount Krizevac. He noticed that the cross was gone and in its place stood a large, white, bright column. Soon the column changed into "a statue with the contour of a woman." He called the associate pastor, Father Tomislav Vlasic, who went and got some binoculars. Then Fathers Janko Bubalo and Stanko Vasilj came and the four priests took turns looking through the binoculars.

Father Luka looked through the binoculars twice. He was excited by what he saw. This "statue of a woman" had her hands extended. All Father Luka could see was her general contour. He could not distinguish her eyes, mouth, hair, nor other details.

The lady was looking towards the parish church. At times it seemed as though she was bowing, now to the left, now to the right. The appearance lasted about half-an-hour.

Father Luka was not only excited; he also experienced joy. The thought came to him: "This is a reward from Our Lady for the long and exhausting four months of hearing confessions in Medugorje."

Many pilgrims, those around the church as well as those who came out of the church, witnessed the appearance. All were kneeling, praying, singing, shouting with joy as they looked toward Mount Krizevac. "Their faces were aglow with exultation."

Father Luka ended his signed statement with the words: "I am willing to confirm the truthfulness of this testimony by oath at any time."

Father Janko Bubalo was with Luka Vlasic on October 22. He, too, has described what he saw on that day. It was a little after five p.m. when he looked out the rectory window and saw two of the nuns of the parish kneeling on the wet ground with their arms wide open. Near them were some seventy men and women, kneeling and quite oblivious of the rain that was falling. Some were crying, some praying, and others singing religious hymns. They were all looking toward the cross on Mount Krizevac. Father Janko looked in that direction but the cross had disappeared. "In its place was a strange pale rose-colored light without equivalent in real life." As his eyesight is poor he looked through Father Tomislav's binoculars and in the place of the cross he saw "the silhouette of a woman." Her arms were open and her feet were hidden in a luminous cloud near the base of the pedestal of the cross. He could not make out any details, such as the face, the eyes, or the hair. As he feasted his eyes on the sight, he was filled with joy. He affirms that the other priests who were with him saw the same thing and that all the people in the village who looked at Mount Krizevac at that time also witnessed it. It lasted about forty minutes. He adds that people prevailed on the seers to ask Our Lady about the significance of this happening and she told them that "she was the one who was on the mountain."

Here is Father Stanko Vasilj's account of what he saw on October 22. He went to the sacristy of the church and then outside. The rain had stopped but the sky was dark. He looked toward Mount Krizevac and noticed that the cross had disappeared. Shortly after that he saw a "white column" in place of the cross. He went back into the sacristy and told Sister Ignacia Bebek to go out and look. She replied, "That's Our Lady! Yesterday the people of Miletina saw it several times at the same place." He then left for the rectory and on his way encountered two sisters and the fourth priest from Humac, Father Vinko Dragicevic. He asked them if they could see anything. Father Vinko retorted, "You aren't blind are you! Don't you see?"

In the rectory, Father Stanko took the binoculars and looked toward Mount Krizevac. Now, in place of the white column, he saw the silhouette of a woman with a cape. The cape was grey, but a very light and luminous grey. At a certain moment, a ray of sparkling light issued from her right cheek. He left the rectory to tell the people who were in the church, but found them behind the church, on their knees, looking toward Mount Krizevac, praying, singing, and shouting for joy.

As this was going on, a car from the old cathedral city of Split arrived at the church. In it were three Carmelite priests and four nuns. They joined the others in praying. When it was all over, they stated that they had witnessed this phenomenon from Tromedja to Medugorje, a distance of a mile-and-a-half. One of the nuns, however, said she had not seen anything, neither on the way, nor at the church.

At the end a cloud rose up from the site of the cross. "It was clear and transparent and divided in two, in the form of a fan." It was followed by another cloud, dark and somber, that came down like a curtain on each side of the cross. The cross finally resumed its usual appearance.

Father Stanko ended his account with these words: "I affirm all this, fully aware of my great responsibility before God and the Church."[8]

Another sign that would seem to have been given as much for the government as for the people occurred on October 28, 1981. On that day a fire of unknown origin broke out at the site of the first apparition. It lasted about fifteen minutes and was seen by several hundred people, including a number of priests and sisters. A guard who was on duty at the foot of the mountain to stop people from going up and who was there when the fire started did not see anything. Another guard who replaced him while the fire was still in progress did see it. When it was over, he examined the place thoroughly and could not find a trace of scorched matter. The fire had burned without consuming anything.

Some of the signs have had to do with the stars. On the Feast of the Sacred Heart, June 18, 1982, and on the Feast of the Immaculate Heart, June 19, stars were seen rotating in the sky. They were also alternately lit and extinguished for more than an hour. The stars involved in this way looked like the ordinary stars that are seen in the sky every summer night. This phenomenon repeated itself again later. An American priest witnessed phenomena similar to the above in 1984.

Regarding the signs associated with the cross on Mount Krizevac, Father Tomislav Vlasic has said, "Several times, with my own eyes I have seen the cross vanish, and instead of the cross, there appeared a white figure, like a silhouette of Our Lady." He affirms that Our Lady told the seers that all of these signs are meant to reawaken the people's faith. "Every day," she also said, "I pray to my Son in front of the cross, asking Him to forgive the world."[9]

The greatest of all the signs is yet to come. It will be left permanently on the mountain of the first apparitions and will be visible to everyone. According to Father Tomislav, all the seers say they have seen this sign in the course of the apparitions and they know the date when it will occur. It will be the source of many miracles and healings. Three warnings will be given to the world before this great sign makes its appearance. They will follow each other within a brief period of time. Three days before each of these warnings, Mirjana will notify a priest of her choosing. The three warnings and the great sign are all a call to faith; to non-believers a call to believe, to believers a call to deepen their faith. The permanent sign will also be a testimony to the authenticity of the apparitions.

Mirjana says that these events are close at hand and that people should open their hearts to God and convert as quickly as possible.[10]

What has been said above about the signs and wonders witnessed at Medugorje does not exhaust the information that has been gathered about the manifestations that have taken place. Enough has been given to convey an adequate notion of this particular means, among the several, that God is using to authenticate the apparitions of the Blessed Virgin at this Yugoslav village.

The rather large number of signs during the first months of the apparitions were given to make these happenings known in Yugoslavia. To judge by the thousands of people who were streaming into Medugorje in a matter of days, this is certainly what has happened. The less frequently seen signs in the sky since the first months would seem to occur more for the benefit of the pilgrims from various countries around the world who have been coming in ever-increasing numbers. Worthy of note is the fact that signs in the sky have been seen not only by Roman Catholics but also by Orthodox Christians and by Moslems.

Because so many of the signs have involved the cross on Mount Krizevac, it has taken on new importance for the people. They began climbing the mountain — a surprising number in their bare feet — to pray there. At the open-air Mass celebrated there on the Feast of the Exaltation of the Cross in 1981, there may have been as many as 70,000 people present. Eventually the police intervened and forbade anyone to go there. In May 1983, however, the ban was lifted. Both the site of the first apparitions on Mount Podbrdo and the cross on Mount Krizevac have become sacred places that are visited by the local people and by pilgrims from other areas and countries. It is no easy climb to reach these places. Given the stress on penance in the Medugorje message, it is easy to discern the providential nature of the selection of these two sites as important parts of the Medugorje event.

Chapter 14

Healings And Conversions

In addition to the exceptional signs described in the preceding chapter, Medugorje has also known the more traditional ones that have always accompanied authentic apparitions. These more traditional ones are healings and conversions.

Physical cures are especially valuable since they can be medically ascertained as humanly inexplicable. It must be clearly understood at the outset that none of those to be presently described have undergone the rigorous sort of medical scrutiny to which healings are subjected by the Lourdes medical bureau. The procedure followed for the examination of physical healings at Lourdes is long and laborious. It is to be hoped that something of this nature will eventually be established at Medugorje, but it is simply out of the question at this time when the apparitions are still going on. The burden on the parish staff is presently very heavy and exhausting.

Some of the cures that are said to have taken place at Medugorje are presented here very simply, without any claim as to their miraculous nature. To declare that any healing is miraculous is a prerogative of the local bishop. The healings that are being reported at Medugorje are nevertheless so numerous and so very definitely a part of the total event that is unfolding there that it is important to include them in this account.

One of the first healings which occurred in the early days of the apparitions is that of "little Daniel." His is one of the better-known cases.

Daniel was born normal and healthy on September 21, 1978, the third child of John and Anda Setka. Four days after his birth, he came down with septicemia. He turned blue, became rigid, and had convulsions. He was taken to the children's hospital in Mostar where he remained for a month. Because his father worked in West Germany, he was taken there for a month. Nothing seemed to help.

The parents also turned to heaven for help. Pilgrimages were made to Saint John of Jace in Bosnia and to Saint Roko. After two years and nine months there was no change in the child's condition. It was then that the parents heard of Medugorje. The whole family, including Daniel, immediately went to the hillside where the apparitions were taking place. His mother and father carried him up Mount Podbrdo, and the father asked the seers to intercede with Our Lady for little Daniel. They replied that they already had too many requests to submit to her and to come back the next day. They did on June 29, 1981, the sixth day of Our Lady's appearances. Afterward Jakov reported that the Blessed Virgin had said that Daniel's parents were to believe firmly and the boy would be healed.

On the way home the family stopped at a restaurant. Up to that time Daniel had not been able to talk, his head had always been tilted to the right, and he could only take one step or two without falling. To everyone's amazement, Daniel tapped on the table with his hand and said, "Give me something to drink." From that time on his speech gradually improved. He began putting words together better and to speak even if not perfectly yet. Then he started to stand up and to walk on a level surface. His walking continued to improve to the point that he could go up stairs normally and run down. He was eventually able to sing.

As of April 3, 1983, although much improved, Daniel was still not able to use his right hand as well as his left, and though he could say anything he wanted, he still could not pronounce his words distinctly. When Father Svetozar left Daniel's house on that April day, after interviewing the parents, he saw the boy kicking a soccer ball in the yard. [1]

In his book Father Rupcic describes fifty-six healings that have been reported at Medugorje. One case he mentions involved two different healings. Jozo Vasilj was born in Medugorje in 1896. Eight years ago he suffered an attack of apoplexy which resulted in loss of sight in his left eye. During the next four years he progressively lost sight in his right eye and became totally blind. He asked Vida Vasilj to bring him two plants, the everlasting and the sage, from the mountain side of the apparitions. That night he placed them under his head. The next morning he put the plants in water and washed himself with it, reciting the Creed all the while. As he dried himself with a towel afterward, he told his wife he could see and proved it by telling her that she did not have her stockings on. For some time his hands had been covered with painful ulcers. One day he went to the parish church and the ulcers disappeared. This took place before the apparitions had moved into the church.

Both of these healings happened in the early days of the apparitions and Father Stanko Vasilj gathered the above information on September 14, 1981. [2] Jozo Vasilj's use of plants from the mountain side of the apparitions as sacramentals is noteworthy. In a good number of the physical healings reported in Father Rupcic's book, plants, flowers, and soil taken from the mountain side and placed or crushed in water were used.

At Lourdes many healings occur when people are bathed in water from the spring which Our Lady pointed out to Bernadette. At Medugorje there is a well near the rectory. People take water from it and put the water in bottles which they place on the table in the room of the apparitions prior to the seers' coming in for the daily apparition. It would be interesting to know the blessings that have come through the use of this water.

An infinitely wise God is not confined to a single way of doing things, and so it is with healings. At Lourdes they do not all take place through the "Lourdes water." Many occur through the Eucharist, at Mass and at the blessing of the sick with the Blessed Sacrament during the afternoon ceremonies. They are also known to have taken place while people were making the Way of the Cross. It happens likewise at Medugorje, where healings have occurred through attendance at Mass and through the Sacrament of Reconciliation.

The most important healings are the spiritual ones, and of course, most of these come about through the Sacrament of Reconciliation.

Grapes and tobacco are the two main products of the region; so it is not surprising that excessive use of both was prevalent. There has however been a significant change in this regard since the apparitions began. More striking is what happened regarding the deep divisions and animosities in the hamlet of Bijakovici where all six seers were born. Small groups of people who live in close proximity to each other frequently develop dislikes and even real hatreds, some of which manifest themselves in acts of violence. Bijakovici had fallen victim to this affliction, but it has cleared up since the apparitions. Father Tomislav Vlasic gives the following description of the spiritual transformation that developed at Medugorje as a result of the apparitions:

> Before the apparitions the people of the parish . . . were annoyed when Mass lasted more than forty-five minutes. After the apparitions they remained in church for three hours or more and after returning home prayed some more. They prayed in the fields, in their cars — everywhere. On the average, all families pray one hour a day.
>
> The churches everywhere here are always full, full of people and especially young people.
>
> Thursday we have an hour of adoration of the Blessed Sacrament after Mass.
>
> The people here fast every Friday on bread and water. Many people and many families fast twice a week. There are some who make a total fast, eating and drinking nothing all day. The only food they take is the Eucharist; yet they work, sometimes at hard labor.
>
> The young people lead the way. They pray and fast more than others.
>
> The people who live here do not ask themselves whether or not the apparitions are true. They say, "We no longer believe; we know. We now have a new life. We do not want to

retrogress. We do not want our previous life with its pains and litigations. Now we are happy and we definitely want to continue this way." [3]

In a subsequent chapter there will be described a meditation prayer group composed of about fifty young people, from fifteen to twenty-five years of age, who have committed themselves to delay any decision on their life's calling for four years, to pray three hours each day, and to fast twice a week on bread and water. In how many parishes could one expect to find young people promising to do this today? The extraordinary spiritual change that has taken place among the young people of Saint James parish has to be one of the most powerful witnesses to the explosion of grace that has occurred at Medugorje.

"You will know them by their deeds" (Mt.7: 16). The spiritual fruit that has come from the apparitions is the best proof of their authenticity. The deep spiritual conversion, the change of heart that manifests itself in a change of life, is the greatest of all the many signs that have been given at Medugorje. As Father John Bertolucci stated after spending five days in Medugorje: "As far as I am concerned, the most powerful thing I witnessed over in Yugoslavia was hundreds of thousands of lives changed for the better. That is the sign that moved me."

Chapter 15

Mirjana Dragicevic No Longer
Sees Our Lady Each Day

An important development occurred on December 25, 1982, when Mirjana Dragicevic experienced her last regular daily apparition of Our Lady. The other five seers to whom Our Lady began appearing in June 1981 continue to see her on a daily basis. The cessation of Our Lady's daily visits was a traumatic experience for Mirjana. She told Father Tomislav Vlasic about this in an interview she gave him on January 10, 1983, while she was still hurting from what had happened. Most of what follows is in Mirjana's own words:

> I was with the Blessed Virgin for eighteen months and became very close to her. I felt she loved me with a motherly love. I was able to ask her questions about anything I wanted to. I asked her about heaven, hell, and purgatory, to explain some things that were not clear to me.
>
> I saw heaven. I did not see hell because I did not want to. I did not see purgatory either, but Our Lady described it to me.
>
> Two days before Christmas 1982, she appeared to me in my room at the usual hour, as she had been doing every day. She said that she would be with me for the last time on Christmas. On Christmas she was with me for forty-five minutes and we talked about many things. We really put everything together into a unified whole. I questioned her about many people, asking her what they should do.
>
> Then she presented me a very precious gift. She said she would appear to me on each of my birthdays for as long as I live. [1] Independently of the sign [2] or anything else *(sic)*, she will

also appear to me when something very difficult happens to me, something that "hurts me bad." She will come then to help me.

But from now on, I have to live my life without her visits, her help, her advice.

I asked her why she has to cease appearing to me and why I had to be the first to stop seeing her. She said she had stayed "pretty long, longer than she needed to . . . *(than)* she intended to." But I have to understand that I am like any other young person, any other girl and that I have to return to living without her.

She also said that I am more mature than the other seers, that I have to help them a lot. I have to be with them, to speak to them. We should understand each other, be united and stay together.

Mirjana feels that Mary's gift of coming to her on every birthday is "something great, marvelous." Our Lady pointed out to her that if questions arise about which she would like answers, she can take them up with her on each birthday. Mirjana experienced much difficulty in adjusting to the decision of Our Lady. It turned out to be a very great trial which saddened and depressed her. It is worthwhile to quote her at length, for the cross which chosen souls are called to carry is a sign of the authenticity of their special mission:

When Our Lady left after her apparition on Christmas day, I sat there. I don't know. Somehow I felt very strange. I thought: It isn't true; she will come again. I will pray again at the usual time and she will come. I experienced a certain restlessness. For example, I preferred that everyone leave me alone. I locked myself in my room and these thoughts would come to me: She will come again; she won't come again. Everything was so distressful. What am I going to do? How am I going to get along without her? What am I going to do?

Then I would pray and pray for a long time. It was as though I was in some kind of a trance. Then, when I would come to myself, I would say: What am I doing this for? She is not there. She will not come. It was terrible, terrible.

In school, everybody was telling me that I had gone crazy. I did not want to talk with anyone. Before this, I would not allow anybody to see that I was suffering about something. But now, since this happened to me about fourteen days ago, I just wanted to sit alone.

In the classroom, I did not know what was going on. If a professor called me, I did not know what was happening. If he said a word to me and asked why I was not listening, why I was doing certain things, I would start crying without knowing why. I was terribly sensitive.

It has been really terrible. Now, little by little, it is getting easier, but it is still difficult.

I am always thinking about her. I will smile, but then immediately I say to myself, She will not come, and this makes me sad. I keep doing this, reminding myself that she will not come and this makes me sad. Really, something is hurting in my soul.

Since Our Lady stopped appearing to me, I pray as follows. If I go to school in the morning, then in the afternoon, at the time when Our Lady used to come, I go to my room, take a rosary, and pray for an hour or two, according to the time that is available to me. Generally, it is never less than an hour.

I ask God to give me the strength to behave normally again. I also pray for unbelievers, for their conversion, and I pray for the secrets.

At this point in Mirjana's interview with Father Tomislav, he asked her if she read Scripture. She said that she did. Then she went on to explain how she prays. A careful reading of her reply indicates that there are two parts to her prayer. She starts with some formal prayer *(she mentions the rosary),* and when she has become immersed in this she finds herself in a simple conversation with God. Then she goes back to the formal prayer which again leads to a conversation with God, and so on for the duration of her prayer time. All her praying is done out loud: her formal prayer and her conversing with God. This is how Mirjana describes her prayer:

When I pray, something comes to me in prayer. I really immerse myself in prayer *(formal prayer such as the rosary),* and this leads me to a point where it is as though I am speaking with somebody. Then I converse and talk with God. Then I go back to praying *(formal prayer)* and from there to conversing. I do all this out loud.[3]

Mostly, I pray alone. Sometimes, my mother comes when

she is home. She works. Also, Sister Marinka and I get together and pray.

The interpretation of Mirjana's prayer as a two-movement process that alternates formal prayer and simple conversation is confirmed in another section of Father Tomislav's interview with her in which she talks about the partial healing of a man from Sarajevo who could not walk. This man wrote to her and she prayed to Our Lady for him.

> Our Lady said that he is a very good believer, but he should pray. He prays, but not for himself. He has to pray precisely for himself, for his healing. Then he prayed and I prayed too. Three months later he wrote to me that he could walk a little. He got on his feet and walked a little with one crutch.
>
> A person must emphasize the particular thing that is being prayed for: "Dear God, I am praying for my healing." You must pray for that. But you must pray from your heart, from the bottom of your soul, with feeling. It does not have to be a *(formal)* prayer, but a conversation with God: "Dear Lord, you see my suffering. You see my condition. I am not complaining. My cross is not too heavy for me, but I would like to be on my legs once again so that I too might see the world." You pray like that. I mean, there should be conversation, then again prayer.
>
> I would recommend that sick people close themselves in with God, speaking with him and praying for an hour every day. I think that would help their souls very much and would bring them grace from God.

Our Lady always recommends faith, prayer, and penance to all the sick. She never requires anything special of a particular sick person; she says the same thing to every sick person. She pointed out that what the person should emphasize is this, "I am praying for this and this." The sick person should pray with his or her soul. Praying should be done devoutly. The Our Father should not be prayed rapidly; it should be prayed devoutly. The main thing is not only to say the Our Father, but to feel it.

Concerning fasting and the sick, Our Lady said that the sick do not have to fast. They could perform some other good deed. For those who could fast, however, because they are not sick, it is not enough to perform some other good deed instead. It is just those whose health does not permit them to fast who can replace the fast with some good deed.

Mirjana was asked if Our Lady demanded that everybody fast on bread and water alone, or if she allowed or recommended different kinds of fasting. She answered as follows:

> We did not talk about that. She simply said that fasting consists of taking only bread and water. We did not discuss whether it has to be like that always. But probably it should be only bread and water for everybody, that is, for those who would like to receive something from God, who would like to have him help them. *(It is clear that Mirjana was only expressing an opinion concerning the need for everyone to fast only on bread and water.)*

Mirjana was asked one other question concerning prayer: does she, now that Our Lady has stopped appearing to her, experience a feeling of her presence in her inner self. Her answer is revealing. It shows that even after Our Lady has stopped appearing to her she is blessed with mystical graces of prayer. In appraising the authenticity of Medugorje it is important to gain a sense of the the spiritual benefits that Mirjana has derived from seeing Our Lady. She states:

> Oh, I do. I did last night while I was saying the seven Our Fathers, etc. I felt that *(presence)* beautifully. It was as though I was praying with her. It was as though I was hearing her voice in my heart, as though it was echoing in me and praying with me. I did not notice anything around me. I simply immersed myself, praying exactly as she does. I heard my voice and hers echoing. I heard this in my soul and not in my ears.

What Mirjana has said about prayer of petition, whether the person praying be sick or well, can be summarized as follows. There are two parts to this prayer. It starts with some formal prayer, that is, with set forms or formulas of prayer such as the rosary or seven Our Fathers, etc. These should not be recited rapidly but devoutly, that is, with one's heart, with feeling. When one has become immersed in this formal prayer, one should engage in a conversation with God, talking with him in one's own words and telling him very simply what one is seeking, whether it be health or something else. This conversation with God should be simple but it should also be done with feeling, with one's heart. Then one may go back to formal prayer and from that to conversation, alternating formal prayer and conversation according to the time available. Mirjana said she prayed like this from one to two hours every day.

Will the other five seers undergo a similar painful experience when Our Lady stops visiting them on a regular daily basis? It would seem that they will and that Mirjana, the "most mature" of the six, has the mission of "helping them" by sharing with them and having them benefit from her experience.

Chapter 16

New Apparitions And New Seers
Jelena And Marijana

A unique happening in the annals of Marian apparitions took place at Medugorje a year-and-a-half after the event started. Without ceasing to appear in the village church, Our Lady began manifesting herself in a completely new way to two new seers.

It all began on December 15, 1982. Ten-year-old Jelena Vasilj[1] was attending a biology class. As she was wondering about the time, she heard a voice that said, "It is a quarter past ten." Mystified, she looked around to find out who had spoken to her. Not having discovered the person, she asked her neighbor what time it was, and her neighbor answered, "A quarter past ten." The teacher then asked a question, and as Jelena was about to raise her hand, she heard the same voice say, "Don't raise your hand; she won't call on you."[2] As before, Jelena did not know where the voice had come from.

A week later Jelena discovered who had spoken to her in the classroom. "By December 22," she said, "I saw and heard the angel who prepared me for the coming of Our Lady . . . He didn't say so, but I knew he was my angel, my guardian angel." He appeared to her for a full week, calling her to prayer and penance.

Our Lady came on December 29, and her first communications with Jelena were like those of the guardian angel in the classroom; they were in the form of locutions. Our Lady spoke to Jelena but did not appear to her. It was not long, however, before she did appear to Jelena and then continued to appear on a daily basis, sometimes even two or three times a day. For these visits Jelena was required to prepare herself by prayer. The first apparitions took place in her room. Some still occur there; others, as will be seen shortly, take place in the sacristy of the church.

On the Feast of Saint Joseph, March 19, 1983, Our Lady began appearing to another very young girl, Marijana Vasilj.[3] Though their family names are the same, she and Jelena are not related. Marijana said that Our Lady's first apparition to her took place in Jelena's house. She and Jelena are close friends. Marijana stated that Our Lady was preceded by a white cloud that disappeared when she came. She was all in white. She wore a crown of stars held together by themselves "without a wire." A rosary was suspended from her folded hands. Marijana said that Our Lord has accompanied Our Lady "maybe three or four times." He had long black hair and wore a grey robe with a red cape. She and Jelena saw his body only from the waist up. He has appeared with a smile on his face, and also without. He has never spoken. Our Lady is the only one who speaks and gives messages.

All of the above information about these two young girls comes from interviews conducted separately with each of them in August 1984. What follows comes from a sermon and a talk, both given by Father Tomislav on August 15, 1983. He is the person closest to the two girls.[4]

The apparitions to Jelena and Marijana differ from those to the other six seers. The first two have "another type of apparition," an "inner" one. They "see with the heart" whereas the other six see the same thing with eyes shut or open. Jelena and Marijana "see Our Lady like in a film."[5] The first vision of Our Lord that Saint Teresa of Avila mentions in her *Life* seems to have been similar to the apparitions that Jelena and Marijana are experiencing. The great Spanish mystic and Doctor of the Church wrote:

> I was once in the company of a certain person, right at the beginning of my acquaintance with her, when the Lord was pleased to make me realize that these friendships were not

good for me, and to warn me and enlighten my blindness. Christ revealed himself to me, in an attitude of great sternness, and showed me what there was in this that displeased him. *I saw him with the eyes of the soul* (emphasis added) more clearly than I could ever have seen him with those of the body and it made such an impression upon me that, although it is more than twenty-six years ago, I seem to have him present with me still.[6]

The present mission of these two girls is complementary to that of the 1981 group, but they were told that later it would be different. Our Lady is using these two girls now for a deeper work of the Holy Spirit. She is not giving them secrets that contain important messages for the world. She speaks to them of holiness. When asked what Our Lady says to her, Jelena replied, "Nothing special. Everything is simple that she tells me — to pray and to fast. Our Lady just tells me that every Christian should try to be holy."

On May 1, 1983, Our Lady began giving Jelena teachings concerning the spiritual life, and told her to write the teachings down because she is to entrust them later to the authorities of the Church. Throughout the entire day, Our Lady guides her in her spiritual life. Jelena can communicate and speak to Our Lady at will. She can ask questions, but only those related to the field of faith. Our Lady told her that all she needs to know is written in the gospel, that she should read and believe it, and that she would find all the answers there.

Our Lady told Jelena that she wanted to bless her each day. "When she comes to bless me," Jelena says, "light flows from her hands. There is something special that emanates from her." What has just been described is a mystical experience that this young girl has difficulty expressing.

Jelena and Marijana pray together every day along with a third young girl who is a close friend of theirs. All three live very near each other in the same hamlet which is on the opposite side of the church from Bijakovici. The third girl does not see Our Lady nor receive messages from her. They pray out loud when they pray together. Someone who knows Jelena well and has heard her pray says that her prayer is beautiful and has very great depth to it.

Our Lady told the girls that in the winter they should pray an hour each day, and they do so late in the afternoon. Because of their work in the fields during the summer, she said that at that time of the year it was sufficient to pray for half-an-hour. In the interview Marijana was asked when she prays during the day. She answered, "In the morning, at noon, and from five-thirty to six." Jelena also prays morning, noon, and late afternoon.

When their late afternoon prayer is over, the three girls go to the church for Mass and the evening services. When these are concluded, they help the sister put away the candles and microphones and then they go into the sacristy, kneel before the two statues that are there, and begin to pray. Our Lady appears to Jelena and Marijana and speaks with them. After she departs, they say three Our Fathers in thanksgiving. The two girls, with the help of the sister who has been with them during the apparition, put on tape Our Lady's message for the parish. Messages that they receive for themselves are not recorded on the tape.

At the end of May 1983, Our Lady told Jelena to inform the priest that she wanted a prayer group in the parish and that she would give rules or guidelines for the sanctification of its members. Others throughout the world could also use these guidelines.

Father Tomislav is the priest who gathered together the members of this prayer group.

Our Lady said she preferred young people because they are free "to totally consecrate themselves to God and to my Heart." Married people have time-consuming family and work obligations. However, anyone who wants to participate in this program can at least follow parts of it.

Our Lady allowed one month for the selection and preparation of the group. Fifty-six young people joined and were told what she expected of its members.

They would have to pray at least three hours a day. They should not be surprised by this. They had not hitherto been able to fulfill their duties because they prayed too little. They should pray at least half-an-hour in the morning and half-an-hour at night. The remaining two hours could be completed at other moments of the day, for example, in the church at the evening service. "I recommend that you go to Mass frequently, every day if possible," she emphasized.

They would have to put off for four years any decision concerning their calling in life.

They would have to renounce everything and put themselves totally at the disposition of God. They must renounce all fear, because if they are abandoned to God, there is no room for fear. All the difficulties they will have will be for their spiritual growth and for the glory of God.

They must fast twice a week on bread and water. When problems arose they would be asked to fast and pray more. (On June 3, 1984, Father Tomislav told Italian pilgrims that the group had been fasting three days a week during the previous three months.)

Finally the group must meet once a week.

The prayer group is made up of young people between fifteen and twenty-five years of age. Marija Pavlovic is the only member of the group of six seers who prays with this group which Father Tomislav calls the meditation prayer group. As mentioned above, she is the most deeply spiritual of the six seers, the one Our Lady has especially called to prayer.

The group meets on Tuesday nights in the basement of the rectory. Jelena and Marijana do not attend the meetings. Until Father Tomislav was transferred from Medugorje to Vitina in the latter part of 1984, he passed on the instructions they received from Our Lady. When he could not attend a meeting, the group prayed by itself.

For the first meeting, Our Lady said that the members of the group should love their enemies. They should not judge, nor bear rancor, nor curse anyone, but bless and pray for them. "I know that you are not able to love your enemies, but I beg you to pray every day at least five minutes to the Sacred Heart and to my Heart and we will give you the divine love with which you will be able to love even your enemies."

For the second meeting, she said: "You have begun to pray three hours a day and this is good. But you keep looking at your watches and worrying about the numerous things you will have to do after the meeting. If you continue doing this, you will not be able to fulfill these duties properly nor will you be able to advance spiritually. You must renounce your preoccupations and be ready so that the Spirit can lead and guide you interiorly. Only in this way can you advance spiritually. When you do this, you will discover that you have the time to complete all your duties and also have time left over."

Our Lady has frequently asked the members of the group to consecrate themselves to her Heart and to abandon themselves completely to her. She also added, "You must begin to pray much for the Holy Spirit to descend on the earth." She has asked the group to spend at least half of the time of their daily prayer petitioning the Holy Spirit to guide the Pope, the Bishop, and all those in positions of authority in the Church.

A month-and-a-half after the beginning, Our Lady told the group: "You have decided to follow Jesus, to consecrate yourselves totally to him. Now, when people decide to follow God totally, Satan comes along and tries to remove them from the path on which they have set out. This is the time of testing. He will try by all means to lead you astray. Satan will tell you: 'This is too much. This is nonsense. You can be Christians like everybody else. Don't pray, don't fast.' I tell you, this is the time when you must persevere in your fast and your prayers. You must not listen to Satan. Do what I have told you. Satan can do nothing to those who believe in God and have totally abandoned themselves to him. But you are inexperienced and so I urge you to be careful."

Our Lady also told them: "Continue your prayers. I shall lead you into more profound experiences. These are limited to this group."

"As of now," says Father Tomislav, "we can write nothing about these experiences and things that the Blessed Virgin is confiding to us. When she tells us, we will then be able to write to anyone who wants to follow this path. Our Lady said she would be happy if all the world followed this path. If it is at all possible, follow this path."

On one occasion when Jelena recited the rosary with Our Lady, she prayed it "as she was taught it in church." Our Lady chided her, "This is not the rosary. You prayed only with your lips. You must concentrate. You must sit down without moving and enter inside." This is basically the same advice Our Lady repeatedly gave the other seers about the importance of praying "with your heart."

Our Lady has given Jelena "a new type of rosary," a Jesus rosary. Our Lady actually recited this rosary with her. It is to be "offered for those in positions of authority in the church." It is prayed at each Tuesday meeting.

A lad who is about sixteen years old and a member of the meditation prayer group has described the Jesus rosary as consisting of reflections on seven mysteries, each of which deals with some aspect of the life of Jesus.

The prayers of the first six mysteries comprise five Our Fathers, one Hail Mary, and one Glory Be. Those of the seventh mystery comprise only three Our Fathers, one Hail Mary, and one Glory Be. For each mystery, there is a short meditation on it, the invocation "O Jesus, be my protection and my strength," a little spontaneous prayer, and singing.

The topics of the mysteries are: 1. The birth of Jesus; 2. Jesus' love for the sick; 3. Jesus' complete surrender to his Father; 4. Jesus' complete surrender of himself in suffering; 5. Jesus' complete trust in the Father; 6. Jesus' victory through the resurrection; 7. The descent of the Holy Spirit upon the apostles.

The above information was obtained in August 1984 by some Americans who attended two of these meetings. They were not admitted inside the room while the meetings took place, but were allowed to stand in the doorway. They said that the meditation associated with each mystery lasted about five minutes, the spontaneous prayer was of short duration with only two or three of the members speaking out, and Father Tomislav spoke to the group at the conclusion of the rosary. They added that during the prayer the lights were dimmed and a quiet meditative atmosphere prevailed throughout the meeting. Even the spontaneous prayers were spoken softly, almost in a whisper.

When asked how much he prayed each day, the young sixteen-year-old lad replied: "Half-an-hour morning and evening, the Angelus at noon, Mass and Bible reading." He added that Father Tomislav's advice to the group was, "Pray, pray, pray, whether you feel like it or not."

Humanly speaking, one would never expect two young girls to be chosen to guide a meditation prayer group. It would seem to be utter folly. God's purpose in doing this is evidently to show us that what is taking place in and through this group is His work.

That which follows has been taken from interviews with Jelena and Marijana:

Interview with Jelena

Did your life change since you have seen Our Lady?
Yes and no. Yes — I pray more and go to church more. No — We are still like other children.

Does Marijana have different messages than you?
They are not the same but they are similar.

Do you hear what Our Lady says to Marijana?
No. *(Each hears only her own message.)*[7]

Do you see Our Lady for the same amount of time every day?
It is never the same. Sometimes it is longer and sometimes, shorter. Sometimes it is only for a few seconds. *(Our Lady can tell her in a few seconds what it would take us a very long time to tell.)*

Do you have any special prayers to say?
The Mass is the best prayer.

Why does Our Lady appear to you?
She didn't say, but I don't think it is because I am especially good.

Interview with Marijana.

What does Our Lady say to you?
Most of all she tells me to pray and fast. And she talks to me about the conversion of people. She says to pray hard for peace in the world because the world is not at peace. She says that prayer is everything and without prayer we can do nothing. These are the most important things she talks about.

Can you ask Our Lady questions?
Sometimes I can. Almost all the time her answer is to pray, fast, and have a strong faith.

Does Our Lady ever tell you to do something for other people or to show them something?
No, except to give them the message to pray and fast and to tell them that prayer is most important.

Does Our Lady tell you how to pray?
You must desire to pray.

Do you write what Our Lady tells you in a book?
No, we tell it to the priest.

What has changed in you since this started?
Now that we see her, we pray more and go to church more. We have more desire to pray.

What would you say to Americans?
To pray and to fast.

Our Lady's messages to Jelena and Marijana must be seen in conjunction with her messages to the other six seers. The very special focus of the messages to the two girls has been prayer and fasting, with a special emphasis on prayer. Jelena: "She said that prayer is everything and without prayer we can do nothing." Marijana: "*(Our Lady tells me)* to give them the message to pray and fast and to tell them that prayer is most important."

Through the six seers Our Lady is seeking to alert the world to the catastrophe toward which it is so rapidly heading and also giving it the means to avert or at least alleviate that disaster. Through Jelena and Marijana, she is issuing a call to personal holiness: "I will carry you on the road to holiness. I want to sanctify you." Those who join the meditation prayer group "have to renounce everything and put themselves totally at God's disposition."

Both series of messages require a conversion, a turning to God. The messages to Jelena and Marijana are a call to a more complete and total turning to God than the messages to the other seers. The call to a deeper interior life seems to be symbolized by the more interior nature of the charism being bestowed on Jelena and Marijana who see Our Lady "in their hearts."

One thing is clear. God is preparing a prayerful people in Yugoslavia. This was already apparent from the original phase of the Medugorje event that began on June 24, 1981. It is being powerfully confirmed through the later phase of that event which started on December 15, 1982. This is a challenging message, for there is nothing the church needs more today than a prayerful people.

Chapter 17

Our Lady's Two Thousandth Birthday

At the end of May 1984, Our Lady told Ivan that August 5 would be the two thousandth anniversary of her birthday.[1] She said that to "console" her, her Son Jesus would present her with "a special gift" of many conversions throughout the world. In preparation for this day, she asked for three days of prayer and fasting.[2]

On July 29, Our Lady spoke again to Ivan about August 5, saying that the important thing was not to talk about it and publicize it, but to pray and fast. If this were done, "her Son would take care of every heart that comes to Medugorje." What Our Lady probably meant by this last phrase was that to be blessed by Jesus it was not necessary to be present bodily at Medugorje, but that it was sufficient to be there spiritually, with one's heart.

The people of Saint James parish responded magnificently to Our Lady's request for prayer and fasting. News about August 5 spread with amazing rapidity in the United States and there were a good number of people in this country who fasted on bread and water for three days prior to that date.

Besides praying and fasting in preparation for August 5, Our Lady told the seers to make that day a day of prayer:

I have dedicated all my life to you through the centuries. Let it not be too much to give that day to me. There will be conversions, changes in the lives of people, in those who are psychologically ill, in sinners. Young people especially will accept me.

August 3

To give the reader some idea of what happens at Medugorje on important occasions, to impart something of the "feel and flavor" of the place at such times, nothing is more appropriate than a report written by Margie Karminski who spent nine days there at the time of Our Lady's two thousandth birthday. While there, she kept a daily log of what happened and wrote her report soon after she returned to the United States.

Margie was accompanied by her husband Stan and daughter Katie and a priest friend. They flew into Split where they hired a car and drove off with their baggage and heavy video equipment.

They arrived in Medugorje on Friday, August 3. As they approached the village, they saw new construction lining the road. On nearing the church, they had to weave their car carefully through the pilgrims that crowded the roads which were lined with buses and cars. The parking lot near the church was packed with buses, cars, campers, and tents.

The church was filling rapidly when they entered at five p.m. and it was becoming difficult to find seats. Confessions were being heard in the confessionals and along the side aisles. Their priest friend was pressed into service for English confessions.

Some pilgrims came in singing hymns in Italian. The aisles were soon clogged with people. So was the wide area between the front pews and the altars, and the steps leading up to the main altar. Pilgrims were streaming in and out of the room of the apparitions, where they prayed, took pictures, and placed articles on the table over which Our Lady appeared.

Loudspeakers allowed the thousands who were forced to remain outside to follow and participate in what was going on within the church. Priests were hearing confessions in a number of places outside the church.

At about six-thirty, Father Tomislav Vlasic led the congregation in the recitation of the rosary. The seers were in the sacristy. After the rosary, they crossed the sanctuary and entered the room of the apparitions. Ivan, Marija, Jakov, and

Ivanka were the only ones there. Vicka, who had a tumor in her head, was not feeling well enough to be present, and Mirjana no longer sees Our Lady. Only priests and sisters were allowed in the room of the apparition. While the seers were in the room, a priest in the church led the people in the recitation of the rosary.

The apparition lasted only a minute or two. When it was over, the seers came out and led the people in the recitation of the Creed, seven Our Fathers, seven Hail Marys, and seven Glory Be's. Then they went into the sacristy.

There were about fifty-two priests concelebrating that night. After they had vested in the sacristy, the Mass started. Prior to that, Father Slavko Barbaric had been obliged to ask the people to move back from the altar. (This had happened also on the Saturday night in October 1983 when the author had concelebrated with about ten other priests.) It is terribly hot during the day in the summer months and the church was like an oven.

The Mass was followed by the Way of the Cross. Three teen-age altar boys with a cross accompanied the priest from station to station. Participation by the people in the praying and singing was excellent, as it had been during the Eucharist. The entire evening service lasted about three-and-one-half hours. The Karminskis returned to their hotel in Mostar where they stayed for the first three of the nine days they spent in Medugorje.

August 4

When they returned to Medugorje on Saturday morning, August 4, they found many pilgrims already milling around. There was a first Mass in Croatian at seven a.m., followed by others in Italian, French, and German. At ten a.m. the priest with the Karminskis said a Mass in English that was heavily attended. The Karminskis met English-speaking pilgrims from the United States, England, Ireland, Holland, and Rome. Sister Janja Boras, who speaks English quite well, had a briefing session after the English Mass and brought the people up-to-date concerning the most recent events.

After the briefing session, the Karminskis went to Potoci to visit a nun they had met on a previous trip. Late in the afternoon, they returned to Medugorje with the nun. The place was already crowded and the church was filled with people. Thousands were sitting, standing, or kneeling outside, around the church. Loudspeakers carried the praying and singing going on within the church to those outside.

Priests were sitting in the fields, on the hay-strewn lawns, on the walk alongside the church, everywhere, all hearing confessions. People waited patiently, then knelt beside the priests. All was done very devoutly and reverently.

Sixty-five to seventy priests concelebrated at the evening Mass. A number of them had to sit in the body of the church. Some of those in the sanctuary had to leave during the Mass because of the steaming heat. Others were fanning themselves and wiping their brows. Father Jozo Zovko, who had been pastor when the apparitions began, preached an inspiring homily. Prayer petitions were made in Croatian, Slovene, Italian, German, French, English, Polish, Dutch, and other languages that were not identified. Priests brought Communion to the thousands outside the church. A priest informed the people that Our Lady had told the seers that night that she was very happy so many people had come and believed.

After the Mass Fathers Tomislav and Slavko and a French priest prayed for healing. Those outside the church followed the prayers broadcast over the public-address system. The rosary was incorporated into the healing service which lasted for an hour. It was nine-forty-five p.m. when everything was concluded. By then it was refreshingly cool outside.

While the four Americans were driving back to their hotel in Mostar, they encountered pilgrims walking home along the dark road about ten miles outside of Medugorje.

August 5

On Sunday, August 5, the Karminskis once again picked up the sister they knew at Potoci. On their way to Medugorje the sister told them that the nuns often used to walk from Potoci to Medugorje, a distance of about thirty miles, starting at three a.m. and getting there at ten. As they drove along, they encountered a man walking alone on the road. The sister identified him as a priest from Mostar whom she knew. He waved to them as they passed by. The sister said he had a car but wanted to walk — a distance of twenty-four miles. It was two p.m. then and about ninety degrees in the shade. About ten miles from Medugorje, they saw pilgrims walking along the road, reciting the rosary. It is estimated that between thirty and forty thousand people came for August 5.

It was two-thirty p.m. when they arrived at the parish church. The priest in their group went to the church to hear confessions in English and to prepare for a three o'clock English Mass. Another American priest concelebrated with him, and many of the Americans whom the Karminskis had seen the previous day attended the Mass. Preceding this Mass there had been one for a very large number of Germans. Since most of them remained for the English Mass, the Karminskis had to squeeze their way to the front of the church.

The sister from Potoci told Margie Karminski that two teen-age girls from Dubrovnik said that around seven a.m. Our Lady had appeared on Mount Krizevac for about fifteen minutes. Her hands were uplifted and she turned slowly. Some people saw her dressed in brilliant white and some, in colors. Sister at first had doubted their story but later believed it when others reported seeing the same things. [3]

That was not the only sign seen on August 5. Signs in the sun were also witnessed later in the day while the apparition was going on in the church. Two women from the United States were kind enough to give the author written accounts of what they saw:

> We were sitting outside in a large crowd of people when someone tapped me on the shoulder and told me to look at the sun. When I looked, the sun was the size of a large dinner plate and it was spinning furiously. I immediately told my sister to look and we both witnessed this unusual phenomenon. This occurred on August 5, 1984, from 6:45 p.m. to 6:50.

> On August 5, my sister and I were sitting outside. The church was too crowded to enter. I was sitting on the ground next to my sister's wheelchair with my eyes closed. It was approximately 6:45 p.m. We prayed the five decades of the rosary and then the litany began.
> Suddenly, my sister said, "Look! Look at the sun!" I opened

my eyes and looked up. It was the most amazing sight. I looked directly at the sun without it hurting my eyes at all. The glare and the rays that it usually emits were gone. As we watched the outer rim, we could see it spinning furiously. It continued like this for approximately five minutes. And then it was over. The glare returned and none of us could stare directly at it any longer.

These two sisters were privileged to witness another sign during their two-week stay in Medugorje in August 1984. Here is the account one of them gave of it:

> One day, we noticed the nuns and the priests kneeling on the ground and looking towards the mountain where the huge cross is. When we looked, the cross had disappeared. About an hour later, the cross was back on top of the mountain.

Margie Karminski said that the villagers have come to accept the frequency of the signs and wonders as normal. They say that these occur about every three or four weeks and last for two or three days. In her account of August 5, she also affirms that some people in back of the church reported having seen the sun spinning during the apparition. Some saw it, and some did not, even though they looked at the sun at the same time.

A young American boy went up to the site of the first apparitions on August 4. The temperature was about ninety-five degrees. Yet there were about a hundred people there in the scorching sun, most of them barefoot, kneeling on the rocky surface and praying the rosary. There was some commotion to the boy's left, and when he turned to see what it was, approximately thirty people were pointing to nearby Mount Krizevac. He looked and saw nothing unusual. When he inquired what had happened, he was told that the cross on top of the mountain had been spinning for about a minute. [4]

On August 5 Father Tomislav presided at a Mass at which eighty priests concelebrated. He spoke of an eighty-year-old woman who had walked 120 kilometers and of a young man who had walked from Belgium and whom the Karminskis had met earlier in the day. He also told of a criminal who had spent ten years in jail on a murder charge and whom a priest had brought to Medugorje on a pilgrimage. Once there, he had cursed and blasphemed and asked, "What am I doing here?" He was taken to the room of the apparitions where he was completely overcome with intense pain from head to foot. The pain was so bad he had to lie down. The pain went up into his head and he suddenly saw every sin he had committed. He cried out, "O my God, what have I done? Now, I must do something to repair my life." He heard Jesus say to him, "You are mine now." His life has completely changed and he goes to Mass and prays every day.

The seers said Our Lady appeared more brilliant than ever. She was glowing and very happy. She said that she was "very pleased at the response of the people to her request" *(for three days of prayer and fasting in preparation for her birthday).* "Thank you for your coming," she said. "Thank you for all your prayers. Continue to pray. Make sacrifices. Convert yourselves. Pray, pray, don't stop praying."

In the interview with Jelena utilized above, she was asked about August 5. She replied that Our Lady "said she had never cried so much." And she actually shed three kinds of tears. First, "three normal tears," next, "three tears of blood" symbolic of her "sorrow," and finally, "three golden tears" representing her "happiness." She was very happy because the people had carried out her requests and "done everything she had asked them to do."

August 6

From August 6 to August 11, the day of the departure from Medugorje, the Karminski group was lodged and fed in the home of a local family. As Stan Karminski spoke Polish, which, like Croatian, is a Slavic language, this assured good communication. Of course, pantomime was used, too. The family — husband, wife, and three children — was well off and lived in a modern two-story house on a rocky slope of Mount Podbrdo. Outside stairs led to the second floor where two rooms were put at the disposal of the Karminski group. All the water came from a cistern on a cliff above and behind the house. It had to be carried by bucket into the house. The toilet was on the second floor. Water for the sink, for the flush toilet, and for baths was stored in the tub. As it had not rained for almost forty days and the cistern was low, this family was jeopardizing its supply by taking in four extra people.

The group entered its temporary home after the evening service. Typical of the warm hospitality they would experience in the days ahead, they found a delicious meal waiting for them. As is the custom there, the father sat at table with the group and the food was served by the mother and a daughter. After the homemade schnapps and wine, there was soup, a salad of fresh tomatoes, onions and dressing, boiled beef and homemade bread. The group would have all its breakfasts — Turkish coffee or tea, bread and sweet cookies — and evening meals with this kind family.

It was learned that the host's father had been one of the young men who had carried on their backs the material with which the large cement cross had been built on Mount Krizevac in 1933. He had just died a few weeks previously at the age of eighty-four. It was also discovered that the hostess had a sister living in the Karminskis' home state of Pennsylvania.

August 7

On August 7, after the Mass and evening service ended, it began to rain. Lightning struck and the power went off, but the rain was a great blessing as all the cisterns in the area were extremely low. Over the weekend, water trucks had come from Mostar to refill the cistern at St. James church since this was the only source of water for the thousands of pilgrims. The people had to leave the church that night by candlelight.

When the Karminski group entered the driveway of their temporary home, they found their host waiting in the heavy rain with a flashlight. Because of the power failure, he had feared they might have some trouble finding their way in the dark. Power was not restored until the next day. That night dinner was eaten by candlelight.

August 9

Thursday, August 9, was a particularly rewarding day for the Karminskis. They had been preparing a video documentary on the apparitions since their first visit to Medugorje in March 1983. They had been able to tape the seers in ecstasy at that time. On their second visit in October

1983, they had also been privileged to tape the seers in ecstasy on two different nights. In March 1984, their daughters, Katie and Theresa, had come to Medugorje and taped the seers in ecstasy twice. Now on August 9 they were again allowed to tape the seers during the apparition. [5]

The Eucharist that followed the apparition was especially well illuminated because a German film crew was recording the happenings. The Blessed Sacrament was exposed for an hour after the Mass.

August 10

Katie and Margie were a little sick during the night. Although their plan had been to climb Mount Krizevac on the morning of August 10, Margie decided it would be better for her to forego the arduous forty-minute climb and get some extra rest.

As the other three members of the group were coming down the mountain, they met a number of people going up. Some were praying the rosary as they went along. All the women were barefoot. Remarkable among them were two who were around fifty years old. Their hostess was among the number going up barefoot. She later told Margie she had climbed the mountain to pray for her, because she wasn't feeling well. Margie said she had to ask herself if she would have climbed the mountain for a stranger who wasn't feeling well. She had climbed the mountain before and knew how steep and rocky the path was. The fact is that Margie was able to sleep until the other members of the group returned to the house. Then she got up and joined them.

After the evening Mass and healing service that followed it, the family with whom they were living was shown the video tape Katie had made the previous evening in the room of the apparitions. They had never seen the young people during an apparition and were amazed and visibly moved at seeing them in ecstasy.

After the video session, there was a meal of bread and water, for this was a Friday. Then the group climbed Mount Podbrdo to the place of the first apparitions. This would be an eventful last night at Medugorje. What took place belongs to a new phase in the Medugorje event and is the subject of the next chapter.

Chapter 18

Renewed Apparitions
On Mounts Podbrdo and Krizevac

Mount Podbrdo

The climbing of Mount Podbrdo[1] by the three Karminskis on the night of August 10 was in keeping with the Medugorje message. It started with some penance. As there is no clearly defined path to the place of the first apparitions, they lost their way in the dark. They climbed over large stones and crawled on their hands and knees under prickly brush. Then they heard singing and tried to head in the direction of the music. Eventually they found the trail, but not before thorns had torn through their clothing and into their flesh.

Upon arriving they found about twenty young people, including the seers, Ivan and Marija, sitting in front of one of the rustic crosses that marked the place where Our Lady has appeared. In front of the cross was a small shrine with candles burning. Also present were people from the United States and Ireland whom the Karminski group had met during the past few days as well as four members of the parish staff.

One of the young people played a guitar as the group sang hymns. Some of the tunes were familiar to American church-goers. After a while the singing stopped and everyone knelt down as Ivan began to say the Our Father, Hail Mary, and Glory Be. This was followed by a long period of silence. Then Ivan and Marija broke the silence with the Our Father and the

Glory Be. There was no Hail Mary this time, for Our Lady had appeared.

The apparition lasted about thirty minutes, and when it was over, a priest began the rosary. All remained kneeling on the rocky terrain. Among the people present was a young lady who spoke English and reported the following information from Ivan. Our Lady prayed with the group and kissed each one present on the forehead. She said that they should pray for Father Tomislav Vlasic. (Quite soon after this, he was transferred from Medugorje to Vitina.)

The renewal of the appearances at the site of the first apparitions has been going on for some time, at least since March 20, 1984. On that day, during the apparition in the church, Our Lady asked Ivan to go to the mountain of the apparitions. He went after the church service and Our Lady spoke to him for an hour. She prayed with him for the Franciscans and said, "Tell the Franciscans that everything will be all right."

On the feast of Our Lady of Mount Carmel, July 16, 1984, Ivan was on Mount Podbrdo with a group of people and at exactly eleven p.m. he began to lead them in prayer. At the second Our Father his voice stopped and there followed a six-minute period of silence. He then told the people that Our Lady had given him this message: "Pray and fast these days. Satan is pressuring someone. I am praying for the Friars in the parish. Let them not be afraid. I know of changes which are to come and when the changes take place, I will be there. Do not be afraid. There will be signs for the people and for sinners, for those who drink and smoke. Young people will accept me again."

A teen-age American was present at an apparition that took place on Mount Podbrdo on the evening of August 6. Here is his account of what he witnessed:

> There were only about twenty people on the mountain that evening, mostly young people. As I would discover later, it was an evening specially prepared by the Blessed Mother for the young people of Medugorje. Since I was only sixteen, the children (Marija and Ivan) brought me along.

We were sitting, singing and praying. Then suddenly we knelt and prayed, saying an Our Father, a Hail Mary, and a Glory Be. After that silence fell upon us. Seconds after the silence began, a wind came up. Also, there was immediately an incredible peace, a stillness which seemingly quieted everything. Nothing was heard for about twenty minutes.

Finally, the children led us in an Our Father and a Glory Be, at which time I realized that the Blessed Mother was appearing on the mountain, for she is the only one in the entire country who skips the Hail Mary while praying.

After the apparition had ended, we blessed ourselves.

The next day, I discovered what had happened. The Blessed Mother had given the children a message, telling them to pray for non-believers. After this she went around, bending down and kissing each of us. Then she blessed us and prayed for us.

Mount Krizevac

The apparitions at Medugorje are turning out to be full of surprises. Not only has Our Lady appeared again on Mount Podbrdo, the mountain of the first apparitions, but she has also started to appear at a completely new site, Mount Krizevac, the mountain of the cross. Both are part of the same mountain range and are not far from each other.

When did Our Lady begin to appear at this new site? The young American just quoted also mentions that Our Lady made it known that she would appear to Ivan on Mount Krizevac on August 4 at "about twelve midnight," but he was sick and not able to go. She appeared, however, on her birthday, August 5, at seven a.m. and was seen by all those camping around the church of Saint James. In that apparition, which lasted fifteen minutes, Our Lady's hands were uplifted and she turned slowly. Some people saw her dressed in brilliant white and others, in color. This seems to be the same kind of apparition that was witnessed a number of times at the cross of Mount Krizevac.

Another American was present at apparitions that occurred on the mountain of the cross on November 7 and again on November 14. He was kind enough to put in writing what he saw on those two nights:

I spent ten days in Medugorje and on two Wednesday nights

I went up Mount Krizevac. *(It takes a good forty minutes to make the steep climb.)* On both nights the Tuesday night prayer group walked up the mountain with Ivan and Marija, saying the rosary as they went along.

When they reached the top, they all sat down together and started singing hymns to the accompaniment of a guitar. They sang for about half-an-hour. Two of the hymns that I recognized were: "Michael, Row Your Boat Ashore" and "When the Saints Go Marching In." Then, they prayed the rosary until Mary came.

On November 7, the apparition to Ivan and Marija lasted about twenty minutes. It was a beautiful night with a full moon.

The November 14 apparition was only five to ten minutes long. That night, it was cold and wet, with light rain falling. Because of the rain, instead of praying after the apparition, as they did the first night, everyone left immediately. They were all able to get down the slippery, rocky mountain path before it started to pour.

On both nights, the young people asked a few questions which Our Lady answered. She also gave some advice.

On the second Wednesday, Our Lady said, "I am happy that so many of you came. Pray two more rosaries in front of the crucifix before going to bed tonight."

On both Wednesdays Our Lady asked that they pray for her intentions, without saying what these were.

These two apparitions underline the important place the rosary has come to assume in the prayer life of the seers and of the young people of Medugorje.

On December 12, Feast of Our Lady of Guadalupe, Our Lady appeared again on Mount Krizevac. The previous day, December 11, "a dance of the sun" took place shortly after three p.m. An American woman who witnessed it has described it. At the time it happened she was behind the church with her husband, a friend from the United States, and an Irishman.

The Irishman asked us *(the three Americans)* to pray with him the beautiful prayer which the angel taught the Fatima children back in 1916 while the Host was suspended in mid-air and the angel was prostrate on the ground. We prayed with him, "O Most Holy Trinity . . ." three times. We again squinted at the sun. We had been squinting at it since we had come out-side to pray, but lo and behold, we could look at it comfortably.

The sun started to quiver and shake as if it wanted to rip itself loose from the sky. It looked like it had a disc covering it which also shook. The natives call this protective disc "the Host." The struggle lasted about half-a-minute and then the sun started to rotate clockwise toward us. It was spectacular and awesome.

My husband — he came to Medugorje believing that the Blessed Mother appears, but nothing else — kept repeating over and over again, "Well, I'll be! Look at that! Do you see that?"

The Irishman kept praising God. I forgot what my friend did, but I know that I couldn't do anything but sit and cry.

The Irishman finally brought us back to our senses when he fell on his knees and started to pray, "O Most Holy Trinity..." We joined in, all the while watching the sun.

It came toward us and then spun back counterclockwise. Our prayers became more fervent and intensified as we kept watching this miracle.

We were just four people, alone behind the church, and God permitted us to see what the people saw at Fatima in 1917. What an inconceivable blessing. It lasted until about 3:40 p.m.

On December 12 this same woman was privileged to witness "the dance of the sun" once again. She was with her husband, a lady from England, and the Irishman of the previous afternoon. Here is her report:

It was around two p.m. We had told the lady from England about the sun miracle of the day before, and she had joined us in back of the church to pray the rosary. After this we again prayed, "O Most Holy Trinity..."

It was about ten minutes before three p.m. The sky was cloudless and the sun's rays were hot. The sun started to quiver and shake and then spin toward us. We praised God and con-tinually prayed the Angel's prayer over and over. The more we prayed, the more spectacular the sight became.

The sun started to spin faster and faster and all of a sudden we could see a beautiful red glow around it. This changed to yellow, orange, and a most beautiful violet. It started back again and it came toward us, again changing colors around it. I looked at the lady from England next to me and all of a sudden saw that she was bathed in the colors that the sun was throwing off. I also saw the ground bathed in red, yellow, orange, and violet.

But, as if that wasn't enough, suddenly the sun jumped across the sky as if it was going down in the West behind the mountain. But just as fast as it jumped over, it jumped back. After that, it zig-zagged up and down.

But I kept quiet. I guess I couldn't believe my eyes.

My husband and the others all saw it too! This spectacle lasted one full hour. After speaking to the people around us, we found out that only two men didn't see it.

This same American woman described what she observed on Mount Krizevac on the night of that same December 12:

We reached the top of the mountain at ten-thirty or slightly thereafter. Some young people, ages sixteen to twenty-five, were already there. One of them had a guitar. A few older people were there also. A trickle of people kept arriving. It was very cold.

It was not long before Ivan arrived with some of his friends. By this time, there was a total of forty to fifty people, a little more than half of whom were young people. There was also one priest from the parish.

Ivan and his friends sat in front of the cross, facing the church below. They prayed and sang hymns. There was more singing than praying. Quite a few women made their way around the cross, praying on their knees as they moved over the stony terrain.

At one point Ivan fell to his knees and everyone became quiet for people sensed that Our Lady had come. Then Ivan began to pray. Again there was quiet. Finally he got up. It was then about eleven p.m. The apparition had lasted two or three minutes.

Our Lady said she was pleased with us and to keep up what we had been doing. She asked that we pray for sinners, especially big sinners. And she blessed each and every one of us.

On Wednesday, January 2, 1985, Our Lady appeared on Mount Krizevac. It was a significant event. Medugorje ex-

perienced one of its worst snowstorms in forty years on that day. It was almost impossible to see, yet Ivan and some members of the Tuesday night prayer group braved the storm and went up on the mountain. Our Lady told Ivan that she was tremendously pleased because they had done this. She said that their coming had made this the happiest day since she had started appearing and that a large part of God's plan had been fulfilled that night.

On Wednesday, February 20, the government took the names of all those who went up on Mount Krizevac. Because of that, Our Lady told those who were there not to come back for three weeks.

Our Lady's pleasure at the effort made by those who came up on the mountain in the snowstorm of January 2 dramatizes the importance of penance and reparation in the Medugorje message. These apparitions on Mount Podbrdo, as well as those on Mount Krizevac, provide occasions for penance. Climbing the steep mountains, and even coming down, is always difficult, even in the daytime.

Chapter 19

A Most Distinguished Visitor

The end of 1984 and the beginning of 1985 saw a most distinguished visitor come to Medugorje. It was His Excellency, the Most Reverend Frane Franic, Archbishop of Split. He had made an earlier visit on December 19, 1981, when he attended the evening service in the church with a scarf around his neck to conceal his Roman collar. He gave an account of his brief visit in *Vijesnik: The Messenger of the Diocese of Split,* in which he stated: "I returned very pleased."[1]

Archbishop Franic's next visit to Medugorje was on December 16-17, 1984. What made that visit especially significant were two interviews with His Excellency concerning Medugorje. One of these preceded his visit by a week and the other took place at the end of his two-day stay in Medugorje. Both interviews are extremely important. Since they are so closely related in time, they shall be reported together.

The interview that preceded His Excellency's second visit to Medugorje, took place on December 6, 1984. It was conducted by *Glas Koncila, The Voice of the Council,* a Catholic paper published in Zagreb, and appeared in the December 16 issue. The more important part of the interview is quoted below:

Glas Koncila — Most Reverend Archbishop, our readers are showering us with questions about Medugorje. They are puzzled by a variety of news items about the alleged prohibition of pilgrimages to that place by our Conference of Bishops and the Holy See.

Archbishop Franic — I was not personally present at the Bishops' Conference of Yugoslavia which issued the statement to the public.

Concerning the Bishops' statement which says that there should be no officially led pilgrimages to Medugorje, I am in agreement with my brother Bishops. It is my understanding that they wanted above all to abstain from final conclusions before an investigation was made by the Church. I am not in favor of curtailing the pilgrimages, but I do think that the pilgrimages should not be officially organized. I am convinced that the Bishops wanted to say that the pilgrimages should not be led to Medugorje in the name of the Holy See or in the name of some diocese. All other pilgrimages should be considered private. And these pilgrimages, as I see during this month, are not stopping. Instead of lessening, they are intensifying. I consider this as positive.

Here I would like to express my own opinion which I state privately as a believer, not as a Bishop but based on my personal conviction that these events are of supernatural origin. This I conclude from the resulting fruits which no one can deny. That is the great intensified prayer, penance, and conversion that the Blessed Mother recommends as a way to peace. The Virgin said the same thing at Fatima as well as at Lourdes . . .

The Virgin is advising and guiding us once again, repeating that which was forgotten of her message at Fatima: penance, prayer, and conversion. This is what is happening daily at Medugorje.

I cannot accept the fear that it may all end up to be a fraud of the devil and that it all rests on wrong assumptions concerning the supernaturality of the visions. Almost every day, I meet up with many hundreds of Italian pilgrims and among them are professors, medical doctors, and other intellectuals. The other day, November 3, the president of the Italian Demo Christian Group was in Medugorje. He climbed the hill, made the stations of the cross, and went to confession. How could I possibly tell all those intellectuals, theologians, and experts that this is all of the devil. . . How they are all going to confession, praying, and being converted. To me, that seems absurd.

I also consider it absurd to expect that pilgrimages be halted until the Conference of Bishops decides whether the apparitions result from God's action or that of the devil. Namely, if these pilgrimages, prayers, and conversions were to be halted, that is, actually strangled, and if all these were to be extinguished, nobody would care whether or not it is from God, since nothing would be there anymore anyway. We might only want to know if it died off by itself or if it was strangled by an unlawful force.

Many of us are trying to explain these events theologically and scientifically. I myself am one of the smallest of these. I am only a witness of my own personal inner conviction. World experts and specialists of every possible description are studying it, often going there privately. The Bishops' Conference should be thankful to God for already having an abundance of literature on the cases studied and for being able to hear the voice of the theological and scientific experts of the world.

If the members of the Commission *(established by Bishop Pavao Zanic of Mostar, in whose diocese Medugorje is located)* wish to act scientifically, they should adhere to scientific methods, namely, examining sources and literature. This is the fundamental methodology of scientific research. The sources in this case are the child visionaries and their messages, the piety of the pilgrims, and the feeling of the people of faith. The literature is what is being written about it. Interviews are necessary, speaking to the pilgrims and observing their faith or their lack of it.

Glas Koncila — There is some apprehension that the visionaries may be intentionally or unintentionally deceiving us. For example, if they really did see the Virgin, they should already in this world be confirmed in grace. Their every sin thereafter would be proof against the supernaturality of the apparitions.

Archbishop Franic — I always said that it is necessary to examine each message separately since there are not even two messages that are on the same supernatural level. There are human imperfections in the minds and hearts of the young visionaries and their contact with the supernatural depends on how well they are able to overcome those obstacles at that moment. These *(obstacles)* could also be suggestions coming from other people. Rene Laurentin told me that he found a statement of Saint Catherine of Siena that the Virgin appeared to her and said that she was not the Immaculate Conception. Evidently, the saint followed the suggestions of her Dominican teachers who at that time before the proclamation of the dogma held that theological opinion. That suggestion was so powerful in her mind that not even during mystical ecstasy was she able to immerse herself so deeply in God as to overcome it. Thus, she substituted a human suggestion for God's word. This is why the messages need to be studied one by one. For instance, those alleged messages *(received from the Blessed Virgin)* concerning the two Franciscans who were expelled from their order. I spoke with them and advised them to submit. In the same manner, I advised the Franciscans in Herzegovina to turn over those seven precious parishes to the Bishop.[2] It would surely please the Madonna if they did. But then, this is where human weaknesses come in.

It is therefore necessary when making examinations to exclude human imperfection and find out the true nucleus, the essence of the revelations. Each message contains its own meaning depending on the exact moment *(when it is given)* and on the degree of the visionaries' readiness. People have their faults. Children remain children and can, when not in ecstasy, say something untrue. They may cheat on something, they may be disobedient or absent-minded in prayer. They are not saints.

Glas Koncila — Are you requesting that these reported private revelations be approached by the methods of biblical investigation?

Archbishop Franic — Exactly. Scientific exegesis should be applied. I observed *(certain things myself)*. And I spoke with some experts, for example, with *(Father)* Laurentin, with Father *(Michael)* Scanlon, who is president of a Franciscan University *(Steubenville)* in the United States, with Father Teodozije, a great mystic in Rome, and also with some French theologians. They all agree that these phenomena should be seriously investigated and not spoken of beforehand as being an hallucination. An hallucination lasting three years would certainly destroy even the most healthy mind. If the children have been suffering from hallucinations for three years and have remained healthy, this would already be a miracle.

Two days ago, some Italians who were at my place told me that 139 documents relative to healings had already been collected. A Jesuit in Naples, Father Massimo Rastrelli, told me about a lady's healing from cancer for which they were gathering documentation. Of fifty registered cases, twenty-five have been selected for further investigation. Once I had seventeen specialists from Milan with me, some of whom were university professors, who had examined the children during the ecstasies with a variety of electronic instruments. Here then, in a word, is my own personal conviction.

Glas Koncila — It is said that it would be prudent for the church authorities to forbid the children to lead the praying of the seven Our Fathers and the Creed and to prohibit their coming together in the church for the apparitions.

Archbishop Franic — Look, this is not happening in my diocese. The local bishop is the competent and responsible authority. I do not know whether or not the Bishop of Mostar will prohibit the Madonna's appearances in the church and forbid the children from leading the prayers of the Our Father. If he does do this, then I will submit to it. While it is open and free, I take it that any priest as well as any bishop may go there as a private believer and pray.

The interview that took place at the end of Archbishop Franic's second visit to Medugorje was conducted by the Franciscans. Only the more pertinent parts of the lengthy interview are quoted here:

Interviewer — Most Reverend Archbishop, I would like to use this opportunity to talk with you. Every visitor who can help us govern ourselves here is precious to us. Is there anything you would like to say?

Archbishop Franic — The first time I could be present with the visionaries during an apparition was on December 16 and 17 . . . During these two days with you Franciscans, I find you have been accused here and elsewhere in the world of being the main perpetrators in orchestrating and manipulating everything. Some of your adversaries admit that people are coming, receiving the Sacrament of Reconciliation, and converting; but they believe that to be the fruit of the faith of the people of Herzegovina, people of the mountains, who are unspoiled. They believe you Franciscans are intervening in order that, in your disagreement with the Bishop, you may get the parishes you feel you are entitled to. Therefore, you are considered to be manipulating the faith of the people and the pilgrims for your material gain and for your prestige in order to remain the leaders of the people, as in the past, without having to share that role with the Bishop and the secular clergy. I have observed none of these features in the Franciscans of Medugorje, your only goal being to respond to the call which you feel in your souls for conversion and for the glory of God. I have seen a great piety in you. Last night I told a Portuguese priest here that I found the Franciscans to be polite, pious, self-denying, and working only for the glory of God and the salvation of souls. Therefore, I reject these objections . . .

Our Lady is appearing here. That is my conviction. I saw the children twice during the visions and I also visited them in their homes. I must say that these visits to the homes of Vicka, Marija, little Jakov, and Ivan convinced me even more.

I saw Ivan. I saw that he has a life's dream and that he, as a man, will find his way in life. My meeting with the visionaries surprised me very much. My personal impression of them is very good. For example, Ivan did not succeed in the seminary, but I see he knows where he is going. God is showing him the way into the future and, obviously, with his cooperation.

Vicka is a direct and open type. She is sharp, but sincere, in her expressions; and she has her calling. I believe Our Lady is relating her life to Vicka, who is faithfully recording it. She talks about her illness or illnesses as something unessential, even though they are serious. She passes it off lightly — I was surprised. She looks at her calling only in the supernatural light. She is mature for her age and has preserved her own nature. I do not see anything bad in her. I can only say that grace is leading her, Our Lady is leading her.

Visions like these are the lowest kind of charisms. The work of the Holy Spirit is present there. I am convinced by the training of the children. All of them show a great maturity. Little Jakov made a very good impression on me, especially during the apparitions and in his home. He is very sober and, at the same time, very lively. He is a dear little boy, mentally healthy and likeable.

Marija recovered from an illness which could have ended in an unusual way. She is also bearing that as if it is nothing. She speaks about illness and health as if the two are the same. Let only God's will be done. She is so resigned in all this that it is obvious that she is open to the Holy Spirit. I have to conclude that the Holy Spirit is leading her, and leading her according to her own nature.

Interviewer — We were speaking about Marija. She is one of the most precious souls who, like a seismograph, reacts to all the impulses of the Spirit. She is entirely open to God like a glass which receives everything that the Lord tells her.

Archbishop Franic—Yes, that is true. Marija is like that. She is like that by nature. We know every character is capable of holiness. Each has its own expression, and it does not necessarily mean that she is on the highest level of holiness if she is like that. However, she does manifest a greater depth in her relations with people, a greater kindness; or it may be that her behavior pleases us more. Her gentleness is completely feminine and wholly Christian.

She gave me a prophecy. On December 17, the day of my episcopal consecration, she asked Our Lady a question. On that day, very privately, I celebrated the thirty-fourth anniversary of my episcopal consecration with a Mass which I led in Medugorje. I was completely incognito. No one mentioned that I was an archbishop but simply a priest among other priests. I asked Marija if I would be imposing too much to ask Our Lady if she had a message for me. I expressly said that I would be happy if she would give me some admonition for my conversion; if she would point her finger at my weaknesses and tell me where I need to be careful and where I need to improve. However, I received word that, from this day on, greater suffering is expected of me and that Our Lady will be with me in that greater suffering. It will probably be a reaction to my stand regarding Medugorje. I have already seen this in Rome and at home also. However, we will see what happens.

We also visited Jelena and Marijana. They are not in the group of visionaries. They made an even greater impression on me because they have inner locutions. Through these, the truths of the faith are being explained, but in a deeper way. There, everything is together; the visions and locutions are united. But the locutions are on a higher level of experience. They are on an intellectual level and give the impression of a greater reflectiveness and inner experience than *(the apparitions)* of the visionaries.

In a word, I would put all this into the framework of the spiritual renewal in the Church which Mary started in Lourdes and in Fatima. Mary can't do anything without the Holy Spirit. She wasn't able to conceive in her womb and in her heart, without the Holy Spirit. As St. Augustine said, "first she conceived in her heart with her faith, and then in her womb with her body." All this happened in her through the Holy Spirit. And today in the Church, she cannot give Christ to the world without the Holy Spirit. Therefore, the Holy Spirit is leading the renewal of the Church through Mary. She is not a goddess from whom we are expecting salvation. She is only an intercessor, a mediator between us and God and Christ. Her apparitions and the signs of her motherly love come from the Holy Spirit who, together with Christ, is embracing the world. Through the direction of the Father, she is giving love to the world and redeeming it. Therefore, I especially see the work of the Holy Spirit in the charism of locutions, communicating with words and inner messages. I am convinced that the same Spirit which is working in them is working in all the renewal movements in the Church.

I would especially like to emphasize that the young, of whom there are a good number in Split, say that they have received an impetus for prayer in Medugorje. In Split, they have adoration every Thursday at Saint Philip's. They also have Mass every Saturday where they pray in their own way. They say that in Medugorje they have received a call not only to come to the religion classes but also to pray together and celebrate Mass. Therefore, this is something that has grown here, grassroots. This is real faith, real Church — Pentecost. This is de-politicized Church, Church which is looking not only for the glory of God, to give him thanks and praise, but also is endeavoring to save people. This is the Church which, through Christ's saving work, is bringing people to God, spreading his kingdom, and leading them to the eternal kingdom.

We know that the early Church emphasized prayer, prayer meetings, instructions, and catechesis. For many centuries, the Church was led through instruction at prayer meetings. I see the future of the Church in this. And I see a new Church being born in front of our eyes, the Church of the Holy Spirit, the Church of Jesus Crucified and Risen.

However, when the Spirit comes among us, we do not recognize him. We have become so crystallized in our classical pastoral work that when the Holy Spirit brings us new ways, we do not understand them. I do not see any discrepancy between Medugorje and the Holy Spirit who is working in different ways in our Church and in the world. I see continuity in Medugorje and the culmination of all his ways.

I absolutely never expected that the whole world would be attracted to and touched by Medugorje, which, to my great surprise, has become the culmination of the working of the Holy Spirit. I see that Our Lady is calling all of us to come here from different countries to recognize brothers and sisters in each other. In that way, we who are different communicate with each other and, under the embrace of Our Lady, recognize each other as real brothers and sisters. We are becoming one because faith is bringing us closer to each other.

I especially see the importance of the role of Medugorje in the ecumenical work of the Church where Our Lady is bringing us closer, uniting us with our brothers from the Orthodox church, the Moslems, and even our brother Marxists. Our Lady is spreading only love. She is the mother of all and she is teaching us to love even at moments when we feel that our brothers do not understand us and interpret us falsely. One can conclude, according to what is happening here, what is being talked about here, and what the children say, that one universal love is being born here through the gospel, which is recommending that we love all men even when it seems they are our enemies.

I believe the main thing for those of us who respect Our Lady of Medugorje is to strengthen our faith in God and in man. I believe that we have to be ready for suffering and lack of understanding, to spread love even where we do not find it, so that the message and victory of Our Lady are not defeated but become the salvation of everyone.

Personally, I return from Medugorje with a firm conviction that I should never allow anxiety to arise in me toward priests or believers who think differently. I desire to remain always in the frame of mind which I experienced during these two days with you Franciscans who are working here day and night, hearing confessions, preaching, teaching people how to pray to God through meditation and liturgy. The central place is preserved for the sacraments and for evangelism.

Interviewer—I would like to ask a few other things. I would like to return to the dimension of the visionaries' sufferings. Jakov's and Ivanka's mothers died. Vicka and Marija have unusual cycles of illness and attacks. And really, they talk

Mount Podbrdo, site of first apparitions

The path up Mt. Podbrdo

Looking toward Mt. Krizevac (center peak)

The cross on Mt. Krizevac

Fr. Tomislav Vlasic preaching at the cross on Mt. Krizevac

The path up Mt. Krizevac

The lower slope of Mt. Podbrdo overlooking Bijakovici and
the village church of St. James

Church of St. James,
site of daily apparitions
from early January,
1982 until April 2, 1985

Waiting for the seers in the small room of the apparitions

The seers entering the room
of the apparitions

Peeking into the room
of the apparitions

The room of the apparitions

Vicka, Ivanka and Mirjana

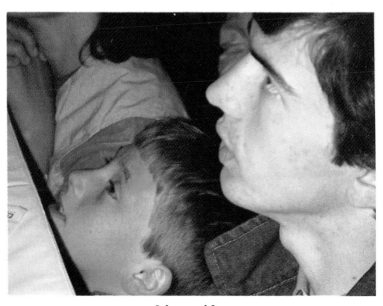
Jakov and Ivan

Jakov, Ivanka and Marija

Marija

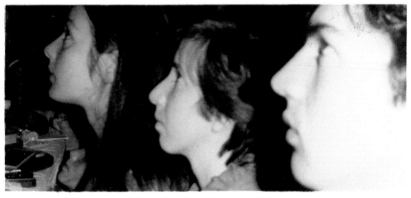

Jakov, Ivanka, Marija and Ivan

Marija and Ivan

Marija, Ivanka, Jakov and Vicka

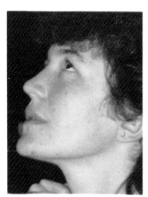

Vicka

Jakov

Jakov, Ivanka and Marija

Vicka and Ivanka

Jakov, Ivanka and Marija
People place articles on table before the apparition

Concelebrated Mass following apparition

Confession in the open

Overflow crowd

Archbishop Frane Franic of Split concelebrates Mass in room of apparitions, January 1985

The rectory (room to the right) where the daily apparitions have been occurring since April 2, 1985

Archbishop Franic speaks with Vicka, January 1985

Vicka, Jakov and Ivanka

Ivan, Marija, Jakov and Vicka

Jelena Vasilj who had a locution (words without any vision) with Our Lady on December 29, 1982 and to whom Our Lady appeared a short time afterwards

Marijana Vasilj to whom Our Lady first appeared on March 19, 1983

about these things as being normal or as what must be.

Archbishop Franic—I see that they look at things in terms of eternity. I was impressed by the way they talk about illness and suffering. It seems to me that they would even accept death in this simple way, with complete self-surrender. And we know they are still very young.

Interviewer—I have personally urged Marija to go with me to a doctor. Almost crying, she responded to me: "God has his plan as well." I told her: "Marija, unless you know that you will rise like a deer tomorrow, I have to tell you to go to a doctor today."

Archbishop Franic—Because they are in contact with the other world, it seems to us that they behave strangely. They should be instructed that God has given us an intellect to use. This should be considered because it might end in fanaticism.

Interviewer—I must tell you about yesterday when Marija said, in a completely incidental manner: "You know, I wish to offer to my dear God, for the intention of the Bishop, all the suffering that comes to me because of him. The Lord is asking me for this sacrifice for him so that peace and love may come among all of us." Her look, her intention, the offering and sacrifice of her own life, of her own sufferings, is something exalted.

What stand should we take toward those who are attacking us? Should we be silent or should we respond?

Archbishop Franic—There should be an information center for events in Medugorje so that people will know what is happening there. Things should be explained in a very peaceful way, with no attacks, but only good information. This would help you, me, and all those of good will. Sometimes we receive information which, in itself, is bad because it is false. We have to find a good solution for this.

Interviewer—You have already said that, globally, you do not see any theological difficulties with the report of the Commission *(of investigation established by the Bishop of Mostar)*. We asked what these difficulties might be. In spite of all our efforts, it seems to me we could not find any difficulties. Laurentin also asked what the difficulties were about. What do you think?

Archbishop Franic—I know that the best experts were not able to find any difficulties. Our Lady has not come to divide parishes. I believe that justice demands that the Holy See be obeyed. I believe that the two Franciscans who were expelled from the Order should submit and start their rehabilitation. After all, the Church has given her discernment.

I think the disciplinary objection is not in direct connection with Medugorje, but some adversaries, outside and within, are connecting the two. If this gets resolved, every objection, and even the possibility of objection, would be removed. Some people cannot understand that the Holy Spirit would be directly engaged in the Church in this extraordinary way. We know that the Holy Spirit is the soul of the Church and that He leads the Church through the hierarchy. That's true. But, He also leads it directly. He gives his active graces and He gives direct inspirations to the people in the form of active graces. These inspirations can be in a visible form, like the visions, or in the form of inner locutions, prophecies, and miraculous healings. It is the same Holy Spirit who gives different gifts.

Again, the Holy Spirit directs everything through gifts, charisms, which were important not only for the early Church but also for our contemporary Church. Some people still do not understand. They think that this is some kind of fiction, fanaticism, or unbalanced piety. But it is, in reality, traditional prayer and piety.

Interviewer — Some who find this a serious objection have posed the question: "How is it possible that Our Lady is appearing every day?"

Archbishop Franic — This is the work of the Holy Spirit and it is not something entirely new. For example, P. Amroth, the editor of the leading Marian magazine in Italy, *Mater Dei,* said that Saint Veronica Juliani had daily visions of Our Lady all her life.

Interviewer—Then wouldn't it be better to ask "Why?" and not "Is it possible?"

Archbishop Franic—Yes, that should be asked. And Mary has answered that already: peace and reconciliation. This is most important to us today, too, because we have been wounded by our contemporary way of life and by the difficulties and ideologies which affect us. Families have been damaged as well as societies and international relations. The danger of a horrible war is threatening. What do you need more than peace and reconciliation? Everything else revolves around that!

Interviewer—Many people, especially our Bishop, are

perplexed by the talk about the great sign in Medugorje. Every week, I speak with the visionaries in the name of the parish. I have asked them a number of times about the sign. They always say: "Our Lady instructed us. We have seen it. We know. There is no need to worry. As for us, we must pray and fast." They say that there would have been other signs if we had accepted the messages better and if Our Lady had not found so much resistance.

Ought we to understand the talk about the great sign in terms of the Apocalypse?

Archbishop Franic—The Apocalypse does talk about the great sign: a woman, clothed in the sun, appears in the skies with a dragon opposing her. Maybe the sign is beginning to be realized in this way. When the prophets spoke, they did not know what they were saying in their prophecies. For example, prophets in the Old Testament spoke about Christ as King of Kings. Were they able to know that He could be a King on the Cross? They did not comprehend properly what God was saying throughout time.

The talk about the great sign is prophetic language. When the children speak, they do not understand many of the things they say since they did not study theology. Therefore, we are here to explain all their expressions about the words, messages, signs, and so on. This cannot be done too literally because that could lead to fanaticism, nor can it be rationalized because that would be from the other world.

Archbishop Frane Franic's next visit to Medugorje occurred on January 23-24, 1985. On January 23, he was in the room of the apparitions during the ecstasy of the seers. Among the other people who witnessed the apparition were some priests from the Archbishop's diocese of Split and a priest from the United States. Ivan, Marija, and Vicka were the only seers present that evening. Our Lady gave a special message for the priests who were there. In the sacristy, Vicka relayed the message Our Lady had given for the priests: "I am pleased with the presence of these priests and assure them of my love, patience, and maternal tenderness." One of the priests from the diocese of Split spoke English and translated it for the American priest who relayed it to the author.

On January 23, a young lady from the United States was

walking near the church when the man of the house where she was staying called out to her and told her to look at the cross on Mount Krizevac. She looked and saw that it was a brilliant white. She saw it that way for about ten seconds. She said that the sky was overcast and for that reason the brilliancy of the cross could not be attributed to the sun. The man told her that the cross had been that way for twenty minutes and that he had been looking for her to tell her about it. He added that he had not seen it like that for six months.

"There will be signs," Our Lady had said on the Feast of Mount Carmel. A number of them have been described in this book. Were there others? It is likely that there were.

On January 24, the Archbishop was once again present at the evening apparition in the church. Our Lady had a special message for him. One of the seers transmitted it to him immediately, while he was still in the room of the apparitions. He was told that Our Lady had come over to where he was sitting, had given him a blessing, and had said that she wanted him to be assured of her continued prayer. The American priest was also present at the apparition. He said that the Archbishop was visibly moved. "Elated" and "like a humble child," he got up and embraced all the priests who were present in the room with him.

Chapter 20

Renewal In The Holy Spirit At Medugorje

What role has the charismatic renewal played in the Medugorje event? It would be easy to assume that the charismatic renewal has manifested itself at Medugorje in the same way it has in the United States and, therefore, to attribute to it a role in what has developed there that it has not really had. To do so would be to misunderstand its role. Perhaps the cause of such a misunderstanding lies in a misinterpretation of the facts or in a too selective choice of them. They did seem, initially, to point to a strong influence of the charismatic renewal; but after careful scrutiny the evidence does not support the theory of an influential role of the charismatic renewal in what is transpiring at Medugorje.

The apparitions can be said to have had their origin in Rome at The International Leaders Conference of the Catholic Charismatic Renewal held in May 1981. The person most involved in this was a "charismatic" priest from Yugoslavia, Father Tomislav Vlasic, who was prayed over for the healing of the Church and was given a prophecy concerning the apparitions. Father Tomislav was later put in charge of the spiritual direction of the group of young people seeing Our Lady. One of his statements on the renewal of the Spirit is very suggestive of strong influence: "Once I asked Our Lady through the seers if it was good to have a prayer group in this parish and to bring them into the renewal of the Spirit. *(Her answer was:)* 'It is good, and not only in the parish of Medugorje, but it should be everywhere in all parishes.' "[1]

A prayer group was started in the parish and all the seers are said to have been baptized in the Holy Spirit.[2]

Some of the priests and sisters who staff the parish of Saint James are also said to have been baptized in the Holy Spirit.

The last group of facts in support of the view of a primary role of the charismatic renewal at Medugorje concerns healing. Teams composed of a seer and a few other persons prayed publicly over people in the church each night after the Eucharistic celebration in very much the same fashion as is done in the United States after charismatic prayer meetings. Finally, Our Lady gave the seers specific instructions on how to pray over people for healing.

On the basis of all these facts, it would seem normal to think that the charismatic renewal has played an important part in what has gone on at Medugorje. It must be recognized, nonetheless, that despite the vital role of the Holy Spirit in all the Medugorje activities, the charismatic renewal as it is known in the United States has not been a significant factor.

It is important to realize that Father Tomislav joined the parish staff only after the apparitions had been going on daily for about two months. Neither Father Jozo, nor any of the Sisters were "charismatic." It is Father Tomislav who introduced the charismatic renewal in Saint James parish. He arrived there only on August 18, 1981, after Father Jozo had been imprisoned. This is the answer to those who have expressed the fear that the apparitions might have been a subjective response to enthusiastic charismatic influences. If Father Tomislav could ever have been described as enthusiastic about the charismatic renewal, that description does not fit him today.

An important characteristic of the charismatic renewal is the manifestation of the charismatic gifts. This usually occurs through the members of a "prayer" group. What is not generally known is that Father Tomislav has some apprehension about these gifts. While admitting that there are "some" of these gifts at Medugorje, but "not many," he says, "It would have been better for us had there been none." His main apprehension concerning the gifts would appear to stem from the special situation in which he finds himself. "The people and the priests are not able to understand these gifts," he explained. "They would only be obstacles for the priests, given that many of them say that the charismatic movement is something parapsychological," and people "would say that priests have brought or imported parapsychological phenomena into Medugorje. So, now they say it is Our Lady and this, according to me, is better. . ." He also raises the issue of the leadership of the prayer group: "If a leader does not pray enough, then to belong to such a group is not very important."

Another danger Father Tomislav sees in the charismatic movement is the danger of an exclusivist or elitist attitude on the part of those who participate in it. This results in exaggerating the importance of the movement and looking down on those who do not participate in it. He believes that this restricts freedom and is not in keeping with the great respect for freedom which Our Lady has manifested at Medugorje. As he has expressed it: "Here, I have seen that Our Lady never brings a recipe to anyone. If a person inquires: 'What shall I do in this situation? Shall I follow this vocation or that vocation?,' Our Lady never replies otherwise than: 'You must decide.' " This was the case of the seers who asked her if she wanted them to follow a religious vocation.

"So," Father Tomislav concludes, "we now work here on universal principles that are fundamental to Christianity: prayer, fasting, love, and peace. It is our wish that everyone be able to participate: the old and the young, all on this wide path. The prayer groups, the charismatic groups, the meditation groups would be groups to deepen faith, to bring all this to the people, to bring them a deeper spiritual life. I say, according to me, it is not important to belong to a charismatic group. It is not very important, but it is very important to let the Spirit live within us."

Although Father Tomislav has reservations about the charismatic movement, he is well aware of the importance of the Holy Spirit in our spiritual life. He pointed out that Our Lady has stressed this in her messages to the seers: "In this year *(1983)*, Our Lady asks us to pray and fast so that the Holy

Spirit will descend on earth. It is a matter of renewal in the Spirit of the entire world. It is not only a matter of prayer groups."[4]

It would seem that Our Lady is counting especially on the "meditation prayer group" for the deeper work of the Holy Spirit at Medugorje. In August 1984 it was definitely the only prayer group in the parish.

Father Tomislav develops this point in his August 15, 1983, interview:

> People wonder why Our Lady told us to pray seven Our Fathers, Hail Marys and Glory Be's, and the Creed and why she says one should pray the rosary. What I have understood is that Our Lady is giving concrete means which are accessible to everyone.
>
> Often Our Lady underlines that it is not good to pray seven Our Fathers or any other prayer, with the lips, but that one has to pray with the heart. So one day she asked the people to pray three Our Fathers, Hail Marys, and Glory Be's in order that the Holy Spirit might descend on the earth, but to pray them at least for fifteen minutes, that is with the heart . . .
>
> Our Lady prayed with one seer *(Jelena)* and taught us a rosary of Jesus Christ. It is a meditated rosary with spiritual songs and spontaneous prayers and also with Our Fathers, Glory Be's, and the Creed.
>
> One can see that Our Lady has given practical means to people *(means adapted to their capacity),* and to those who have advanced in the spiritual life, in meditation, she has also given concrete means *(i.e. the meditated rosary).* [5]

One has to see Father Tomislav's coolness toward charismatic prayer groups in its proper perspective. He finds himself in a very special situation. He is in a parish where, at a moment of great crisis, apparitions bring a message to a world faced with a catastrophe of staggering proportions. Nothing must be allowed to distract from this central fact. The charismatic gifts that manifest themselves in prayer groups could divert attention from the apparitions at Medugorje if they were significantly manifested there. God is doing something unique in this humble village. The charismatic renewal at Medugorje must be viewed in that light.

Father Tomislav's attitude toward charismatic prayer

groups must not be allowed to obscure the fact that Our Lady did say it would be good to have a prayer group at Saint James parish and that all parishes should have one. Also, part of Our Lady's message at Medugorje is "praying and fasting so that the Holy Spirit will descend upon the earth."

The meditation prayer group and the spiritual directives Our Lady gives for the personal sanctification of its members are very enlightening and help put the apparitions to the six young people in proper perspective. Everything at Medugorje seems to encourage personal holiness. During the second phase of the apparitions to the six seers, Our Lady concentrated on giving personal spiritual guidance to all members of the group. That in itself was an indication of what Our Lady was seeking above all at Medugorje.

The simple folk of Saint James parish and indeed of the entire area have evidently sensed this, as is manifested by the almost unbelievable spiritual transformation which has taken place and which so deeply impresses all who go there. The love of these peasants for the Eucharist, as evidenced by their attendance at daily Mass, their monthly three days of intensified prayer, penance, and confession that end with the Feast of Reconciliation, their outstanding practice of the great virtue of love, as shown through forgiveness among themselves and through generous kindness and hospitality toward visitors, their frequent fasting on bread and water, all these things show that these people are rapidly becoming a holy people. None of the major Marian apparitions of our era have produced such results. God is truly doing something new at Medugorje.

This amazing outpouring of God's love has a sobering aspect to it. If the magnitude of this outpouring of God's love is the measure of the catastrophe that menaces the world, then this catastrophe is great indeed. People would do well to remember what happened when the heavenly warning given at Fatima was not heeded.

In an interview which Father Tomislav Pervan graciously gave the author[6] through an English-speaking interpreter, he very clearly attributes what is happening to the parishioners at Medugorje to the work of the Holy Spirit:

Here, we are going back to the Holy Spirit. Here, there is no emphasis on the gifts of the Holy Spirit. The gifts of the Holy Spirit are not as important as the life. You have to live the life according to the Holy Spirit and if you live the life according to the Holy Spirit, you will receive the gifts and the fruits of the Holy Spirit.

Something that indicates that the charismatic gifts have been far from featured is the experience of Father Emilien Tardif at Medugorje in August 1983. Father Tardif is the priest who prayed over Father Tomislav Vlasic in Rome in May 1981 and who received the prophetic message: "Do not worry, I am sending you my Mother." He came with Father Pierre Rancourt, a Canadian missionary of the Sacred Heart, and with Doctor Philippe Madre, a member of the French charismatic community of the Lion of Juda. They arrived in Medugorje on August 23. Their intention was to "stir up the charisms, especially the gift of healing" which had already manifested itself at Medugorje. They planned to spend some time there. They were so successful and there were so many healings that word of their activities quickly reached the police who became alarmed and arrested them on August 25. They were freed the next day at 1:30 a.m. and told to leave the country by midnight or they would be incarcerated. They were also forbidden to return to Yugoslavia for a full year.[7] This episode is more eloquent than words and clearly corroborates what Fathers Vlasic and Pervan said about the low profile of the charismatic gifts in Medugorje. One has to wonder if it were not for the best that the "awakening session" did end quickly; thus attention was not diverted away from the apparitions of Our Lady.

It is certain that the Holy Spirit is very active in Medugorje through the spiritual guidance that is flowing from the apparitions to the original six seers and to Jelena and Marijana. There are, however, two other less evident factors from which much can be drawn out. These are the role of the priests and the devotion of the people to Mary.

The parish staff of priests and sisters forms a single community with the parishioners. The spiritual leadership of this parish family is indisputedly in the hands of the priests who exercise it with wisdom and love. Father Tomislav Vlasic is a key person. He directs the six seers and is very much involved in the various kinds of prayer that go on in the parish. His very important role in the apparitions, and especially in the accompanying outpouring of the Holy Spirit, was prophesied at Rome when he asked to be prayed over for the healing of the Church. It will be remembered that the part of the prophetic message concerning him came in the form of a mental image or vision. He was seen sitting on a chair surrounded by a vast throng and streams of water were seen pouring out to the people from beneath his chair. He was being told that in the forthcoming apparitions of Our Lady at Medugorje he would be used powerfully in bringing to people "the rivers of living water" (Jn 7:38) that would flow so abundantly there.

Although Father Tomislav's role has been very important, the entire parish staff is involved in various capacities in what is taking place. Sister Janja Boras, for instance, is very close to the girls involved in the apparitions. The renewal in the Holy Spirit at Medugorje is an excellent example of what happens when a parish renewal is guided by its official spiritual leaders. It also illustrates how a renewal prospers and bears abundant fruit when Mary is duly recognized and honored, when people involved in the renewal not only have great love for her, but also openly manifest and express that love. This is a vital lesson that is being taught.

Father John Bertolucci was deeply impressed by what he saw at Medugorje in March 1983 when he visited the home of one of the parish families. Shortly after his return to America, he gave a talk on March 26 at the New York General Charismatic Conference. The talk was entitled "The Grace of Pentecost." In it he gave this witness to the new insight he received in Yugoslavia concerning the importance of Mary's role in the plan of salvation:

I have to tell you something burning in my heart. I just came back from Yugoslavia . . . I went over there because of something happening that just awes me . . .

We were asked by the Charismatic Renewal Office in Rome to take our television team which produces the weekly program "The Glory of God" . . . to film the phenomenon taking place in the province of Herzegovina among a whole group of Roman Catholics who are of Croatian ancestry . . . We went to film what is happening in a little parish, Saint James, that is experiencing spiritual renewal.

I want to say something at this point for all of you. There is another grace of Pentecost that we ought to take a good look at. It is the grace of being aware of everyone who was in that upper room. If you go back and look at Acts 1, verse 14, it says "together they devoted themselves to constant prayer." Do you know what it says then? "There were some women in their company." Then it singles out "Mary, the mother of Jesus."

There is a grace of Pentecost, brothers and sisters, that I have come to appreciate. Deeper levels of the charismatic gifts. And one of them is recognizing that that passage is related to what is in John about the wedding feast at Cana (Jn 2:1-11), when Jesus, through a miraculous intervention, created the new wine. The new wine which was served last was better than the wine that was served first.

But there was a very important person there, who motivated that whole process, who collaborated with that whole process, who had something to do with that whole process. She is mentioned too, Mary.

Then, I am conscious that at the foot of the cross, in the Gospel of John, Jesus says something about handing over his mother to John and John to his mother . . . It's more than just a simple thing of saying, take care of her. There is more going on there. One of the graces, one of the facets of this grace of Pentecost that has moved me lately is a *growing appreciation of the proper and authentic grace of Mary in the whole plan of salvation (emphasis added).*

I want to tell you that when I went over to that parish and was experiencing the outpouring of the Holy Spirit, the awesomeness of it all was the fact that it was in connection with apparitions which six teen-age children claim they are receiving.

Now, I submit this and defer publicly to the judgment of the magisterium of the Church. But, I want to tell you what I saw. I want to tell you what my cameras recorded.

I want to tell you that I was in the midst of a parish undergoing spiritual renewal which is revolutionary. I experienced a parish community and the thousands of people in that area coming to the Lord, giving their lives wholeheartedly to Jesus Christ . . .

I saw a Christ-centered parish. *It had proper respect for the Madonna (emphasis added)* . . .

I saw a parish that is being renewed by the Holy Spirit because God sent a very special messenger, who is doing in that parish what she did at Cana, in the upper room and at the foot of the cross . . . pointing to Jesus, saying: "Do whatever he tells you." Now, I *spent one week among these people and will never be the same (emphasis added).*

As far as I am concerned, the most powerful thing I witnessed over in Yugoslavia was hundreds of thousands of lives changed for the better. That is the sign that moved me. [8]

Chapter 21

The Messages And The Secrets

Mary comes to God's people in times of crisis as His very special messenger. She comes to warn them and give them guidance. This is simply a continuation of the policy God followed with His people in Old Testament times. He raised up prophets in times of great need. "Indeed, the Lord God does nothing without revealing his plan to his servants, the prophets" (Am 3:7). The Jews considered this so normal that when God delayed in sending prophets during bad times, the Psalmist complained and cried out in distress: "There is no prophet now, and no one of us knows how long. . ." (Ps 74:9).

God loves the people of today no less than He loved His people of old. When He has had something very special to say in modern times, He has sent the mother of Jesus as His messenger.

It is important to understand apparitions, especially Marian apparitions. They are special means that God provides for exceptional situations and times in history, and yet they are also normal means, in the sense that they are part of God's overall plan for us. They have a definite place in that plan. What we must see in them is God in His love speaking to today's men and women and giving them guidance in times of great need. This is why in more recent times Popes have increasingly given them official recognition in various ways. This is particularly true of Fatima, the most recent of the approved major Marian apparitions. The Popes have participated in important celebrations at Fatima by sending personal radio messages or personal Legates or by coming themselves to these events. [1] Although the Church does not impose belief in such apparitions, she does not regard them as unimportant, as the following words of Pope John XXIII indicate:

> We exhort you to listen with simplicity of heart and honesty of mind to the salutary warnings of the Mother of God. The Roman pontiffs . . . if they have been constituted the guardians and interpreters of the divine revelation contained in the Scriptures and in Tradition, also have the duty, when, after mature examination, they deem it necessary for the common good, of bringing to the attention of the faithful those supernatural lights which it pleases God to dispense freely to certain privileged souls, not for the purpose of presenting new doctrines, but rather to guide us in our conduct. [2]

The most important thing about any apparition is its message. The signs and wonders that accompany apparitions are given to authenticate and draw attention to them so that people may accept and heed their message. Sometimes, all parts of the message are not revealed immediately. Some are to be kept secret until a designated time. At Fatima, several secrets were imparted to the three little shepherds. At Medugorje, Our Lady has imparted more secrets than at Fatima or any of the other well-known Marian shrines.

Why are secrets imparted in apparitions such as Fatima and Medugorje? The word, secret, has a magical effect on people. It arouses curiosity and stimulates interest. God makes use of this to draw attention to the message he wishes to transmit through his heavenly messenger.

Our Lady began imparting secrets quite early at Medugorje. The seers were told that each of them would receive ten. Our Lady has been imparting these secrets progressively to each seer. When Father Rupcic's book was published in 1983, Marija had received six, Vicka seven, Ivanka seven, and Mirjana nine. Jakov and Ivan did not tell him how many they had received. [3] At the present time, Mirjana and Ivanka have received all ten secrets and all the other seers have received nine, with the exception of Vicka who has received only eight. It is interesting to note that Mirjana received the tenth secret on December 25, 1982, which Our Lady told her was the last day on which she would appear to her regularly. Henceforth, she would only appear to her on her birthday *(March 18)* and in times of great need.

Father Rupcic asked the seers questions about the secrets' contents. The responses were quite general and not too revealing.

Marija said they pertain "to us, to the Church, and to people in general."

Jakov said they pertain "to our lives and to people."

Vicka said, "The first has to do with the church in Medugorje," and they also pertain "to the sign, to all humanity, and to everyone; to the Church in general and there are some for us."

Ivanka said they pertain "to us, personally, to the Church, and to the world."

Mirjana said they pertain "to us, to the sign, to the whole world, and to Medugorje."[4]

When asked by Father Rupcic whether the secrets concerning the world had to do with good or bad things, their reply was that there were good things and bad things.[5]

Our Lady will tell the seers when and to whom the secrets are to be revealed.[6]

The best available source of information concerning the secrets is a report Father Tomislav Vlasic sent to the Pope and to the Bishop of Mostar on December 2, 1983. Our Lady requested through the seer, Mirjana, that he do this:

"According to Mirjana, during the apparition on December 25, 1982, the Madonna confided the tenth and last secret to her, and she revealed the dates on which the various secrets will come to pass. The Blessed Virgin revealed many aspects of the future to Mirjana, many more up to now than to the other seers. For that reason, I relate now what Mirjana told me in a conversation on November 5, 1983. I shall summarize the essential things she said, without any literal quotations."

—Before the visible sign[7] is given to humanity, there will be three warnings to the world. The warnings will be warnings on the earth. Mirjana will witness them. Three days before one of these warnings, she will advise a priest of her choice. Mirjana's testimony will be a confirmation of the apparitions and an incentive for the conversion of the world. After these warnings, the visible sign will be given for all humanity at the place of the apparitions in Medugorje. The sign will be given as the testimony of the apparitions and a call back to faith.

—The ninth and tenth secrets are grave matters. They are a chastisement for the sins of the world. The punishment is inevitable because we cannot expect the conversion of the entire world. The chastisement can be mitigated by prayers and penance.[8] It cannot be suppressed. An evil which threatened the world, according to the seventh secret, had been eliminated through prayer and fasting, Mirjana said. For that reason, the Blessed Virgin continues to ask for prayer and fasting: "You have forgotten that with prayer and fasting you can ward off wars, suspend natural laws."

—After the first warning, the others will follow within a rather brief period of time. So it is that people will have time for conversion.

—This time is a period of grace and conversion. After the visible sign, those who are still alive will have little time for conversion. For that reason, the Blessed Virgin calls for urgent conversion and reconciliation.

—The invitation to prayer and penance is destined to ward off evil and war and above all to save souls.

—We are close to the events predicted by the Blessed Virgin.

—Convert yourselves as quickly as possible. Open your hearts to God. This is a message to all mankind.[9]

Father Tomislav gave a little additional information about the secrets during the taped interview of August 15, 1983: "They *(the seers)* say that with the realization of the secrets entrusted to them by Our Lady, life in the world will change. Afterwards, men will believe like in ancient times. What will change and how it will change, we don't know, given that the seers don't want to say anything about the secrets."

"Life in the world will change. Afterwards, men will believe like in ancient times." These few words imply a lot about the extraordinary events that lie ahead and for which Our Lady came to prepare the world at Medugorje.

Chapter 22

Leading The Seers To Holiness

The message of Medugorje could be summarized in a single word—conversion. But the conversion that Our Lady is seeking at Medugorje is of two kinds: the conversion of the sinner who has cut himself off from God through serious sin and then reconciles himself with Him; and the conversion of the one who lives normally in God's friendship, but who at some point in time seeks to seriously deepen that friendship.

At Medugorje, Our Lady's message has to do with both kinds of conversion. She has come to call sinners back to God and to put them on the road to salvation. It is this part of the message of Medugorje that has been made known to a greater degree. Medugorje is also a call to holiness, and this is the special mission of Jelena and Marijana. They have personally been called to holiness and have also been entrusted with leading others to holiness. What about the other six seers? It can be said that they too have personally been called to holiness. Their call to holiness is the object of the present chapter.

A very important place has been given to personal messages for all six of the original seers. Indeed, there has been an entire phase of Our Lady's heavenly visits devoted to messages or instructions that had to do with their personal guidance and spiritual growth. During this period, Our Lady has acted as their spiritual director.

She told the children, "You are like water faucets and can become rusty." It is the understanding of those close to the

young people that God is using them to impart a very important message to the Church and to the world, but that this
message will not come through them as fully as it should
unless they keep themselves in good spiritual condition by
their personal growth in the spiritual life. If they allow
themselves to become spiritually rusty, they will not be good
channels for communicating God's message.

It is precisely to keep the children from becoming spiritually
rusty that she has undertaken to instruct them herself in the
way of perfection. She has been successful in this, as the
young people themselves testify. Father Rupcic asked them if
they had "changed in any way because of Our Lady's apparitions?" They were quite candid in their answers. All indicated
that they felt they had changed for the better, spelling out the
ways in which they felt there had been improvement. All six
specifically mentioned prayer as an area where they had
changed for the better. They used expressions such as: "Now,
it pleases me to pray. . .I like to pray better. . .I pray more,
before I was always in a hurry. . .Now, I am happy to
pray. . . Now, I have more strength for prayer." Four of the
young people specifically said that they "prayed more."
Similar expressions were used to indicate improvement in
regard to going to church, attending Mass, receiving Communion, and going to confession.[1] Very significant is the
mention of improvement in the reception of the sacraments.

At Medugorje there has been considerably more emphasis
on the reception of the sacraments, particularly that of
Reconciliation, than at Lourdes and at Fatima. In those
earlier apparitions, the sacramental message was indirect or
implied. At both places, Our Lady sought "a chapel" where
her Son could be honored in the Eucharist and received.

In 1916 the angel brought communion to the three little
shepherds of Fatima during his last apparition to them on
Mount Cabeco. It was then that he taught them a eucharistic
prayer of reparation which became an important part of their
daily prayer life. Francisco spent long hours of adoration and
reparation before the Blessed Sacrament in the village
church. Jacinta developed a great hunger for the reception of
"the hidden Jesus." Lucia's First Solemn Communion was the

occasion of very special graces. These were all indirect teachings on the Eucharist.

During an apparition, when the Blessed Virgin gives a message for the whole world or for all of the young seers, then all of them are able to hear what she is saying, but if her words are meant only for one of them, only that one will be able to hear her. This happens when she corrects or admonishes one of them. Only the person being admonished will hear her, and the correction will be done while the fault is still fresh in that one's mind.

When Our Lady gives one of them some personal advice, only that one hears what she has to say. "In some situations, where there was no way out," declared one of the visionaries, "she told me how I should act or behave," and another one added, "She told me that I was very naive, that I believe everyone, that I have to correct that."

In her guidance and spiritual direction of the young people, Our Lady has shown herself to be respectful of their free will. This came to light in their answers to Father Rupcic's questioning on whether Our Lady had told them what they should do in life. The replies made it clear that she would like to see them all "become sisters and priests." But this was only "her wish" and "she will not force anyone." Mirjana said she told Our Lady that some of them wanted to become sisters or priests and others wanted to stay in the world. The Blessed Virgin replied that the decision "was our affair" and that "one or the other would be good." And "she explained and gave us advice." She said that to enter the convent and not stay would "bring shame on the Church and everyone."

At the time these answers were given, four of the seers indicated a preference for a religious vocation and the two others said that they were undecided. [2]

It is interesting to note the concrete way in which Our Lady has taught the children. For example, in teaching them about overcoming sin, she used the device of a novena in preparation for the Feast of her Immaculate Conception on December 8. They were asked to renounce a specific sin each day of the novena and to fast on bread and water. A member of the parish staff pointed out that the seers adhere very strictly to these fasts, never taking anything but bread and water.

It has been noticed that, at least occasionally, the events at Medugorje have occurred at liturgically appropriate times. Such, it seems, was the linking of the teaching on sin with the feast commemorating Mary's Immaculate Conception, her preservation from original sin. Such also was the disappearance of Jakov and Vicka from the earth and their vision of heaven on the Feast of All Saints.

Our Lady has used visions, particularly those of heaven, of hell, and of purgatory as means of teaching the young people and of stimulating them to pray and make sacrifices for sinners and the souls in purgatory. All six of them have seen heaven. Four have seen hell and the other two indicated they had not seen it because they have been too fearful of such an experience. The Blessed Virgin said this about hell: "This is the punishment of those who do not love God and many today are going to hell." Five have seen purgatory; the sixth one did not see it, but Our Lady described it to her. Of purgatory, Our Lady stated: "These people are waiting for your prayers and sacrifices."

At Fatima on July 13, 1917, the three little shepherds were given a vision of hell that made a lasting impression on them and had much to do with stimulating their generosity in praying and making sacrifices. This was particularly true of Jacinta, the youngest of the trio who saw Our Blessed Mother.

One must always remember that at Medugorje and at Fatima Our Lady is always teaching the world at large as well as the visionaries. There can be no doubt that she wants all the faithful to pray more and to be generous in making sacrifices, especially for sinners, the "many sinners" who today are on the road to eternal perdition.

Chapter 23

Messages For The Parish

From the early days, Our Lady began manifesting to the six seers a special motherly love. One of the important ways in which she did this was through spiritual guidance.

The people of Medugorje were also the object of her special love. She gave special messages for them, but the specific content and the precise dates of most of the early messages have been lost. At the beginning of 1984, however, Our Lady told Jelena that she wanted the parishioners of Saint James to come together at the church one evening a week so that she could direct them in their spiritual life. The priests chose Thursday.

Since March 1, Our Lady has been giving messages quite regularly every Thursday — and exceptionally on some other days. The messages have not been rigorously restricted to the parishioners. They have also been offered to others, especially to those who go there often. They are a call to all who have an open heart. These Thursday night messages have been coming to the parish through the original group of six seers and almost entirely through one member of that group, namely, Marija. Other messages for the parish have been received through Jelena.[1]

One of the important objectives Our Lady is pursuing is to prepare the parish for the future events which she has been revealing to the seers. In the words of Father Tomislav Vlasic, "As we go along, Our Lady is pushing the parish to improve more and more."

1. Thursday Night Messages Received Through The Original Group Of Seers.

March 1, 1984

Dear children! I have chosen this parish in a special way and I wish to lead it. I am guarding it in love and I wish everyone to be mine.

Thank you for your response this evening. It is my wish that you always be here in greater numbers with me and my Son. Every Thursday, I will give a special message to you.

March 8, 1984

Thank you for your response to my call.

Dear children! In this parish, start converting yourselves. In that way all those who come here will be able to convert. *(Your example will inspire those who come here to convert themselves.)*

March 15, 1984

This evening, dear children, I am grateful in a special way for your being here. Adore continually the Blessed Sacrament. I am always present when the faithful are in adoration. Special graces are then being received.

(Every Thursday evening the faithful worship the Blessed Sacrament after Mass, but this evening it was noticed that many men remained in the church for adoration, although they had worked hard in the fields.)

March 22, 1984

Dear children! This evening I ask you in a special way during this Lent to honor the wounds of my Son, which He received because of the sins of this parish. Unite yourselves with my prayers for this parish so that His sufferings may become bearable. Thank you for your response to my call. Make an effort to come in greater numbers.

March 29, 1984

Dear children! This evening I am asking in a special way for your perseverance in trials. Ponder how the Almighty is still suffering because of your sins. So when sufferings come, offer them as your sacrifice to God.

Thank you for your response to my call.

April 5, 1984

Dear children! This evening I am especially asking you to venerate the Heart of my Son, Jesus. Make atonement for the wounds inflicted upon the Heart of my Son. That Heart has been wounded by all sorts of sin.

Thank you for coming this evening.

April 12, 1984

Dear children! This evening I ask you to stop slandering and to pray for the unity of the parish, for my Son and I have a special plan for this parish.

Thank you for your response to my call.

April 19, 1984

Dear children! Sympathize with me. Pray, pray, pray!

Monday, April 30, 1984

(Our Lady didn't give a message for the parish on Thursday April 26. On April 30, Marija asked her why she didn't give her a message for the parish on Thursday.)

Even though I had a special message for the parish to awaken the faith of every believer, I did not want to force anyone to do anything he didn't want to do. Only a very small number of people have accepted the Thursday messages. At the beginning, there were more who accepted them, but now it seems as if they have become something ordinary. Recently, some have been asking for the messages only out of curiosity and not out of faith and devotion to my Son and me.

May 10, 1984

(Many believers were struck by the last message of Our Lady. Many thought that Our Lady was not going to give any more messages for the parish, but on this evening she did.)

I am still speaking to you and I intend to continue. But listen to my instructions.

May 17, 1984

Dear children! Today I am very happy because there are many here who desire to devote themselves to me. I thank you. You have not made a mistake. My Son, Jesus, wishes to bestow special graces on you through me. My Son is happy because of your dedication.

Thank you because you have responded to my call.

May 24, 1984

Dear children! I have already told you that I have chosen you in a special way just as you are. I, as your mother, love you all. In your moments of difficulty don't be afraid. I love you even when you are far away from me and my Son.

I ask you not to allow my heart to shed tears of blood because of the souls who are being lost through sin. Therefore, dear children, pray, pray, pray!

Thank you for your response to my call.

May 31, 1984

(This was the feast of the Ascension. There were many people from abroad. Our Lady did not give any message. She said to Marija that she would give the message on Saturday to be announced to the people on Sunday.)

Saturday, June 2, 1984

(This is the novena for Pentecost.)

Dear children! During the days of this novena, pray for an outpouring of the Holy Spirit on all of your families and your parish. Pray, and you shall not regret it. God will give you the gifts *(of the Holy Spirit)* and you will glorify Him for them till the end of your life.

Thank you for your response to my call.

Saturday, June 9, 1984

(Again last Thursday, Our Lady did not give any message for the parish. She promised to give it this evening.)

Dear children! Tomorrow night *(Pentecost Sunday)* pray for the Spirit of truth, especially those of you from this parish. The Spirit of truth is necessary for you in order to convey the messages the way I give them to you, without adding or removing anything. Pray that the Holy Spirit grant you the spirit of prayer, that you may pray more. I, as your Mother, tell you that you pray little.

Thank you for your response to my call.

June 21, 1984

Pray, pray, pray!
Thank you for your response to my call.

July 5, 1984

Dear children! Today I wish to tell you: always start your work and end it with prayer. If you do that God will bless you and your work.

These days you have been working too much and praying too little. Therefore, pray! In prayer you will find rest.

Thank you for your response to my call.

July 12, 1984

Dear children! These days Satan is trying to thwart all my plans. Pray that his plan may not be fulfilled. I will pray to my Son, Jesus, that He give you the grace to experience His victory over Satan's temptations.

Thank you for your response to my call.

July 19, 1984

Dear children! You have experienced these last few days how Satan works. I am always with you; do not be afraid of trials. God is always watching over you. I have given myself to you and I sympathize with you even in the smallest trial.

Thank you for your response to my call.

July 26, 1984

Dear children! Today also I would like to call you to persistent prayer and penance. Especially, let the young people of this parish be more active in their prayers.

Thank you for your response to my call.

August 2, 1984

Dear children! Today I am happy and I thank you for your prayers. Pray more these days for the conversion of sinners.

Thank you for your response to my call.

Saturday, August 11, 1984

(Our Lady did not give any message last Thursday. This is what she said to Marija this evening.)

Dear children! Pray, because Satan is continually trying to thwart my plans. Pray with your heart and in prayer give yourselves up to Jesus.

Tuesday, August 14, 1984

(This apparition was unexpected. Ivan was praying in his

house. After praying, as he was getting ready to go to church for the evening service, Our Lady appeared to him and asked him to transmit this message to the people.)

I ask the people to pray with me these days. As much as they can. Fast strictly on Wednesdays and Fridays. Every day, at least one rosary: joyful, sorrowful and glorious mysteries.

(Our Lady asked the people to accept this message with firm will. She asked this in a special way of the parishioners and believers of the surrounding places.)

August 16, 1984

Dear children! I beg all of you, especially the members of this parish, to live my messages and to tell them to whomever you meet.

Thank you for your response to my call.

August 23, 1984

Pray, pray, pray!

(Marija informed us that Our Lady invites people, especially the young, to keep order in the church during Mass.)

August 30, 1984

Dear children! The cross *(on Mount Krizevac)* was in God's plan when you built it. These days especially, go up on the mountain and pray at the foot of the cross. I need your prayers.

Thank you for your response to my call.

September 6, 1984

Dear children! Without prayer there is no peace.

For that reason, I say to you: dear children, pray at the foot of the cross for peace.

Thank you for your response to my call.

September 13, 1984

Dear children! I continually need your prayers. You wonder what all these prayers are for. Look around, dear children, and you will see how much ground sin has gained in this world. Because of that, pray that Jesus conquers.

Thank you for your response to my call.

September 20, 1984

Dear children! Today I ask you to start fasting, putting your heart in it. There are many people who fast only because everyone else is fasting. It has become a custom which no one wants to stop. I ask the parish to fast out of gratitude to God for allowing me to remain so long in this parish. Dear children, fast and pray with your heart.

Thank you for your response to my call.

September 27, 1984

Dear children! Your prayer has helped my plans to be fulfilled. Pray continually for their complete fulfillment.

I beg the families of the parish to pray the family rosary.

Thank you for your response to my call.

October 4, 1984

Dear children! Today I would like to tell you that your prayers delight me, but there are enough people in the parish who do not pray and for that my heart is sad.

Pray, therefore, that I may bring all your sacrifices and prayers to the Lord.

Thank you for your response to my call.

Monday, October 8, 1984

(This message was given for the parish through Jakov in his home. He did not go to the church on that day because he was not well.)

Dear children! Let all the prayers you say in your homes in the evening be for the conversion of sinners because the world is in great sin. Pray the rosary every evening.

October 11, 1984

Dear children! Thank you for offering all your afflictions to God, even at this time when He is trying your patience as you reap your crops. (*Our Lady is alluding to prolonged rain which came in the middle of the harvesting and caused great damage.*)

Be aware, dear children, that He loves you and that it is for that reason that He tests you. Always present your burdens to God and do not worry.

Thank you for your response to my call.

October 18, 1984, Feast of St. Luke, the Evangelist

Dear children! Today I ask you to read the Bible in your homes every day. Place it in a visible place there, where it will always remind you to read it and to pray.

Thank you for your response to my call.

October 25, 1984

Dear children! Pray during this month. God has allowed me to help you every day with graces in order to protect you from evil. This month is mine. I would like to give it to you. Pray and God will give you the graces that you ask for. I will support your requests.

Thank you for your response to my call.

November 1, 1984

Dear children! Today I call you to renew family prayer in your homes. The field work is over. Now, may all of you devote yourselves to prayer. Let prayer have first place in your families.

Thank you for your response to my call.

November 8, 1984

Dear children! You are not aware of the importance of the messages which God is sending you through me. He is giving you great graces and you don't realize it. Pray to the Holy Spirit for enlightenment. If only you knew how many graces God is giving you, you would pray without ceasing.

Thank you for your response to my call.

November 15, 1984

You are a chosen people and God has given you great graces. You do not realize the importance of every message I am giving you.

Now I only wish to say: Pray, pray, pray! I do not know what else to tell you because I love you and wish that in prayer you come to know my love and the love of God.

Thank you for your response to my call.

November 22, 1984

Dear children! These days, live all of my messages and continue to root them in your hearts this week. *(That week marked the end of one liturgical season and the beginning of Advent.)*

Thank you for your response to my call.

November 29, 1984

Dear children! You do not yet know how to love nor do you

listen with love to the words I am giving you.

Be assured, my beloved ones, that I am your Mother and that I have come on earth to teach you how to listen with love, how to pray with love, and not compelled by the cross you are carrying. Through the cross, God is glorified in every person.

Thank you for your response to my call.

December 6, 1984

Dear children! These days, I am calling you to family prayer. Many times, I have given you messages in God's name, but you have not listened.

This Christmas will be an unforgettable day for you, provided you accept the messages I am giving you.

Dear children, do not allow that day of joy to be a day of deepest sorrow for me.

Thank you for your response to my call.

December 13, 1984

Dear children! You know that the day of joy is coming near, but without love you will obtain nothing. Therefore, first of all start loving your family and everyone in the parish. Then you will be able to love and accept all those who will come here.

Let this week be the week of learning how to love.

Thank you for your response to my call.

December 20, 1984

Today I am asking you to do something concrete for Jesus Christ. On the day of joy, I would like every family of the parish to bring a flower as a sign of self-offering to Jesus.

I would like every member of the family to have a flower next to the crib so that Jesus can come and see your offering of self to Him.

Thank you for your response to my call.

December 27, 1984

Dear children! This Christmas, Satan wanted in a special way to thwart God's plans. You, dear children, witnessed Satan even on Christmas day. But God conquered in your hearts. Let your hearts continue to rejoice.

Thank you for your response to my call.

January 3, 1985

Dear children! These days, the Lord granted you many graces. Let this week be a week of thanksgiving for all the graces God has granted you.

Thank you for your response to my call.

January 10, 1985

Dear children! Today I want to thank you for all your sacrifices. I thank especially those who come here gladly and have become dear to my heart. There are parishioners who do not listen to my messages; but because of those who are especially close to my heart, I give messages to the parish. And I will continue giving them for I love you and want you to spread them with love.

Thank you for your response to my call.

Monday, January 14, 1985

Dear children! Satan is so strong. With all his power he wants to thwart the plans I have undertaken with you. You must pray; pray constantly and do not stop for a moment. I will pray to my Son that the plans I have started be fulfilled. Be patient and persevering in your prayers. Do not let Satan discourage you. He is working vigorously in the world. Be cautious.

January 17, 1985

In these days, Satan is fighting deviously against this parish, and you, dear children, have fallen asleep in *(regard to)* prayer. Only some of you are going to Mass. Persevere in these days of temptation.

Thank you for your response to my call.

January 24, 1985

Dear children! These days you have savored the sweetness of God through the renewal in your parish. Satan plans to work even more energetically to take the joy away from each of you. Through prayer you can totally disarm him and ensure your happiness.

Thank you for your response to my call.

January 31, 1985

Dear children! Today I want to ask you to open your hearts

to God, just like the flowers in the spring that yearn for the sun. I am your Mother and I would like you to be ever closer to the Father and that He pour gifts into your hearts abundantly.

Thank you for your response to my call.

February 7, 1985

Dear children! Satan is manifesting himself in this parish in a particular way these days. Pray, dear children, that God's plan be carried out, and that every work of Satan be turned to the glory of God.

I have remained this long to help you in your great trials.

Thank you for your response to my call.

February 14, 1985

Dear children! Today is the day when I give you the message for the parish, but not everyone in the parish accepts my messages and lives them. I am sad and I want you, dear children, to listen to me and to live my messages.

Every family must pray and read the Bible.

Thank you for your response to my call.

February 21, 1985

Dear children! Day after day I have been appealing to you for renewal and prayer in the parish. But you are not responding. Today I am appealing to you for the last time. This is the season of Lent, and you, as a parish in Lent, should be moved through love of my appeal to take the first step. If you do not take this step, I do not want to give you any more messages. God will allow me not to give you any more.

Thank you for your response to my call.

February 28, 1985

Dear children! Today I call you to live these words during this week: I love God.

Dear children! With love, you can achieve everything, even what appears impossible. God wants this parish to belong to Him completely. And I want that too.

Thank you for your response to my call.

March 7, 1985

Dear children! Today I invite you to renew prayer in your families. Dear children, encourage the very young to pray and to go to holy Mass.

Thank you for your response to my call.

March 14, 1985

Dear children! In your life, you have all experienced light and darkness. God gives every person the power to recognize good and evil. I am calling you to light, which you must carry to all those who are in darkness. From day to day, people who are in darkness come into your houses. You, dear children, give them light.

Thank you for your response to my call.

March 21, 1985

Dear children! I want to give you the messages. Therefore I ask you to accept these messages. Dear children, I love you. In a special way I have chosen this parish which is more dear to me than any of the others to which I gladly came when the Almighty sent me. Therefore, dear children, I ask you to accept me for your well-being. Follow the messages.

Thank you for your response to my call.

March 28, 1985

Dear children! Today, I am asking you to pray, pray, pray. In prayer you will experience great joy and the solution to every helpless situation. Thank you for making progress in prayer. Each one of you belongs to my heart. I am grateful to all of you who have begun praying again in your families.

Thank you for your response to my call.

April 4, 1985, Holy Thursday

Dear children! I am thankful that you have begun to treasure more highly in your hearts the glory of God. Today is the day that I wanted to stop giving messages because certain people do not accept them. The parish has responded and I wish to continue to give messages to a degree such as has never before been witnessed in the world since the beginning of history.

Thank you for your response to my call.

April 5, 1985

You, the members of this parish, have a large and heavy cross to bear. But don't be afraid to carry it. My Son is there to help you.

April 11, 1985

Dear children! Today I wish to tell each one of you in this parish to pray particularly to be enlightened by the Holy Spirit.

From this day on, God wants to try this parish in a special way in order to fortify it in faith.

Thank you for your response to my call.

April 18, 1985

Dear children! Today I thank you for the opening up of your hearts. Joy overwhelms me for every heart that opens to God, especially in the parish. Rejoice with me. Pray all the prayers for the opening of sinful hearts. I want this. God wants this through me.

Thank you for your response to my call.

April 25, 1985

Dear children! Today I want to tell you to begin to work in your hearts like you work in the fields. Work and change your hearts so that the Spirit of God may move into your hearts.

Thank you for your response to my call.

May 2, 1985

Dear children! Today, I invite you to pray with your heart and not only through habit. Some come here but do not pray with their hearts. Therefore, as your mother, I beg you to pray that prayer may prevail in your hearts at every moment.

Thank you for your response to my call.

May 9, 1985

Dear children! You do not know how many graces God is bestowing upon you. You are not willing to get moving in these days when the Holy Spirit is working in a special way; you do not want to advance. Your hearts are turned to earthly things and you are preoccupied by them.

Turn your hearts to prayer and ask that the Holy Spirit be poured upon you.

Thank you for your response to my call.

May 16, 1985, Feast of the Ascension

Dear children! I am calling you to more attentive prayer and to greater participation in the Mass. I want you to experience God within yourselves at Mass.

I want to tell young people especially to be open to the Holy Spirit because God desires to draw you to Himself during these days when Satan is active.

Thank you for your response to my call.

May 23, 1985

Dear children! These days, I am calling you especially to open your hearts to the Holy Spirit. These days, the Holy Spirit is acting through you in a particular way.

So, open your hearts and surrender your lives to Jesus so that He may work through them and make you stronger in faith.

Thank you for your response to my call.

May 30, 1985

Dear children! I am calling you again to prayer of the heart. Let prayer, dear children, be your everyday food, especially when work in the fields is exhausting you, and you cannot pray with your heart. Pray and then you will overcome every tiredness. Prayer will be your happiness and rest.

Thank you for your response to my call.

June 6, 1985

Dear children! Many people of all nationalities will come to the parish and now I am calling you to love. Love first of all the members of your own family and then you might be able to accept and love all those who are coming.

Thank you for your response to my call.

June 13, 1985

Dear children! I am begging you, the people of this parish, to pray more until the anniversary of the apparitions. May your prayer be an act of devotion and commitment to God.

I know about your tiredness, dear children, but you don't know how to give yourselves to me. These days, I beg you, make an act of total dedication to me.

Thank you for your response to my call.

June 20, 1985

Dear children! For the coming feast I want to say to you: Open your hearts to the Lord of all hearts! Give me all your feelings and all your problems. I want to console you in all your trials. My wish is to fill you completely with God's peace, joy, and love.

Thank you for your response to my call.

Tuesday, June 25, 1985, Anniversary of the apparitions.

Dear children! I urge you to ask everyone to pray the

rosary. With the rosary you will overcome all the troubles which Satan is trying to inflict on the Catholic Church. Let all priests pray the rosary. Give time to the rosary.

(Our Lady gave this message to Marija Pavlovic in answer to her question, "Our Lady of Peace, what do you wish to say to priests?")

Friday, June 28, 1985

Dear children! Today I give you a message in which I am calling you to humility. These days you have felt great joy because of all the people who came and to whom you spoke with love about your experiences. Now I call you to continue to speak to all those who come, with humility and with an open heart.

Thank you for your response to my call.

July 4, 1985

Dear children! I thank you for each sacrifice you have made. Now I urge you to offer all your sacrifices with love. I want you who are troubled to begin to help pilgrims with confidence and the Lord will give to you in the same measure.

July 11, 1985

Dear children! I love your parish and I protect it under my mantle against every satanic enterprise. Pray that Satan will flee from your parish and from everyone who comes to your parish. In that way you will be able to hear each appeal from God and to respond to it with your life.

Thank you for your response to my call.

July 18, 1985

Dear children! Today I invite you to put more blessed objects in your homes and may every person carry blessed objects on himself. Let everything be blessed. Then, because you are armored against Satan, he will tempt you less.

Thank you for your response to my call.

July 25, 1985

Dear children! I want to shepherd you but you do not want to obey my messages. Today I call you to obey my messages and then you will be able to live everything that God tells me to relate to you. Open yourselves to God and God will work through you and give you everything you need.

Thank you for your response to my call.

August 1, 1985

Dear children! I wish to tell you that I have chosen this parish. I guard it in my hands like a little flower that does not want to *(that I do not want to let?)* die. I beg you to give yourselves to me so that I can offer you as a gift to God, fresh and without sin. Satan has undertaken one part of his plan and wants to possess it *(your parish?)*. Pray that he does not succeed because I desire to have you for myself so that I can offer you to God.

Thank you for your response to my call.

August 8, 1985

Dear children! Today I am calling you to begin your struggle against Satan with prayer. Satan wants to work more now that you know he is active. Dress up, dear children, in clothes of armor against Satan; with rosaries in your hands you will conquer.

Thank you for your response to my call.

August 15, 1985

Dear children! Today I bless you and I wish to tell you that I love you. I appeal to you at this moment to live my messages. Today I bless you all with the solemn blessing which the Almighty has granted me.

Thank you for your response to my call.

August 22, 1985

Dear children! Today I wish to tell you that the Lord wants to put you to the test, which you can overcome by prayer. God puts you to the test in your daily activities. Pray now that you pass every test peacefully. Come through every test from God more open to Him and approach Him with greater love.

Thank you for your response to my call.

August 29, 1985

Dear children! I am calling you to prayer, especially now that Satan wants to make use of the grapes of your vineyards. Pray that he does not succeed.

Thank you for your response to my call.

September 5, 1985

Dear children! I thank you today for all your prayers. Pray continually and pray more so that Satan will go far away from this place. Dear children, the plan of Satan has failed. Pray that every plan of God be realized in this parish. I especially thank young people for the sacrifices they have offered.

Thank you for your response to my call.

September 12, 1985

Dear children! I wish to tell you these days to put the Cross at the center of your life. Pray especially before the Cross which is the origin of great graces. In your homes make a special consecration to the Cross of the Lord. Promise that you will not offend Jesus and that you will not insult Him, nor the Cross.

Thank you for your response to my call.

September 19, 1985

Dear children! Today I am calling you to live in humility all the messages I give you. Dear children, when you live the messages do not glorify yourselves by saying: "I live the messages." If you carry the messages in your heart and live them everyone will notice it. So, there is no need for words which serve only those who do not *(wish to)* hear. For you it is not necessary to speak. For you, my dear children, it is necessary to live and witness by your lives.

Thank you for your response to my call.

September 26, 1985

Dear children! Thank you for all your prayers. Thank you for all your sacrifices. I want you to renew the messages that I am giving you. Heed the call to fasting because by fasting you will ensure that the total plan of God here in Medugorje will be fulfilled. That will give me great joy.

Thank you for your response to my call.

October 3, 1985

Dear children! I want to say to you, be thankful to God for every grace that God gave you. For all the fruits of grace be thankful to the Lord and praise Him.

Dear children, learn to be thankful for little things and then you will be able to be thankful for great things.

Thank you for your response to my call.

October 10, 1985

Dear children! Today I call you to live the messages in this parish. I especially call the young people of this parish which I cherish so much.

Dear children, if you live the messages you will live the seed of holiness. As a mother I call all of you to holiness, so that you may give it to others because you are like a mirror for other people.

Thank you for your response to my call.

October 17, 1985

Dear children! Everything has its time. Today I invite you to start working on your hearts. All the work in the fields is finished. You manage to find time to clean the least looked-after places but you leave your hearts aside. Work more and clean all the recesses of your hearts with love.

Thank you for your response to my call.

October 24, 1985

Dear children! I want to dress you from day to day in holiness, goodness, obedience, and love of God so that from day to day you may become more beautiful and be better prepared for your Lord.

Dear children, listen to my messages and live them. I desire to lead you.

Thank you for your response to my call.

October 31, 1985

Dear children! Today I wish to call you to work in the Church. I do love you all equally. I want each one of you to do as much as he can. I know, dear children, that you can work but do not want to take on this work because you feel that you are unworthy of the duties. You must be courageous. Like little flowers you enrich the Church and Jesus so that we can all be happy.

Thank you for your response to my call.

November 7, 1985

Dear children! I am calling you to love your neighbors and to love those people from whom evil comes to you, so that in the power of love you will be able to judge the intentions of the heart. Pray and love, dear children. In the power of love you can do even those things that seem impossible to you.

Thank you for your response to my call.

November 14, 1985

Dear children! I, your mother, love you and I wish to urge you to prayer. I am, dear children, tireless and I call you even when you are far away from my heart. I feel pain for everyone who has gone astray. But I am a mother and I forgive easily; I rejoice for every child who comes back to me.

Thank you for your response to my call.

November 21, 1985

Dear children! I wish to tell you that this time is special for you who are from this parish. In the summer you say that you have a lot of work to do. Now that there is no work in the fields, work on yourselves personally. Come to Mass because the time has been given to you.

Dear children, there are many who come regularly to Mass in spite of bad weather because they love me and they wish to show their love in a special way. I ask you to show me your love by coming to Mass; the Lord will reward you abundantly.

Thank you for your response to my call.

November 28, 1985

Dear children! I want to give thanks to everyone for all that they have done for me, especially the young ones. I beg you, dear children, to engage in prayer conscientiously and in prayer you will come to know the majesty of God.

Thank you for your response to my call.

December 5, 1985

Dear children! I call you to prepare yourselves for Christmas by penance, prayer, and works of charity. Don't concern yourselves only with material things because then you will not be able to experience Christmas.

Thank you for your response to my call.

December 12, 1985

Dear children! For Christmas I invite you to give glory to Jesus together with me. I will give Him to you in a special way on that day, and I invite you to join me in giving glory and praise to Jesus at His birth.

Dear children, pray more on that day and think more about Jesus.

Thank you for your response to my call.

December 19, 1985

Dear children! I want to invite you to love your neighbor. If you were to love your neighbor you would experience Jesus' love more, especially on Christmas day. God will give you a great gift if you abandon yourself to Him. I want to give to mothers, particularly on Christmas day, my maternal blessing and I will bless the others with His blessing.

Thank you for your response to my call.

December 26, 1985

Dear children! I want to thank all of you who have listened to my messages and who have lived on Christmas day what I have told you. From now on you are cleansed of your sins and I want to continue to guide you in love. Abandon your hearts to me.

Thank you for your response to my call.

(On Christmas day Mary appeared with the Infant Jesus)

January 2, 1986

Dear children! I invite you to decide completely for God. I beg you to surrender yourselves completely and you will be able to live everything I say to you. It will not be difficult for you to surrender yourselves completely to God.

Thank you for your response to my call.

January 9, 1986

Dear children! I invite you to prayer so that by your prayer you will help Jesus to accomplish all that He has begun in this parish. By offerings and sacrifices to Jesus all that He has planned will be fulfilled. Satan will not be able to do anything.

Thank you for your response to my call.

January 16, 1986

Dear children! I invite you to pray. I need your prayers so much in order that God may be glorified through all of you. I beg you to listen, dear children, and to heed your mother's call because I am calling you out of love for you so that I can help you.

Thank you for your response to my call.

January 23, 1986

Dear children! Again I invite you to prayer of the heart. If you pray from your heart, dear children, the ice-cold hearts of your brothers will be melted and every barrier will disappear. Conversion will be easily achieved by those who want it. You must intercede for this gift for your neighbors.

Thank you for your response to my call.

January 30, 1986

Dear children! Today I invite all of you to pray in order that God's plan for you and all that God wants to achieve through you may be realized. Help others to be converted, especially those who come to Medugorje.

Dear children, do not allow Satan to reign in your hearts, because then you would become the image of Satan and not of me. I call on you to pray so that you may be witnesses of my presence. God cannot fullfill His will without you. God gave everyone free will and it is up to you to respond.

Thank you for your response to my call.

February 7, 1986

Dear children! I have chosen this parish and so it is special. It is different from others and I am giving great graces to all who pray from their hearts.

Dear children, I give the messages first of all to you parishioners and then to all others. You should be the first to accept them and after you all the others. You will be responsible to me and to my Son, Jesus.

Thank you for your response to my call.

February 13, 1986

Dear children! Let this Lent be a special incentive for you to change. Start from this moment. Turn off the television and renounce other things which are useless.

Dear children, I am calling you individually to conversion. The present time is for you.

Thank you for your response to my call.

February 20, 1986

Dear children! My second message for the Lenten days is

that you renew your prayer before the cross.

Dear children, I am giving you special graces and Jesus is giving you special gifts from the cross. Accept them and live them. Reflect on Jesus' passion and unite yourselves to Jesus in life.

Thank you for your response to my call.

February 27, 1986

Dear children! Be humble. Live in humility.

Thank you for your response to my call.

March 6, 1986

Dear children! Today I call you to open yourselves more to God so that He can work through you. Inasmuch as you open yourselves to Him you will bear the fruit of it. I wish to call you again to prayer.

Thank you for your response to my call.

March 13, 1986

Dear children! Today I call you to live this Lent with your little sacrifices. Thank you for every sacrifice you have brought me. Live in that way continually and with love, dear children. Help me to bring the offering of your sacrifices to God; He will reward you for them.

Thank you for your response to my call.

March 20, 1986

Dear children! I am calling you to an active approach to prayer. You wish to live everything I tell you, but you do not get results from your efforts because you do not pray. I beg you to open yourselves, dear children, and begin to pray. Prayer will be a joy, if you begin. It will not be boring because you will pray out of pure joy.

Thank you for your response to my call.

March 27, 1986

Dear children! I wish to thank you for your sacrifices and to invite you to the greatest sacrifice of all, the sacrifice of love. Without love you are not able to accept me nor my Son. Without love you cannot bear witness of your experience to others. That is why I invite you, dear children, to begin to live the love in your hearts.

Thank you for your response to my call.

April 3, 1986

Dear children! I am calling you to live the holy Mass. There are many of you who have experienced the beauty of the Mass but there are others who go unwillingly. I have chosen you, dear children, and Jesus is giving you His graces in the holy Mass. Let everyone who comes to Mass be joyful. Come with love and rejoice in the holy Mass.

Thank you for your response to my call.

April 10, 1986

Dear children! I wish to call you to grow in love. A flower cannot grow without water. Neither can you grow without God's blessing. You should pray for His blessing from day to day so that you can grow normally and carry out your activities with God.

Thank you for your response to my call.

April 17, 1986

Dear children! You are now preoccupied with material things and in the material you lose everything that God wants to give you. I invite you, dear children, to pray for the gifts of the Holy Spirit that you need now, in order that you may give witness to my presence here and to everything I am giving you.

Dear children, abandon yourselves to me so that I can lead you totally. Do not be preoccupied with the material things of this world.

Thank you for your response to my call.

April 24, 1986

Dear children! Today I am calling you to prayer. You are forgetting that everyone is important, especially the elderly in the family. Incite them to pray. May all young people be an example by their lives and may they testify for Jesus.

Dear children, I beg you to start transforming yourselves through prayer and then you will know what you have to do.

Thank you for your response to my call.

May 1, 1986

Dear children! I ask you to begin to change your life in your families. Let your family be a harmonious flower which I wish to give to Jesus. Every family should be active in prayer. It is my wish that the fruits of prayer be seen one day in the family.

Only in that way will I give you as petals to Jesus in fulfillment of God's plan.

Thank you for your response to my call.

May 8, 1986

Dear children! You are responsible for the messages that I give here. The fountain of all graces is here and you are the vessels which must carry them. That is why I am calling you to fulfill your duties with great responsibility. Everyone is responsible for carrying these messages in the measure he has received them. I am calling you, dear children, to carry these gifts to others with love. Do not keep them just for yourselves.

Thank you for your response to my call.

May 15, 1986

Dear children! Today I ask you to give me your heart so that I may change it and your heart may become like mine. You keep wondering: why can't we respond to what you ask of us? You cannot respond because you have failed to give me your heart so that I may change it. You speak much but do not act. I am calling you to do all that I ask of you. Only in that way can I abide with you.

Thank you for your response to my call.

May 22, 1986

Dear children! Today I want to give you my love. You do not know how great it is and you do not know how to accept my love. In all kinds of ways I want to prove my love to you, dear children, but you do not recognize it. You do not understand my words with your hearts and so you cannot take my love seriously either.

Dear children, accept me in your life. You will then be able to accept and welcome all that I tell you and everything to which I invite you.

Thank you for your response to my call.

May 29, 1986, Feast of Corpus Christi.

Dear children! Today I am calling you to a life of love toward God and toward your neighbor. Without love, dear children, you cannot do anything. That is why, dear children, I am calling you to live in mutual love. Only in that way can you love and accept me and everyone else around you, and also those who will come to your parish. Everyone will feel my love through you. That is why I beg you to start as of today to love with the burning love with which I love you.

Thank you for your response to my call.

June 5, 1986

Dear children! Today I am calling you to decide whether or not you want to live my messages. I am calling you to become active in living and carrying my messages to others. I desire that all of you become the living image of Jesus and bear witness to this unfaithful world. I desire that you become a light to all and that you witness to everyone around you.

Dear children, you are not called to darkness; you are called to become a light. So be a light by the way you give witness with your lives.

Thank you for your response to my call.

June 12, 1986

Dear children! I am calling you to begin to pray the rosary with a living faith. Only in that way will I be able to help you. You wish to receive many graces but you do not pray. I cannot help you if you do not undertake the task of prayer seriously.

Dear children, I am calling you to pray the rosary. This prayer is a must and you should pray it with joy. Only then will you begin to understand why I am with you for such a long time. I wish to teach you how to pray.

Thank you for your response to my call.

June 19, 1986

Dear children! In these present days Our Lord has permitted me to intercede for extra graces for you. For this reason I again wish to invite you to pray. Pray without ceasing. In this way I can give you the joy that Our Lord gives me. Through these graces, dear children, I want your suffering to be transformed into joy. I am your mother and I want to help you.

Thank you for your response to my call.

June 26, 1986

Dear children! God has allowed me to share with Him in establishing this oasis of peace. I invite you to take care of this oasis so that it remains always pure. There are some who through their thoughtlessness ravage peace and prayer. I call you to testify and to help by your own way of living to see that peace is preserved.

Thank you for your response to my call.

July 3, 1986

Dear children! Today I call on all of you to pray. Without prayer you cannot feel my presence, nor God's, nor the graces I am giving you. Therefore, I call you to always begin and end each day with prayer.

Dear children, I wish to lead you evermore in prayer, but you cannot grow if you do not wish to. I invite you to let prayer have the first place.

Thank you for your response to my call.

July 10, 1986

Dear children! Today I invite you to holiness. You cannot live without holiness. Overcome all sin with love. Overcome every difficulty with love.

Dear children, I beg you to live love within yourselves.

Thank you for your response to my call.

July 17, 1986

Dear children! Today I invite you to meditate on why I have been with you such a long time. I am the mediator between you and God. For that reason I would like to invite you to live always, out of love, what God is expecting of you. Live all the messages that I give you in complete humility.

Thank you for your response to my call.

July 24, 1986

Dear children! I am happy about all of you who are living in the way of holiness and I beg you to help, by your witness, all those who don't know how to live in a saintly way. For that reason, dear children, your families should be the place where holiness is born. Help everybody to live in a sanctified way, especially your own family.

Thank you for your response to my call.

July 31, 1986

Dear children! Hatred creates division and blinds one to everybody and everything. I invite you to create unity and peace. Especially, dear children, act with love in the place where you live. Let love always be your only tool. With love turn everything to good that the devil wants to destroy and take to himself. Only in this way will you be completely mine and I will be able to help you.

Thank you for your response to my call.

August 7, 1986

Dear children! You know that I promised you an oasis of peace here but you may not be aware that around every oasis is a desert where Satan is lurking. He wants to tempt each one of you.

Dear children, only by prayer are you able to overcome every influence of Satan in your area. I am with you, but I can't take away your free will.

Thank you for your response to my call.

August 14, 1986

Dear children! I invite you to have one purpose to your prayer: that it become the joy of an encounter with the Lord. I cannot guide you to that point until you find joy in the act of prayer. I want to guide you every more deeply into prayer but that is something I cannot impose on you.

Thank you for your response to my call.

August 21, 1986

Dear children! I am grateful for the love that you show me. You know that I love you without limit and that I daily ask the Lord to help you to understand the love that I show you.

Dear children, pray and pray and pray.

Thank you for your response to my call.

August 28, 1986

Dear children! I want you to be an example to everyone in all that you do, especially in prayer and witnessing. I cannot help the world without you. I want your cooperation with me in everything, even in the smallest things. Therefore, dear children, help me by your prayer from the heart and by surrendering completely to me. In that way I will be able to teach you and lead you along the road upon which I have set you.

Thank you for your response to my call.

September 4, 1986

Dear children! I am calling you to prayer and fasting. Be assured, dear children, that with your help I can do everything: prevent Satan from inducing you into error and force him to leave this place. Satan, dear children, lies in wait for each one of you; he particularly wants to sow the seed of doubt in each one of you. Therefore, dear children, I invite you to make of each day a prayer and a total surrender to God.

Thank you for your response to my call.

September 11, 1986

Dear children! During these days when you joyfully celebrate the Feast of the Holy Cross, I desire that your own cross become for you a source of joy. Dear children, pray that you will be able to accept sickness and suffering with love just like Jesus did. Only in that way can I experience the joy of giving you the graces of healing which Jesus will allow me to give you.

Thank you for your response to my call.

September 18, 1986

Dear children! I am grateful again today for everything you have done for me in recent days. I thank you in the name of Jesus especially for the sacrifices you offered this week. Dear children, you are forgetting that I want your sacrifices in order to help you and to keep Satan away from you. It is for that reason that I invite you to offer sacrifices to God with a deep reverence.

Thank you for your response to my call.

September 25, 1986

Dear children! I am calling you to help others, through the peace that exists in you, to recognize what peace is and to begin seeking it for themselves. Because you are at peace, dear children, you cannot conceive what it must mean to be without it. I call upon you again to help everybody by your prayer and your way of living to destroy all that is evil in their lives and to unmask Satan's deceptions. Pray for truth to prevail in every heart.

Thank you for your response to my call.

October 2, 1986

Dear children! Today, again, I invite you to pray. You will not realize, dear children, the value of prayer until you say to yourselves, "Now is the time for prayer; nothing else is more important to me. There is no one more important to me now than God." Dear children, dedicate yourselves to prayer with special love; only in that way can God give you graces.

Thank you for your response to my call.

October 9, 1986

Dear children! You know that I wish to guide you in the way of holiness and not to force you. I wish to see everyone of you help yourselves and help me by your little sacrifices so that I can guide you to be more holy day by day. Dear children, I do not want to force you to live the messages but rather I want you to realize that the long time I have spent with you shows that I love you without limit and that I want every single one of you to be holy.

Thank you for your response to my call.

October 16, 1986

Dear children! Today I wish to show you again how much I love you. It saddens me that I am unable to help each and every one of you to understand the depth of my love. That is why, dear children, I invite you to pray and to surrender yourselves completely to God, because Satan wants to conquer you in daily affairs and to take first place in your lives. That is why, dear children, you must pray without ceasing.

Thank you for your response to my call.

October 23, 1986

Dear children! Again today I call on you to pray: to pray particularly for peace, dear children. Without your prayer, dear children, I cannot help you to understand the message that my Lord has given to me to give to you. That is why, dear children, you must pray so that in prayer you may recognize the peace that God is giving you.

Thank you for your response to my call.

October 30, 1986

Dear children! Today I would like once again to ask you to accept and live with all seriousness the messages that I am giving you. It is for your sakes, dear children, that I have stayed so long with you; it is so that I might be able to help you put into practice all the messages I give you.

Thank you for your response to my call.

November 6, 1986

Dear children! Today I would like to invite you to pray every day for the souls in Purgatory. Every soul needs prayer and grace in order to reach God and His love. By praying for these souls you will gain intercessors for yourselves who will be able to help you recognize in this life that earthly things hold no importance; that heaven is the only goal worth aspiring to. For this reason, dear children, pray without interruption so that you may help yourselves and those to whom your prayers will bring joy.

Thank you for your response to my call.

November 13, 1986

Dear children! Again today I appeal to all of you to pray with your whole heart. Reform your lives a bit each day. I am especially calling you, dear children, to begin, through your prayer and sacrifices, to live in a holy manner. I want each one of you who has been to this holy place *(Medugorje),* this spring of grace, to come to paradise with the special gift which you will bear with you: the gift of holiness. Pray and reform your lives, dear children, so that you may become holy. I will be forever close to you.

Thank you for your response to my call.

November 20, 1986

Dear children! Today I invite you to live all the messages I give you and to follow them with special love. God does not want you lukewarm and indecisive, but totally committed to him. You know that I love you and burn with love for you. For that reason, dear children, you too must commit yourselves to love so that daily you may burn with the love of God and experience it for yourselves. Dear children, commit yourselves to love so that it may prevail in all of you. Not human love, but God's love.

Thank you for your response to my call.

November 27, 1986

Dear children! Today, also, I invite you to dedicate your life to me with love, so that I may be able to guide you with love. It is a very special love that I bear for you, dear children, and it is my desire to lead all of you to God in heaven. I want you to realize that this life is very short compared with that in heaven. Therefore, dear children, commit yourselves to God today. Only in that way can I show you how dear you are to me and how much I want all of you to be saved and to be with me in heaven.

Thank you for your response to my call.

December 4, 1986

Dear children! I call upon you again today to prepare your hearts at this time, when the Lord's chief wish is to purify you from all the sins of your past. You cannot do this by yourselves, dear children, and for that reason I am here to help you. Pray, dear children, for only thus will you be able to recognize all the evil that dwells in you and abandon it to the Lord so that he may purify your hearts completely. So, dear children, pray without ceasing and prepare your hearts through penance and fasting.

Thank you for your response to my call.

December 11, 1986

Dear children! Today I invite you to pray during this special season so that you may experience the joy of meeting the new-born Jesus. Dear children, I desire that you experience these days with the same joy that I have. I wish to guide you and show you this joy to which I want to bring all of you. For that reason, dear children, pray and surrender yourselves completely to me.

Thank you for your response to my call.

December 18, 1986

Dear children! Today I call you again to prayer. When you pray you are so much more beautiful, like flowers that show forth all their beauty when the snows have gone and all their colors become indescribable. In the same way, dear children, after prayer, you also unfold before God everything that is beautiful and can please Him. Therefore, dear children, pray and open your inner self to the Lord so that He may make of you a harmonious and beautiful flower for paradise.

Thank you for your response to my call.

December 25, 1986, Christmas Day

Dear children! I am grateful to my Lord today for all that he has given me and especially for this gift of being with you again today. Dear children, these are days in which the Father is giving special graces to all who open their hearts to Him. I bless you and I wish that you also might know these graces and that you might place yourselves at His disposal so that He might be glorified through you. My heart follows your progress with close attention.

Thank you for your response to my call.

January 1, 1987

Dear children! Today I wish to call you all to live throughout this new year all the messages I give you. You know, dear children, that it is for your sake that I have stayed with you so long, so that I could teach you to walk on the road of holiness. Therefore dear children, pray without ceasing and live the messages I give you for I do it with a great love for God and for you.

Thank you for your response to my call.

January 8, 1987

Dear children! I want to thank you for your response to my messages; especially, dear children thank you for all the sacrifices and prayers you have presented to me. I want to continue, dear children, to give you messages, no longer every Thursday but on the 25th of each month. The time has come when all that my Lord wanted has been fulfilled. From now on I will give you fewer messages but I will still be with you. Dear children, I ask you to listen to my messages and to live them so that I can guide you.

Thank you for your response to my call.

2. Monthly Messages Given Through Marija

January 25, 1987

Dear children! Today I want to appeal to all of you to start living a new life from this day forward. I want you to understand that God has chosen each one of you to have a part in His great plan for the salvation of mankind. You cannot grasp fully how great your role is in God's plan. For that reason, dear children, pray so that through prayer you may penetrate more deeply into an understanding of God's design for you. I am with you so that you can fulfill it completely.

Thank you for your response to my call.

February 25, 1987

Dear children! I want to wrap all of you in my mantle and lead you along the way of conversion. I beg you, dear children, to surrender all your past life to the Lord and all the evil that has accumulated in your hearts. I want each one of you to be happy, but with sin nobody can be happy. Pray and in prayer, dear children, you will come to know a new way to happiness. All the joy in your heart will shine forth and so you will be joyful witnesses of what my Son and I want you to be. I am blessing you.

Thank you for your response to my call.

March 25, 1987

Dear children! Today I thank you for being present in this place where I give special graces. I call upon each one of you to start living the life which God seeks of you and to start doing good deeds of love and mercy. I do not want you, dear children, to live the messages while at the same time displeasing me by committing sins. For that reason, dear children, I want each one of you to live a new life such that you will not destroy everything God creates in you and gives to you. I give you my special blessings and I remain with you on your way to conversion.

Thank you for your response to my call.

April 25, 1987

Dear children! Today I invite you to pray. You know that God grants special graces in prayer. Therefore, dear children, seek and pray in order that you may be able to understand all that I give you here.

I call upon you to pray with your hearts. You realize that without prayer you cannot comprehend all that God is planning to accomplish in and through each one of you. So pray! It is my wish that God's plan be fulfilled in and through each one of you and that all He has placed in your hearts will increase. So pray that God's blessing may protect you from all the evil that threatens you.

I give you my blessing, dear children.

Thank you for your response to my call.

May 25, 1987

Dear children! I invite everyone of you to start living in God's love. You are always ready, dear children, to commit sin and to place yourselves in Satan's hands without stopping to think. I call on each one of you to make a personal choice to be on the side of God and against Satan.

I am your mother and so I want to lead all of you to total holiness. I want everyone to be happy here on earth and then to be with me in heaven. This, dear children, is my purpose in coming here and my desire.

Thank you for your response to my call.

June 25, 1987

Dear children! Today I thank you all and would like to call you to the peace of God. I wish that each one of you may experience in his life the peace that God gives.

Today I want to bless you all. I bless you with God's blessing, and I ask you, dear children, to follow and live my way. I love you all, dear children. That is why I have called you so many times. I thank you for all that you do for my intentions. Please help me so that I may offer you to God, save you, and guide you on the path to salvation.

Thank you for your response to my call.

July 25, 1987

Dear children! I ask you to accept, beginning today, the road to holiness. I love you and so I desire that you become holy. I do not want Satan to block your progress along this road.

Pray, dear children, and accept everything God offers you on this hard road. Everyone who must walk this road experiences the great joy that God gives and is able to respond more eagerly to His every call. Pay no attention to trifles and make Heaven your goal.

Thank you for your reponse to my call.

August 25, 1987

Dear children! Today I appeal once again to each one of you to commit yourself to the living of my messages. God has permitted me, during this year that the Church has dedicated to me, to speak to you and to encourage you along the road of holiness.

Ask God, dear children, for all the graces He wishes to confer on you through me. I am ready to intercede with Him for everything you seek so that your sanctification may be complete. Ask then without fail, seeing that God has made it possible for me to obtain for you the graces you desire.

Thank you for your response to my call.

September 25, 1987

Dear children! Again today I wish to invite all of you to pray. Let prayer become your life.

Consecrate more of your time, dear children, to Jesus Himself and He will grant you everything you seek; also He will reveal Himself to you more and more fully.

Satan is powerful, dear children, and he lies in wait to tempt every one of you. So pray — and he will be unable to harm you or to hamper your progress on the road of holiness. Day in and day out, come as close as you can to God through prayer.

Thank you for your response to my call.

October 25, 1987

Dear children! I wish to invite each and every one of you today to make paradise your goal. The road leading there is difficult for those who have not made a decision for God.

So, make your decision, dear children, and you can rest assured that God will offer Himself to you in all fullness. You are being called and you must respond to the Father who is calling you through me.

Pray, for it is in prayer that each one of you will become able to attain perfect love. I give you my blessing and I want to gather every one of you under my maternal cloak.

Thank you for your response to my call.

November 25, 1987

Dear children! Today also I invite each one of you to decide all over again to abandon yourself completely to me. Only then will I in turn be able to offer each one of you to God.

You realize, dear children, that I love you immensely and want each one of you to belong to me. However, God has endowed everyone with free will and I respect it with all my heart and I humbly accept your free choice.

I seek your help so that the plan that God has conceived for this parish will be realized. But if you do not pray you cannot perceive my love nor God's designs for this parish and for each one of you personally. Pray lest Satan seduce you with his pride and his power to deceive.

I am by your side and want you to believe in my love for you.

Thank you for your response to my call.

December 25, 1987

Dear children! Rejoice with me! My heart rejoices because of Jesus and today I wish to give Him to you. Open your heart to Jesus, dear children, and I will give Him to you lovingly. I want Him to change you, to teach you, and to protect you. Today I pray in a special way for each one of you and present you to God. He will then reveal Himself to you.

I am calling you to sincere prayer of the heart so that your every prayer may be a meeting-point with God. In your work and in your daily life may He come first. Today I appeal to you in all earnestness to obey me and do as I ask.

Thank you for your response to my call.

January 25, 1988

Dear children! Today I invite you once again to a total change of heart — an act which is difficult for those who have not opted for God. It's a total conversion to God that I invite you to, dear children.

God wants to give you everything you ask of Him, but you only turn to Him when sickness, problems, or hard times beset you, and you think that He doesn't hear your prayers nor answer them because He is far away. No, dear children, that is not the case. You cannot receive His graces if you are far away from Him, because in that case you are not able to ask for them with firm confidence.

I want to bring you closer and closer to God but I cannot do so if you do not want that. If you do, then place your life in God's hands.

I bless you all!

Thank you for your response to my call.

February 25, 1988

Dear children! Today I want to invite you once again to give yourselves to prayer and total surrender to God. You know that I love you and it is on account of this love that I come here to show you the road to peace and to save your souls. I want you to obey me and not allow Satan to seduce you. He is strong enough to do that, dear children. I ask you for your prayers. Offer them to me for those who are under Satan's power so that they may be saved.

Give witness by your life; sacrifice your life for the salvation of the world. I am with you and I wish to thank you. In heaven you will receive from the Father the reward He has promised you. Therefore, dear children, do not worry about anything. If you pray, Satan cannot hinder you in the least because you are God's children and He watches over you. Pray and may the rosary be always in your hand as a sign to Satan that you belong to me.

Thank you for your response to my call.

March 25, 1988

Dear children! Today I invite you to complete surrender to God. You are not conscious of the great love God has for you. Because of this He allows me to be with you, to help you find the path to peace; but you cannot find this path if you do not pray. So, leave everything, dear children, and devote all of your time to God alone. He will give you everything and will bless you.

Do not forget, dear children, that your life fades away like that of a little spring flower which is beautiful today and yet by tomorrow has gone without leaving a trace. Because of this, pray in such a way that your prayer and your total surrender become a road sign. Then your testimony will not only be of value to you but of value for all eternity.

Thank you for your response to my call.

April 25, 1988

Dear children! God wants to make you holy. That is why He is inviting you through me to complete surrender. Let Holy Mass become your life. Understand that a church is God's palace, the place in which I gather you and seek to show you the way to God. Come and pray. Do not look down on others nor speak ill of them. Let your life become a signpost along the road to holiness.

Churches deserve respect and are sacred because God-who-became-man dwells there day and night. Therefore, little children, believe and pray the Father to increase your faith — and then ask for whatever you need.

I am with you. I rejoice at your change of heart and I shelter you under my maternal mantle.

Thank you for your response to my call.

May 25, 1988

Dear children! I invite you to complete surrender to God. Pray, little children, lest Satan shake you like branches in the wind. Be strong in God. Through you I want the whole world to come to know the God of joy. May your lives bear witness to His joy. Do not be anxious nor allow yourselves to be disturbed. God Himself will provide help and show you the way ahead.

It is my desire that you love everybody, good and bad alike, with my own love. Only in this way will it be possible for God's love to reign in the world. You are mine, dear children. I love you and want you to entrust yourselves to me so that I can lead you to God.

Pray without ceasing so that Satan will be prevented from taking advantage of you. Pray that you may come to realize that you are mine. I bless you with a joyous blessing.

Thank you for your response to my call.

June 25, 1988

Dear children! Today I am calling you to a love that is loyal and pleasing to God. Little children, love accepts things which are bitter and difficult for the sake of Jesus who is love itself. Therefore, pray to God to come to your aid — not, however, according to your desires, but according to His love. Surrender yourselves to God so that He may heal you, console you, and forgive everything inside you which is a hindrance to the way of love. In this way, God can mold your life and you will grow in love. Little children, glorify God with a canticle of love so that God's love may be able to grow in you day by day to its fullest.

Thank you for your response to my call.

3. Messages Received Through Jelena

Our Lady has spoken to the parish on many important occasions through Jelena.

March 1, 1984

On this day, Our Lady invited the parishioners of Saint James to read the gospel of Saint Matthew, 6:24-34. She asked them to read it every Thursday. In this passage of the gospel, Jesus asks us to put God first in our lives and to trust completely in Him, and He assures us that if we do this, He will provide for all our needs.

A number of Our Lady's messages to Jelena are invitations to the parishioners to prepare for important liturgical events. She asked them to prepare themselves in a special way for Holy Saturday, the Sacrament of Confirmation (by a novena), the Feast of Pentecost, and the third anniversary of the apparitions.

December 21, 1984

I want you to be a flower that will bloom for Jesus at Christmas, a flower that will not cease blooming when Christmas is over. I want your hearts to be *(like those of the)* shepherds for Jesus.

4. Various Undated Messages

Dear children! If you only knew how great is my love for you, you would cry for joy.

Dear children! When someone is standing before you asking you for a favor, you respond by granting it. Yet, I stand before many hearts and they do not open up to me. Pray that the world may receive my love.

Dear children! The love of God has not flowed over the whole world. Therefore, pray!

Dear children! I want the whole world to become my children, but people do not want to. I want to give them everything. Therefore, pray!

We are fortunate to have so many of these parish messages. They are very important and could be called guidelines to holiness for Christian families. It is obvious that Our Lady did not intend them solely for the parishioners of Saint James. Notable is the theme of prayer that runs through so many of them. It is interesting to see how Our Lady stresses preparation for special events, such as Pentecost, the Sacrament of Confirmation, June 24, the anniversary of the first apparition, and August 5, her birthday. This is in keeping with the tradition of the Church and the former vigils of prayer and fasting. So many things are touched upon in these messages! Noteworthy also is the tremendous effort Satan is making to disrupt what the Queen of Peace is trying to do at Medugorje and through Medugorje. This should alert everybody to how much is at stake here!

Chapter 24

Catastrophe And The Crisis Of Faith

The message of Medugorje is essentially a message for the world and for a world that is undergoing a critical crisis of faith. Because of that crisis the world finds itself on the edge of catastrophe. This can be called the basic message of Medugorje and it is meant for the world at large. It is a message that is addressed to all men and women since all are affected in some way or other by this crisis of faith.

In addition to this broad basic message of Medugorje, there are a number of specific messages that are addressed to various categories of people. There are messages for the Church at large, for the parish of Medugorje, for the Pope, for the Bishop of Mostar, for priests, for the seers themselves, and there have also been messages for certain individuals, such as the replies to requests for healing and to questions addressed to Our Lady through the seers. The concern of the present chapter will be principally with the messages for the world and the Church.

In a general way, it can be said that there have been three phases to the Medugorje messages. The first phase had to do with the world and the Church. The second phase consisted in a personal spiritual formation program for the seers in which Our Lady corrected them of their faults and told them how to improve their lives, that is, how to grow in Christian maturity and holiness and prayer. In the third phase, Our Lady talked about her own life.

Our Lady has said that the world is now on the edge of catastrophe. There is a sense of urgency about the Medugorje message that sets it apart from that of other apparitions. The crisis which has brought the mother of Jesus to Medugorje is very great, far greater than most people suspect. The present crisis of faith has resulted in widespread rejection of God and of His law. We are living in a sinful world and these sins are so serious and numerous that they cry to heaven for redress. It is significant that all of the first messages of the early days of the apparitions speak of faith.

The first day on which Our Lady spoke was June 25, the second day she appeared. She joined the seers when they said seven Our Fathers, Hail Marys *(Our Lady was silent during the Hail Marys)*, and Glory Be's. She told them that these prayers pleased her and to continue to pray them. Then, she asked them to join a Creed to these three other prayers. The Creed is of course a profession of faith. In subsequent apparitions, Our Lady presented the recitation of the Creed as a means of strengthening the faith and she said that the recitation of the Creed and seven Our Fathers, Hail Marys, and Glory Be's should be the minimum of one's daily prayer. The seven Our Fathers, Hail Marys, and Glory Be's are a devotional prayer recited in honor of The Seven Sorrows of Our Lady.

When Our Lady finally took leave of the seers on June 25, her words of farewell were, "Go in the peace of God." We are in God's peace when we believe in him and live according to our faith.

The message of faith becomes more explicit from the third day on. On that day, June 26, when asked why she had come and what she wanted, Our Lady replied, "I have come because there are many believers here. I want to be with you to convert and reconcile everyone." Her words of farewell were once again, as henceforth they will always be, "Go in the peace of God."

As Marija was returning home after the June 26 apparition, Our Lady appeared to her again when she was halfway to the village. She stood in front of a cross that did not have the body of Christ on it. She was crying and tears streamed down her cheeks. After asking where the other girls were, she said, "Peace, peace, peace. Reconcile yourselves." Her last words were, "Go in the peace of God."[1]

This was an important apparition. It made clear that people were being called to reconcile themselves with God. Peace would result from that reconciliation. The cross without the body of Christ is rather uncommon in Catholic piety and so may have special significance. It could be that the absence of the corpus was meant to symbolize the rejection of Christ and of faith in him, and this is what caused the great sorrow and weeping of Mary, the mother of Jesus.

On the fourth day, when Our Lady was asked to prove that she was appearing, she replied that those who do not see her should believe as though they were seeing her; and when asked if she had a message for the parish and the priests, she said, "The Friars should believe firmly."

The fifth day saw new insistence on faith. When the seers asked Our Lady what she wanted of them, she replied, "Faith and respect for me." When they asked her what she wanted from priests, she said, "That they believe firmly." The reason for this answer is evident. The priests are the shepherds of the flock. To lead their sheep in their faith, they themselves must be staunch believers. Finally, when the seers asked Our Lady what she wanted of "these people gathered here," she replied, "That they believe without seeing."

Our Lady disappeared for a short while. When she returned, the seers resumed their questioning: "What do you want of these people here?" She replied, "That those here who do not see me, believe like the six of you who see me."

Again on the sixth day, the message of faith was reiterated in a powerful way. When the seers for the second time asked Our Lady what she wanted "from these people," her reply was, "There is only one God and one faith. Believe firmly!" On that same day, the seers asked another question very similar to the one above, "Dear Blessed Virgin, what is it that you want here?" Her answer was, "That you have firm faith and confidence." Finally, when Our Lady was asked to heal little Daniel, she replied, "Let them *(his parents who had carried him up the mountain side to the place of the apparitions)* firmly believe that he will be healed." Our Lady will continually stress faith as important for obtaining a healing.

The message of faith came through in a rather unusual way during an apparition that took place at Vicka's house in the middle of October 1981, exactly two days before Father Jozo's trial. Marinko and a few others were present. Our Lady smiled at Marinko. Then she came to where he was, kissed, embraced, and blessed him and said, "Marinko, do not give up your faith. Keep your faith."

There is another apparition which took place in the relatively early days of the Medugorje event that helps us understand the magnitude of the crisis of faith that the Catholic Church and all Christian churches are experiencing. This occurred on the Feast of Our Lady of the Angels, 1981. While Marija was in her room at home after the church service that evening, Our Lady appeared to her and said, "The devil is trying to infiltrate himself here in order to get something. He is making every effort and wants at any price to infiltrate among you."

In a report that Father Tomislav Vlasic sent to the Pope and to the Bishop of Mostar at the end of 1983, he gave some important information on the role of Satan in what we are witnessing in the Church and in the world today. The pertinent section of that report reads as follows:

> Mirjana says that in 1982 she had an apparition which, according to us, throws rays of light on the history of the Church. She tells of an apparition in which Satan came to her disguised as the Blessed Virgin. Satan asked Mirjana to renounce the Madonna and to follow him if she wanted to be happy in love and in life, whereas with the Blessed Virgin she would have to suffer. Mirjana repelled him. Immediately, the Blessed Virgin came and Satan disappeared.
>
> Then, the Blessed Virgin gave in substance the following message:
>
> —Excuse me for this, but you must know that Satan exists. One day, he presented himself before the throne of God and asked permission to try the Church for a period of time. God permitted him to try it during one century. This century is under the power of the devil, but when the secrets which have been confided to you have been fulfilled, his power will be

destroyed. Already now, he is beginning to lose his power and he has become aggressive: he destroys marriages, stirs up division between priests, brings about obsessions and murders. You must protect yourself by fasting and prayer, especially community prayer. Carry blessed objects with you. Place them in your houses. Return to the use of holy water.

According to certain Catholic experts who have studied these apparitions, this message of Mirjana would clarify the vision which the supreme Pontiff, Leo XIII, had. According to them, it was after having had an apocalyptic vision of the future of the Church that Leo XIII would have introduced the prayer to Saint Michael which priests recited after the Mass up until the Council. These experts say that the century of trials foreseen by the Supreme Pontiff, Leo XIII, is about to end.

At the conclusion of his report, Father Tomislav says that he "gave it to the seers so that they might ask the Blessed Virgin if its content was exact." Ivan brought him her reply: "Its content . . . is true."[2]

What we are witnessing in the world today is a particularly violent moment in the Christian warfare of which Saint Paul speaks in his *Epistle to the Ephesians:* "Our battle is not against human forces but against the principalities and powers, the rulers of this world of darkness, the evil spirits in regions above. . .In all circumstances, hold faith up before you as your shield; it will help you extinguish the fiery darts of the evil one" (6:12, 16).

Loss of faith can be said to be the ultimate cause of the impending catastrophe that menaces the world. But, what will this catastrophe consist of? The seers have been silent on this point. The most that can be surmised draws heavily on Father Tomislav's 1983 report to the Pope and the Bishop of Mostar. A section of that report was quoted in an earlier chapter. The last part of that quote seems to allude to this catastrophe although it should be noted that the word is not mentioned. Because of its importance the pertinent section is quoted once again, drawing the reader's attention to this particularly ominous phrase: "After the visible sign, *those who are still alive* (emphasis added) will have little time for conversion."

—The ninth and tenth secrets are grave matters. They are a chastisement for the sins of the world. The punishment is inevitable because we cannot expect the conversion of the entire world. The chastisement can be mitigated by prayers and penance. It cannot be suppressed. An evil which threatened the world, according to the seventh secret, has been eliminated through prayer and fasting, Mirjana said. For that reason, the Blessed Virgin continues to ask for prayer and fasting: "You have forgotten that with prayer and fasting you can ward off wars, suspend the laws of nature."

—After the first warning, the others will follow within a rather brief period of time. So it is that people will have time for conversion.

—This time is a period of grace and conversion. After the visible sign, those who are still alive will have little time for conversion. For that reason, the Blessed Virgin calls for urgent conversion and reconciliation.

—The invitation to prayer and penance is destined to ward off evil and war and above all to save souls.

—According to Mirjana, we are close to the events predicted by the Blessed Virgin. Because of this, Mirjana says to mankind: "Convert yourselves as quickly as possible. Open your hearts to God."[3]

Many of Our Lady's messages have made it clear that the reason for her appearances at Medugorje was the imminence of some great disaster that menaces the world. And this calamity was so terrifying and so close at hand that her motherly love for her children of the earth was prompting her to come and warn them so that they might do something about it. Father Tomislav writes of "a chastisement for the sins of the world." This retribution is close at hand because sins are multiplying at such a rapid rate; they have become so numerous and have been going on for such a long time that people have become hardened to them and have been lulled into a false sense of security. This has happened a number of times in the past and always with the same tragic results.

Examples abound in both Testaments of the Bible according to which the evil that people commit almost invariably leads to pain and destruction. It is not difficult to recognize in the present-day world sinful activities which are surely paths to destruction. Today, invoking constitutionally-guaranteed rights to free speech, the pornography industry—with only the most thinly veiled ties to organized crime—exploits practically every communications medium in its promotion of sexual promiscuity and wantonness. The natural relationship between love and sex, established by God at the time of the creation of man and woman *(Genesis 2: 23-25)* is treated as irrelevant and outdated.

But society is paying a terrible price for those mistakes. Sexually transmitted diseases are at epidemic levels, causing unprecedented concern among national health officials regarding the nation's ability to address the problem before millions of deaths ensue. It is not God who brings death to the sinner; it is godless behavior which leads to deadly excess. As it is explicitly stated in Proverbs (5:22-3): "By his own iniquities the wicked man will be caught, in the meshes of his own sin he will be held fast. He will die from lack of discipline, through the greatness of his folly he will be lost."

Families as well as individuals are being seriously affected by the lawlessness of the present times. The ever-increasing divorce rate in the U.S. has now reached the point where there is one divorce for every 1.8 families. The repercussions of this are tremendously harmful. More than a million children a year are involved in divorce cases.

Then, there are the millions being slaughtered each year by abortion and infanticide throughout the world. There are the evils of alcohol and substance abuse. Both of these are reaching more and more young people. And there are the crimes of violence, which in the United States are becoming more and more numerous within the family.

All of this has reached such proportions that it staggers the imagination. There seems to be no end of it in sight. It keeps increasing and increasing.

But these things cannot go on indefinitely. There comes a time when they call out to God for justice. Ralph Martin has described the situation in which the world finds itself at the present time in these terms:

> I believe that time is running out for our generation. I believe that our generation will see the fire of God. Our generation

faces a choice: repentance or judgment. Time ran out for Sodom and Gomorrah. Time ran out for the generation of Noah. Time tragically ran out for the city of Jerusalem. And time is running out for us.

I believe that God gives warnings to his people to turn back to him before it is too late. God warned the city of Jerusalem before the Roman armies destroyed it. He warned Nineva and he warned Noah's generation. Jesus indicates in Luke (13: 1-5), that God also gives people warnings by means of natural disaster.

Ralph Martin goes on to mention among these signs and warnings, "the various kinds of incurable diseases" and "the strange weather of recent years," the droughts and floods and earthquakes and volcanic eruptions that have occurred throughout the world. And one must not forget the ever-present threat of extinction by nuclear bombs.

During the present time of grace God calls us to repent and turn back to him. This is a time of visitation, a time of choice. At Medugorje, Our Lady had been repeating in her own words what Isaiah said to Israel in his day: "Seek the Lord while he may be found, call him while he is near" (55:6).

Just as the destiny of Noah's generation lay in the hands of that generation, and that of Jesus' generation lay in its own hands, so does the destiny of the present generation lie in its own hands. Will it be the peace that flows from repentance and reconciliation with God and one's fellowmen, or will it be the catastrophe Our Lady has frequently warned about at Medugorje?

Coming within sight of the city, he wept over it and said: "If only you had known the path to peace in this day...Days will come upon you when your enemies will encircle you with a rampart . . . will wipe you out, you and your children within your walls, and leave not a stone within you, because you have failed to recognize the time of your visitation" (Luke 19: 41-44)

At Fatima, Our Lady prophesied World War II as a punishment for the sins of that era. At Medugorje, she tells the world that its lack of faith and consequent sinfulness are about to exact a costly toll.

Chapter 25

Our Lady Queen Of Peace And Conversion

Our Lady Queen of Peace

In addition to faith, peace is another topic that stands out in the words spoken by Our Lady during the first days of the apparitions on Mount Podbrdo.

On June 25, the second day Our Lady appeared and the first on which she spoke, her parting words were: "Go in the peace of God." From that day on, her farewell would always be those very same words that feature the ultimate purpose of her coming to Medugorje, to bring the peace "of God," the peace that comes from living in His friendship.

On June 26, in the apparition to the six seers on Mount Podbrdo, Our Lady declared, "I have come to be with you to convert and reconcile everyone." In the subsequent apparition to Marija on her way home, she said, "Peace, peace, peace. Reconcile yourselves."

These two June 26 apparitions make it clear that the peace Our Lady is seeking is above all the peace of heart and mind that comes from conversion and reconciliation between God and men.

In addition to the frequent return of Our Lady to the topic of peace during her apparitions, three very special things have underscored how important she deems it to be.

There is the day on which she first chose to appear, June 24, the Feast of the Birth of Saint John the Baptizer, the precursor of Jesus Christ. It was John's mission in life to preach penance and reform of life which brings about peace of heart and mind. The next thing Our Lady did was to make it clear that a major objective in coming to Medugorje was the spiritual or inner peace that comes from reconciliation with God; this she did by stating that she wanted a new feast, Our Lady Queen of Peace, to be instituted in the Church on June 25, the day following the Feast of Saint John the Baptizer. Finally, there was the blazoning of the word *Mir* (Peace) in the sky above the cross on Mount Krizevac.

Peace in the world among nations would come about when men are reconciled with God and with each other.

Conversion

Because of the great decrease in faith and consequent prevalence of sin in the world, Our Lady has spoken frequently at Medugorje of conversion and of confession; conversion which includes reconciliation with both God and man, and confession which is the sacramental way through which reconciliation is effected in the Catholic Church.

On the third day on which Our Lady appeared, when Ivanka, at the suggestion of Marinko, asked her what she wanted at Medugorje, her reply was, "I want to be with you to convert and reconcile everyone." On that same day, after the apparition on the mountain side during which Our Lady gave the above reply, and as Marija was walking home from that apparition, she saw her again. Our Lady stood weeping in front of a cross that did not have a body of Christ on it. She said, "Peace, peace, peace. Reconcile yourselves."

On December 7, eve of the Feast of the Immaculate Conception, Our Lady said, "Many people are on the way to conversion, but not all of them." The next day, December 8, the seers had expected Our Lady to be joyful, as she usually was on her feast days, but to their surprise, Our Lady appeared very serious. She knelt down, opened her hands toward heaven, and began to pray, "My dear and beloved Son, please forgive those serious and numerous sins by which humanity is offending You." She continued to pray in this fashion, but the seers do not remember the exact words she used.

After she finished her prayer, she said the Our Father and the Glory Be with the young people. Then she told them that she prays daily at the foot of the cross on Mount Krizevac, asking her divine Son to forgive sinful humanity. [1]

Part of Father Tomislav Vlasic's August 15, 1983 interview deals with conversion, as the following paragraphs reveal:

> Already with the specific name with which she presented herself to the seers, "I am the Queen of Peace," Our Lady gave her main message, namely *mir,* which means peace.
>
> Several times, Our Lady told the seers that the world is living in great tensions and that it cannot be saved if it continues like this.
>
> The world has to find peace to be saved. But it will not find peace without God. It will only find peace in God.
>
> Therefore, Our Lady asks for conversions . . . The call to conversion has been strong, especially in recent times.
>
> A message was given to one of the seers in the following words: "Tell my sons and daughters, tell all the world as soon as possible that I desire their conversion. The only word I give to the world is: 'Convert—and do not wait.' I will ask my Son that he not punish the world, but that the world be saved. You don't know, nor can you know, what God will send to the world. Convert yourselves, renounce everything, be ready for everything, because all this is part of conversion."
>
> A few days ago *(a few days before August 15, 1983),* Our Lady repeated her call to conversion, saying: "Tell the world not to wait. It needs to convert itself. When God comes, he will not joke with anybody. I tell you that you have to take my messages seriously." [2]
>
> Our Lady has promised to leave a sign on the mountain of the apparitions. This sign will be given for atheists . . . Regarding the sign, Our Lady said: "You faithful must not wait for the sign to convert yourselves. Don't delay in converting yourselves. This is a time of grace for you. You can never thank God *(enough)* for this grace He has given you.

This time is for a deepening of faith and for your conversion. When the sign comes it will be late for many."

On April 20, 1983, one of the seers saw Our Lady crying for sinners and heard her make an important plea on their behalf: "I would like to convert them, but they don't convert themselves. Don't wait . . . I need your prayer and your penance."

"I need your prayer and your penance." This plea for sinners was addressed specifically to the seers, but there can be no doubt that Our Lady intended it for all of us. If for no other reason than our own self-interest, we should take this plea to heart. It is only through prayer and penance that the catastrophe that hangs over the world will be mitigated.

Our Lady made a similar plea at Fatima. In the course of the fourth apparition, in August 1917, she said to the three little shepherds, "Pray, pray very much and make sacrifices for sinners, for many souls go to hell because they have no one to make sacrifices and to pray for them."

At Medugorje, the specific form of penance that Our Lady asks for is fasting: the austere form of fasting on bread and water. The efficacy of that form of penance was indirectly brought out on August 15, 1983, when Our Lady said that "Satan is furious with those who fast and convert themselves." In many of her messages fasting was particularly linked with conversion. Father Tomislav Vlasic has said, "From the beginning, Our Lady has underlined that conversion can only come about through prayer and fasting."[3]

Chapter 26

Monthly Confession And The
Triduum of Reconciliation

On August 6, 1982, Our Lady made this statement which has been so marvelously taken to heart and so effectively applied by the priests of Saint James parish: "If Christians started to go to confession every month, reconciling themselves with God and their neighbors, soon whole Christian regions would be spiritually healed."[1]

The key to the spiritual transformation of Saint James parish that deeply impresses all who go there is the Triduum of Reconciliation which is held each month.

When on July 1, 1981, the eighth day of the apparitions, the pastor, Father Jozo Zovko, introduced the first rosary at five p.m. and the first Mass at six p.m., he could not have foreseen what this would ultimately lead to. The jammed church which greeted him when he went in to celebrate that Eucharist was the first of the many overflowing churches that would follow.

When the Sacrament of Reconciliation was made readily available at the daily evening Mass, an important step toward the Triduum of Reconciliation was taken.

The Triduum is a montly event that starts at the evening service on the last Thursday of the month. On that day, the regular daily schedule of rosary, apparition, seven Our Fathers, and Eucharist is immediately followed by a Holy Hour in the presence of the Blessed Sacrament. On Friday the hour of Eucharistic adoration after the Mass is replaced by an hour of veneration of the Cross. On Saturday it is replaced by devotions to the Blessed Virgin. On all three days confessions are heard, and many more priests come to help.

Sunday is the Feast of Reconciliation and features reconciliation between families. Families in the same neighborhood get together for a meal. The focus on this day is the joy that comes from reconciliation.

Speaking of the Triduum of Reconciliation, Father Tomislav says it is "not just a monthly confession to pass in front of a priest." In other words it is a confession in depth. An American priest of Croatian extraction went to Medugorje in the summer of 1983. Because he spoke Croatian he was asked to hear confessions, which he did outside of the church. He heard confessions for four-and-a-half hours and was deeply impressed with the depth or quality of the confessions. This was true of all who came to him, irrespective of their age, the young as well as the older people. As he expressed it, "These were not the usual shopping-list confessions."

The Sacrament of Reconciliation is being used as it was meant to be used, as a tool or means of growth in holiness as well as a means of forgiveness, of reconciliation. In addition to the forgiveness of the sins confessed, the Sacrament of Reconciliation brings the penitent special help or grace to overcome and eradicate these sins.

Thanks to the device of the Triduum of Reconciliation, the people are regularly reminded of Our Lady's request for monthly confession and they are helped by their priests to derive maximum benefit from this important and presently neglected sacrament. It is not without reason that Medugorje is said to be something unique.

The strong emphasis on confession in the Medugorje message may well be one of the reasons why Our Lady chose to appear in the parish of Saint James. There are a considerable number of Franciscan priests in that area who can be called upon to help with the confessions. There is a large monastery at Humac, which is only a dozen miles from Saint James church. Several priests from that monastery have been coming daily to hear confessions. Then there are a number of Franciscan-staffed parishes within reasonable proximity of Medugorje. That explains how at times there have been thirty or more priests hearing confessions there.

The parish staff has not had to introduce new devotions to renew the parish. It has had the vision to see that all the tools needed were already at hand. All that was needed was to make these tools available to the people.

Chapter 27

Prayer And The Sacraments

Prayer

Prayer is a theme that is woven through the entire fabric of the Medugorje apparitions. Since the first days, it has come back many times. It is the solid rock upon which firmly rests the spiritual structure Our Lady has been building. Prayer is the life blood of the soul, keeping it healthy and vigorous. Without it, the soul is weakened and eventually exposed to the death of serious sin. Never was man more in need of prayer than today, when sin invites him on every side. That is why Our Lady has so frequently asked for prayer at Medugorje.

Our Lady began asking for prayer from the very first days of the apparitions. On the second day, June 25, 1981, the seers recited seven Our Fathers, seven Hail Marys, and seven Glory Be's in the presence of Our Lady. She joined them in saying these prayers[1] and told them to continue, asking that they also say the Creed once. On another occasion she stated that these prayers are the minimum a person should say each day. They have been a much used prayer at Medugorje and constitute a part of the daily liturgy held in the church each evening. It should be noted that prayer was the very first thing Our Lady recommended at Medugorje. That alone reveals how much importance she attaches to this devotion.

On the fifth day of the apparitions, the seers asked Our Lady if she preferred that they pray or sing. Her reply was that they "do both, pray and sing." The singing of religious hymns is, of course, a form of prayer.

It is significant that with the exception of the first and the second day of the apparitions, which were unusual ones, Our Lady appeared only after the young people had started praying. And it has continued that way ever since.

Not only has Our Lady requested prayer but she has frequently prayed with the seers during the apparitions. This usually occurs when the young people ask Our Lady to pray for some intention, such as a healing. Our Lady will say, "Let us pray together for this." When she prays with them this way, the seers' voices become audible. It is the only part of their conversation with Our Lady that is ever heard by the spectators. It has also happened occasionally that when a seer was praying somewhere for the healing of a certain person, Our Lady appeared and prayed with the seer.

All of the seers have received what could be called graces of prayer. They pray more; they pray better. This is true not only of the original group of seers but also of Jelena and Marijana. Their personal prayer life has improved. Also, prayer is the heart of the messages these two seers have been asked to transmit to others. When asked if Our Lady ever told her to do something for other people or to show them something, Marijana answered, "No, except to give them the message to pray and fast and to tell them that prayer is the most important."

Our Lady's request for prayer has frequently been a joint request for prayer and fasting for the conversion of sinners. As already mentioned, one of the seers saw Our Lady on April 20, 1983, crying for sinners and pleading on their behalf: "I would like to convert them, but they don't convert themselves. Don't wait...I need your prayer and your penance."

In her pleading for the world, Our Lady also linked fasting with prayer, reminding us of how pleasing to God this can be: "You have forgotten that with prayer and fasting you can ward off war and suspend natural laws." It is a fact that fasting and penance are pleasing to God and strengthen our prayer when they are joined to it.

The meditation prayer group which Our Lady told Jelena she wanted established is a powerful indication of the importance Our Lady attaches to prayer.

There has never been any let-up in Our Lady's request for

prayer. Indeed, her plea for prayer only seems to have become more frequent and more insistent as time has gone on.

On July 20, 1984, Our Lady gave the seers instructions on how to pray. The following information concerning this apparition was given by Marija:

> Our Lady said, "Open your hearts and come. Pray your prayers out loud." We used to say our prayers for ourselves, in our hearts. But the Blessed Virgin said, "Speak, speak. I know your pains. When you express them to me out loud it is going to be easier for you."
>
> Then we started. As we were saying those prayers, she was following each of us with her eyes and she looked as though she were feeling with each one who was praying, each one in the group. Someone was praying for the Bishop.[2] Then, a large tear came from Our Lady's eyes. She had her hands together and she started crying even more. Then, she said to us: "You are my little flowers. Be my light."
>
> Then, with her hands she indicated that we should kneel and she said a prayer which we could not understand.
>
> Then, she blessed us with her cross and said: "Pray, my children. It will be easier for me," and she went away crying.[3]

"Pray, my children. It will be easier for me." Apparently, something was causing Our Lady deep sorrow and the prayers of the children would alleviate that sorrow. We are reminded of Francisco of Fatima, who delighted in spending hours before the tabernacle "consoling" Jesus.

"Speak, speak. I know your pains. When you express them to me out loud it is going to be easier for you." Our Lady does not need to have the seers speak out their needs. She knows them even before they express them. The seers are the ones who will benefit from praying out loud. It will be recalled that in her January 10, 1983, interview with Father Tomislav Vlasic, Mirjana, the seer from Sarajevo, spoke at some length about praying out loud. It was evident that she derived benefit from this manner of praying.

It would be interesting to know how frequently Our Lady spoke about praying aloud and what other things she might have said about this manner of praying.

In a talk to a group of Italian pilgrims on June 3, 1984, Father Tomislav said Our Lady gave the following message on Holy Saturday, April 21, 1984. It would seem that the message was received by Jelena:

"Open your hearts and raise your hands because Jesus wants to give you a special gift, which is also my gift. It is this: The trials you will have to go through, you will go through easily. We will show you the way out, if you follow us.

"Don't say that the Holy Year is finished and that you can stop praying. Rather, increase your prayers. Let the Holy Year be a stepping stone ahead."

And the seer saw the Resurrected Christ. From His wounds came a brilliant light that fell on all the people. . . "Tell all the people they can be happy only with me."

An interesting message was addressed to the members of the parish staff in March 1984. Our Lady said that they were wasting a lot of time giving information to people. She asked them not to do this. "Please make this a place of prayer."

In response to a question which a priest had asked the seers to submit to Our Lady, she explained her role as an intercessor. Her answer was: "Please pray to Jesus. I am His mother and I intercede with Him. But all prayer goes to Jesus. I will help, I will pray. However, everything does not depend on me, but also on your strength and that of those who pray."[4]

As previously seen, Our Lady has especially recommended certain prayers, but she has also taken into consideration the varying needs and capacities of different types of people and has offered many options.

Without any attempt to establish any order of importance among them, the following is a list of prayers and devotions Our Lady has mentioned at Medugorje: the seven Our Fathers, Hail Marys, and Glory Be's, and the Creed, the traditional rosary of Our Lady, the rosary of Jesus Christ, prayer for healing, meditative prayer, devotion and consecration to the Hearts of Jesus and Mary, the Sacrament of Reconciliation, the Mass, and Communion.

One should not be misled into believing that Our Lady, favors only these prayers and devotions. She has emphasized the fact that every prayer is pleasing to God if it comes from the heart.

Prayer for Healing

Prayer for healing has played a significant role at Medugorje. For a long while, people were prayed over individually as well as collectively each night at the conclusion of the evening Mass. The seers were involved in the small groups that prayed individually over people. When this became too great a burden because it sometimes went on until midnight, it was greatly reduced.

Father Rupcic asked the six seers what Our Lady required of people who wanted to be healed. From the answers they gave, it is clear that especially four things are required: faith, fasting, prayer, and penance. Faith is very important. "She requires strong faith most of all," one of the seers replied. [5]

In his report on Medugorje, Father Thomas Forrest gives the following information concerning what Our Lady has told the seers about praying for the sick and for healing:

> The answer to such prayers depends not only on the one who does the praying, but also on the one being prayed for. The sick person himself must also be praying and even fasting.
>
> The surest paths to healing are those of faith and of abandonment to God.
>
> In praying for the recovery of the gravely sick, not just one but a whole group of people should undertake the prayer, continuing to pray daily for the sick person, fasting for him as well. The Madonna has said for the healing of the sick: "I need the help of your prayers and sacrifices."
>
> The shortest daily prayer for a sick person, according to the Madonna, is an Our Father, a Hail Mary, and a Glory Be to the Father. But, she adds that any kind of prayer for them is good.
>
> The Madonna has stated: "I myself cannot heal you. Only God Himself can heal you."
>
> Priests who wish to grow in this gift, must learn to pray and to fast a great deal.
>
> The Madonna speaks about two things that are very useful in praying for healing: the imposition of hands, and the anointing with blessed oil.
>
> She also ties in closely the Sacrament of Reconciliation with healing, and Medugorje has seen even physical healings take

place through the making of a good confession.

The Sacraments

Although Our Lady does not seem to have spoken with as much frequency about the Eucharist as about some other topics, there can be no doubt that it is an extremely important part of the Medugorje message. It is the more uncommon parts of her verbal message that have been publicized. This is quite understandable but it would be most unfortunate if this were to result in neglecting that greatest channel of God's grace.

As more and more information has come forth, it has become increasingly clear that the Eucharist holds center stage in Medugorje and that from the very start Our Lady spoke to the six seers about the Eucharist and its importance with more frequency than was suspected. This helps to understand why the parish staff has placed so much emphasis on the Mass and public adoration of the Blessed Sacrament in the church services that have been made available to parishioners and pilgrims.

It is also a fact that Our Lady herself has brought the Eucharist into her messages and requests in a new and more insistent way as time has gone on. She has done this through the new seers, Jelena and Marijana: through the personal messages she gave them and through the messages intended for the parish. One should recall Jelena's statements to the effect that Our Lady never spoke to her about the rosary but spoke to her about the Mass, saying that it is "the best" and that the people should "go to Mass more and more and to Communion." Moreover Our Lady recommended that the members of the meditation prayer group go to Mass "frequently, every day if possible."

One of the strong signs pointing to the authenticity of the Medugorje message is its emphasis on the Sacraments of the Church, particularly Reconciliation and the Eucharist.

Chapter **28**

Penance, Fasting, And Reparation

The strong focusing on penance and specifically on fasting in the message of Medugorje is certainly one of the things that differentiate it from other Marian apparitions. The Fatima message places much emphasis on penance and sacrifice, but of quite a different kind. Sister Lucy has made it clear that at Fatima Our Lady was not seeking austere forms of penance, such as fasting on bread and water. Rather, she was asking for the smaller and more humble penances and sacrifices that are involved in willingly and lovingly accepting the pain and hardship that so often accompany the fulfillment of our daily occupations and duties.

An important aspect that the penance messages of Fatima and Medugorje have in common with each other is reparation or atonement. Reparation was explicitly mentioned many times at Fatima, as when Our Lady asked the three children to pray and make sacrifices for sinners because there are none to do this for them. All three children responded generously to this request. This was especially true of little Jacinta, the youngest of the trio. She became a real heroine of reparation, seemingly never able to do enough for poor sinners.

Reparation is an important facet of the Medugorje message. Our Lady frequently requested prayer and fasting. Extreme times require extreme measures. Our Lady's message that the world is on the edge of catastrophe is the key to understanding the austere message of Medugorje, particularly the often repeated request that we fast on bread and water. One cannot understand the extent of Our Lady's pleading for fasting on bread and water except in the light of the perilous times in which we live.

Maybe it is because of the great need for reparation at this particular moment of history that Yugoslavia was chosen for these apparitions. Living under a Communistic regime that harasses believers, the Croatian Catholics would be disposed to accept at face value their heavenly Mother's disturbing message, including its austere requests. It cannot be denied that the request for fasting on bread and water is austere; nor can there be any doubt that Our Lady deems fasting on bread and water very important in the present crisis, for that request has been repeated and even intensified and broadened.

She began by asking for fasting on bread and water once a week, on Fridays. Then she requested a second day, Wednesday. All of the six seers have complied and fast on bread and water twice a week. So too has the parish staff of priests and sisters. The people of Medugorje have also responded generously to Our Lady's plea. A good half of the parish began fasting once a week on bread and water, and since Our Lady asked for a second day of fasting, some have been doing this. Among the seers, Marija and one or two of the other girls have added a third day of fasting, which is Saturday. But on this third day, the fasting is not so severe and some potatoes are taken along with the bread and water.

A new dimension was added to the fasting when Our Lady asked the seers to prepare for the Feast of the Immaculate Conception by a novena which includes nine days of fasting on bread and water. More recently she asked not only the seers but everyone to prepare for her birthday with three days of fasting on bread and water.

There is considerable focus on reparation in the messages Our Lady has given for the parishioners of Saint James. It is especially clear in the following messages that were received during lent:

> I ask you in a special way during this Lent to honor the wounds of my Son which He received because of the sins of this parish. Unite yourselves with my prayers for this parish so that His sufferings may become bearable. *(March 22, 1984)*

> I am asking you to venerate the Heart of my Son, Jesus.
> Make atonement for the wounds inflicted upon the Heart of my
> Son. That Heart has been offended by all sorts of sins.
> *(April 15, 1984)*

Fasting is a powerful means of reparation, but to be effective it must be done with the proper motivation. Our Lady reminded the parishioners of Saint James of this in her message of September 20, 1984:

> Today, I ask you to start fasting, putting your heart in it.
> There are many who fast, but only because everyone else is
> fasting. It has become a custom that no one wants to stop. I
> ask the parish to fast out of gratitude to God for allowing me to
> remain this long in this parish.
> Dear children, fast and pray with your heart.

At Medugorje, Our Lady's request for fasting was almost always joined to a request for prayer, because fasting and other forms of penance render our prayer more pleasing to God. Aware of this, the saints, who are our models, frequently joined penance to their prayers, especially when they prayed for important things. Fasting in the early or apostolic church seems to have always been linked to prayer when important issues were at stake *(Acts 13: 2-3; 14:23)*. Fasting liberates the mind and the spirit, disposing us to pray.

Many people need to get rid of false notions and prejudices about fasting that create a psychological state which makes it much more difficult than it would be if fasting were approached in the proper state of mind.

The generous response of the local people to fasting on bread and water is striking. Another form of penance that is less sensational but still noteworthy is that practiced by those who come to daily Mass. Most of them walk considerable distances. They do this in all kinds of weather. The rainy and cold days are not the only ones that involve hardship. The summers are intensely hot in the Medugorje area. It will be remembered that three of the girls were overcome by heat during one of the June 1981 apparitions.

The stipulation that those who join the meditation prayer group must fast twice a week on bread and water and may later be asked to add more fasting and prayer, if problems arise, is just one more bit of evidence of the important place this form of penance holds in Our Lady's messages at Medugorje.

The Feast of the Exaltation of the Holy Cross on September 14 is one of the days that draws great crowds to Medugorje. A large number of people, including young people, climb up and down Mount Krizevac barefooted, in order to attend the Mass that is always celebrated there at the concrete cross on that day.

Since Our Lady began appearing on Mount Krizevac in 1984, it has become a popular place for those who wish to pray and do penance. Mount Podbrdo has never ceased to attract people. Although the distance to the site of the apparitions is not quite as great as that to the cross of Mount Krizevac, the path is more difficult and painful.

Although Our Lady has said that "the best" form of fasting is on bread and water alone, she is well aware that this is not possible for everyone, for example those who are too sick or too weak to do so. These people can renounce different things. She said: "First of all, renounce television programs. They are a great source of sin for your families. After these programs, you are incapable of praying. Renounce alcohol, cigarettes, and various pleasures. Everyone can make these renunciations."

Our heavenly mother's insistence on penance, especially on fasting on bread and water, indicate her evaluation of the magnitude of the catastrophe that awaits the world if people do not repent and reconcile themselves with God and neighbor.

Chapter 29

Miscellaneous Messages

A considerable number of the messages which Our Lady imparted at Medugorje were for special categories of people. Among them have been messages for priests and a few specifically addressed to the priests of St. James.

The Bishop of Mostar

There have been messages for the Bishop of Mostar, His Excellency the Most Rev. Pavao Zanic. In response to a question by Father Rupcic, Marija mentions a message for the bishop which the seers communicated to him at the time it was received. [1]

In the summer of 1983, Our Lady told the seers to fast twice a week for the Bishop because he carries a heavy responsibility. She added that, if necessary, she would ask for a third day of fasting. She also asked them to pray for the Bishop every day. Since then Our Lady has frequently requested prayers for the Bishop.

The Pope

There have also been messages for the Pope. Some of these are secrets which the seers cannot speak about until Our Lady tells them they can, and some are not secrets. For example, the Pope should consider himself as the father of all peoples and not only of Christians. And he should tirelessly and bravely spread the message of peace and love towards all people. [2]

Poland and Russia

In October 1981, Our Lady gave Marija the following messages that were in reply to questions asked by a priest from Mostar. There was a message concerning Poland to the effect that there would soon be great conflicts there but that the just would be victorious. There was also a message which stated that Russia is the nation where God will be the most glorified.[3] This last message brings to mind the prophetic message of Fatima in which Our Lady asked that Russia be consecrated to her Immaculate Heart by the Pope in union with all the bishops of the world, stating that the nation would eventually be consecrated to her Immaculate Heart and converted, and a period of peace would be granted to the world.[4]

False Prophets

In Mirjana Dragicevic's interview with Father Tomislav Vlasic on January 10, 1983, she told him that Our Lady had spoken to her about the false prophets of our day. She told her that there are "a great number of false prophets in the world in our time. There are many who lie, claiming that they see her or Jesus." She said that "this is a great sin" and that we should pray a lot for these people. They don't understand how grave a sin it is to lie about seeing someone from heaven. Mirjana added that she and the Blessed Virgin prayed for fourteen days "only for false prophets."

October 13, 1984, message for priests

In October 1984, about six thousand priests from all over the world attended a charismatic retreat in Rome during which they were privileged to hear Pope John Paul II and Sister Teresa of Calcutta among other speakers. After the retreat, one hundred and ten American priests went to Medugorje. On October 13, they met in late afternoon with four of the seers in the hall under the rectory. A few French and Italian priests were there also and during the meeting Our Lady appeared to the seers and gave this message:

> My dear sons, today the Lord has permitted me to gather you here to give you the message which is for all those who love me.

My dear sons, pray and always ask God to continue to inspire you. In everything you do in the future, always seek the will of God.

My dear sons, thank you for having answered my call to come here.

Like most of the messages of Our Lady at Medugorje, this one is short and simple, but it is vitally important and bears close scrutiny. It contains much more than appears at first sight.

"Today, the Lord has permitted me to gather you here." Our Lady is saying that the priests she is talking to are a very special group. They are not there by chance but have been specially picked and called by her from three foreign countries. Although the priests have come mainly from one country, the message of this day is for all priests, "for all those who love me."

Then the core of the message is a reminder to all priests of their call to holiness without which they will be simply "noisy gongs and clanging cymbals" *(I Cor. 13:1)*. That holiness is not complicated: "Pray and always ask God to continue to inspire you. In everything you do in the future, always seek the will of God."

It is fitting that this account of the happenings at Medugorje close with this message addressed to priests. Our Lady has appeared there because of a crisis of faith. Ultimately, it is the priests who are the guardians of the faith in the day to day life of the Church.

Epilogue
Mary Our Mother

What must be seen first in any apparition, Marian or other, is the goodness of our heavenly Father; for Mary, like any heavenly visitor, comes as His messenger, as one sent by Him.

Mary is not just any messenger. She is the Father's very best messenger, the one He reserves to bring His most important messages to His children of the earth. And so it is that when Mary appears somewhere and gives us proof that it is indeed she, we must take notice for we know that there is something significant at stake for us.

One of the foremost things that the Father wants to teach us when He sends Mary as His messenger is that she is no ordinary person in His plan for our salvation. This apparently is something that we have difficulty in understanding, for He keeps sending Mary to us again and again. This is especially true of the last 125 years, starting with Lourdes in 1858.

The Father sends Mary because she is important and He wants us to know it, but He also sends her because she is our mother, our spiritual mother, given to us by Jesus from the Cross as a last testament and proof of His love.

There is no role that Mary delights in more than that of being our spiritual mother. In the apparitions where she is involved, the seers immediately perceive this. Medugorje is no exception. One of the ways in which she manifested the tenderness of her affection for the seers was by calling them "her angels, her dear angels." She lost no time in doing this, using the expression for the first time on the fourth day she appeared.

Allowing people to touch her was an unusual manifestation of Our Lady's love, one that could be readily understood by both the seers and the people. On the sixth day she appeared, Our Lady allowed Dr. Glaumuzina, the observer sent by the authorities at Citluk, to touch her. She allowed spectators to touch her on other occasions, as was seen. I know of no other Marian apparition where Our Lady submitted to such a thing.

Our Lady was even more condescending than this in her manifestations of motherly love at Medugorje. We recall her apparition to Jakov and Vicka that occurred in the latter's house in the fall of 1981. Marinko, a few children, and some adults were present. Our Lady "smiled" at Marinko. Then she "came" to him, "kissed, embraced and blessed" him. A little later, she "blessed" the children and the adults. She had blessed and kissed people on other occasions also.

For a long while, Our Lady allowed the seers to transmit questions to her on the part of people and she answered many of these questions. The seers said that she blessed all the articles that were on the table over which she appeared in the church.

There was a powerful teaching in all these many kindnesses of the Blessed Virgin and it was basically the same teaching for all the recipients of these loving acts, whether they were seers or others: "I am your mother, the most tender and considerate of all mothers. I want to establish a warm, loving relationship with each and every one of you. I want you to be simple and childlike in your dealings with me. My son, Jesus, told you that you had to become like 'little children' *(Mt 18: 3)*. That is the way I want you to be with me."

All of the seers of Medugorje would undoubtedly subscribe to what Mirjana said about Our Lady:

> At the beginning, I looked on her as something inaccessible, but now when she is with me, I look on her as a mother, as my best friend who helps me.
>
> I . . . became very close to her. I felt she loved me with a

motherly love. I was able to ask her questions about anything I wanted to.[1]

Devotion to our Blessed Mother has suffered greatly in the last twenty years. This has been a tremendous loss for the Church. To restore love of her and confidence in the power of her intercession is one of the important purposes for which the Father sent her to Medugorje. Certainly one of the reasons why these apparitions have been going on for so long is the low ebb that our love of her and recourse to her have reached.

We saw that Our Lady asked that the members of the meditation prayer group consecrate themselves to her Heart and abandon themselves completely to her. Consecration to Mary is not something new. It was popularized by Saint Louis de Montfort (1673-1716) during his life time of preaching and bequeathed to posterity through his spiritual classic, *A Treatise on the True Devotion to the Blessed Virgin.*[2] Saint Maximilian Kolbe was a modern day apostle of total consecration to Mary. It was undoubtedly through the influence of the writings of this Polish Franciscan, that Pope John Paul II came to consecrate himself to Mary and took as a motto, both as Bishop and as Supreme Pontiff, *Totus tuus Maria* — I am all Yours, Mary. Our recent Popes, Pius XII, Paul VI, and John Paul II have all consecrated the world to the Immaculate Heart of Mary.[3]

At Fatima Our Lady asked for the consecration of Russia to her Immaculate Heart, promising the conversion of that country and a period of peace for the world through the consecration. It was a particular form of consecration that she requested, namely, a consecration of Russia by the Pope in union with all the bishops of the world. This remains to be done.[4] It would seem that there has not been enough prayer and penance to bring this about and that to obtain these prayers and penance is one of the reasons why Our Lady has come to Medugorje.

The Hail Holy Queen has been one of the most popular prayers in the Church. Mary is reminding us at Medugorje that she is still "our Queen, our Mother of mercy, our life, our sweetness and our hope."

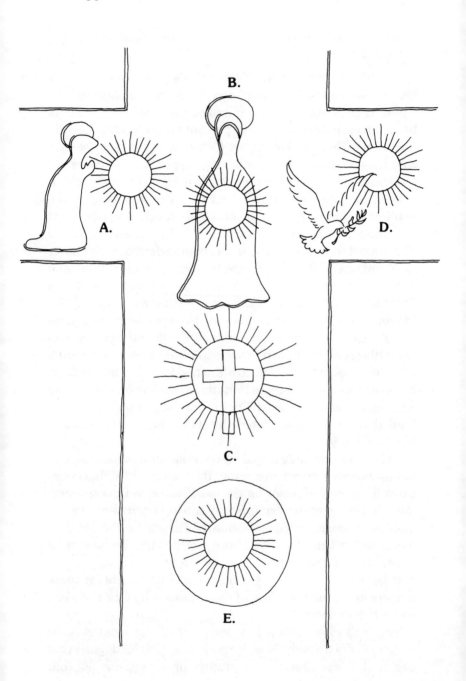

Appendix 1
A Recent Witness Speaks Out
The Christian Life As It Was Meant To Be Lived

John Craig and his wife, Joan, were part of a group of 175 people from Chicago and Cleveland who were in Medugorje from March 29 to April 4, 1985. John has written a moving account of what he and his wife experienced. Fortunately this report can be included as an appendix before going to press. The report has been shortened and a few editorial changes have been made.

Joan and I returned joyfully on Holy Thursday, April 4, from our pilgrimage to Medugorje, Yugoslavia, and we feel compelled to share our experience as it will profoundly influence our future lives.

We went to Yugoslavia as believers based on our reading the accounts of several authors. We returned with the deepened conviction of the blind man of the gospel who testified: "I know this much: I was blind before; now I can see" *(Jn 9: 25)*. Thus, our report is intended to testify only to what we saw, what we experienced, and what we learned. We leave the resolution of the question of authenticity to the Church.

PHYSICAL PHENOMENA INVOLVING THE SUN

We personally observed two remarkable phenomena involving the sun, and received the testimony of Father John O'Malley *(a visiting Irish missionary from Argentina)* about a third, separate phenomenon.

1. Gyrations of the Sun

During the period of time immediately preceding, during, and following the apparition to the seers (which occurred at 6:45 p.m., each day we were there) we observed the sun spinning, pulsating, and throbbing in the sky. This phenomenon was observable to the naked, unprotected eye.

Here is how this phenomenon was specifically observed. One looked directly into the sun. In approximately two to three seconds, a yellow halo formed around the sun, framing it. The sun viewed through the rimmed halo was then as clear as a full moon. The halo then faded away leaving only the sun.

The sun then did things in no particular sequence:

a. It spun in a clockwise direction so fast it gave the impression there were two suns.

b. It pulsated like a beating heart.

c. It throbbed as if moving closer to the earth and returning to its place.

These phenomena occurred on all four days of our visit and were visible from many different places throughout the surrounding geographic area.

2. Spiritual Figures Surrounding the Sun

The second, even more remarkable, phenomenon of the sun was also observable only during the time described above.

Here is a description of this phenomenon. The sun was viewed initially as described above, that is, through a halo, until it was as clear and as well defined as the moon. Then, five individual unique "overlays" became clearly visible on or near the sun *(See the drawings at the head of the appendix).*

a. The kneeling silhouette of the Blessed Mother to the upper left of the sun, at approximately "11 o'clock" on the sun.

b. The standing silhouette of the Blessed Mother *(front facade)* encompassing and blocking the sun.

c. A cross overlayed on and emanating from the sun.

d. A three-dimensional dove directly below the sun.

e. A perfectly round, white host encompassing and blocking the sun.

Again, these phenomena were observed by Joan and me and by many others of our group.

THE CROSS ON THE HILL

The following account was given by Father John O'Malley, Irish missionary from Argentina.

On one of the first mornings in Medugorje, the housekeeper in the home where he was staying came excitedly to his room to bring him to the front of the house. She pointed to the cross on Mount Krizevac. The horizontal member had disappeared. The base and the vertical members were present. The horizontal member returned to view in several minutes. There were no clouds in the sky.

The next morning at 7:30, Father O'Malley arose to observe the cross again. On this occasion, under sunlight conditions and a cloudless sky, both the vertical and the horizontal members were gone, leaving only the base visible to the viewer. Both members reappeared in several minutes.

THE FRUITS EVIDENT IN THE PARISH OF SAINT JAMES

Although less physically sensational, we believe that the most marvelous sign in Medugorje is the intense environment of prayer and Christian service that is evident throughout the community.

The parish holds devotional services every evening from six o'clock to nine. Joan and I attended these services for four consecutive evenings. They are offered in Croatian and consist of the following parts:

1. The recitation of the sorrowful and joyful mysteries of the rosary.

2. The Eucharist. This is the center of the devotional services. The Mass is profoundly devout. Every person sings every song. No song books are used and no hymn numbers posted. The entire church is a choir.

The consecration was the most devout community experience of my Christian life. Every knee in every crowded aisle and corner bends to the floor in adoration. At the words of the consecration, the faithful, in almost perfect spontaneous unison, can be heard to utter, "My Lord and my God", at the elevation of the Host and "My Jesus mercy" at the elevation of the Precious Blood. The experience must be lived to appreciate its full beauty and impact.

3. The blessing of religious objects. This centers around the recitation of the Litany of the Saints.

4. The prayers for healing. The principal celebrant prays over the entire congregation asking the Lord's healing for those who seek it.

5. The prayers for conversion. The principal celebrant leads the congregation in these prayers. The Blessed Mother asks that these prayers be said around the world: the Apostles' Creed, seven Our Fathers, seven Hail Marys and seven Glory Be's.

6. The recitation of the glorious mysteries of the rosary. This concludes the devotional services.

7. Confessions. These are heard throughout the entire three hours of the services.

Having described the sequence of the evening services, we now add our notes and observations regarding them.

1. Confessions are being heard perpetually. There is hardly ever a time, while the church is open, that they are not being heard. We would suggest that far more confessions were heard in the four days we were in Medugorje than we have seen heard during our lifetime.

2. The church is filled to overflowing every night and we saw no one leave early.

3. The services are packed with teen-agers and young adults.

4. The homilies are delivered with obvious conviction. Everyone listens with keen attention.

THE FRUITS IN THE VILLAGE COMMUNITY

We observed and received the simplest of loving care among the villagers as they went about their daily activities.

The recitation of the rosary was evident everywhere as one strolled the streets and fields of the village.

The peasant villagers received us and our fellow pilgrims, and, in spite of the language difference, treated us with spontaneous Christian care. We saw no frowns, only smiles, and evidence of great interior and exterior peace.

CONCLUSION

This simple report can only begin to convey all that one experiences in Medugorje.

We believe that the fruits evident in the parish of Saint James are the principal sign of Our Lady's presence and influence.

Our group agreed that what it saw in Medugorje was the living expression of what the Church has wanted to create in parishes since the Second Vatican Council.

Appendix 2
Two More Recent Witnesses Speak Out
A People Living According To The Gospel

In early March, 1985, John Franklin's wife went to see a video tape on Medugorje entitled: "Message for Peace." She was deeply moved and shared her experience with her husband. Two months later, John Franklin and his mother-in-law, Rita Schleker, were in Medugorje. They arrived there on May 10 and stayed eleven days. Happily the reports of both can be included in this book as an appendix. Both reports have been shortened and some editorial changes have been made.

John Franklin's Report

I know of no words to accurately describe Medugorje, the place and the people.

The people there were living the gospel as you might imagine it was lived shortly after the death of Jesus. It was evident in their happinesss, their generosity, and their peace. You could feel the presence of Jesus and Mary so strongly in these people and in this place.

I found it overwhelming that you could attain such closeness with so many people in so short a time. It seemed that in that place the fear of vulnerability was gone, your defenses were down. The stone walls built around our hearts after so many years of mistrust, fears, and worries were no longer needed.

People were genuine and openly honest. Most of them were truly seeking to repair and renew their relationships between themselves and with Jesus and Mary.

The church was alive, full of the Holy Spirit. Rarely had I

witnessed such Spirit-filled Masses. I found this to be true especially in the English-speaking Masses we shared most mornings with a few people in the chapel of the apparitions. All of the visiting priests were so spiritually moved. You could see it on their faces and detect it in their homilies.

Somehow, while there, all you had been taught or learned about God and the Church became so real. I could feel the peace of Christ in myself and in my brothers and sisters around me. We had nothing to fear. God was with us.

This is the miracle of Medugorje. It shows you to be free, to let go, to joyfully give yourself, your worries, your crosses, your free will, the gifts God had given you, back to him, knowing that He will provide, as only He can do.

I feel the urgency of spreading the message Mary has brought us at Medugorje, which is the gospel message of her Son, Jesus. The people of Medugorje are living this gospel message, as we are asked to do.

I was privileged to witness the dance of the sun twice and to be present at two apparitions.

On May 13 at about six-forty-five p.m., I witnessed it. I had been saying the rosary behind the rectory and on finishing it, walked around to the rear by the well. I noticed some people I had met looking up at the sun. I looked myself for an instant and noticed nothing more than the bright sun. Then I looked again and saw the sun quite clearly. It appeared to be closer than it normally is, and within the perimeter of the sun was a disc slightly smaller in diameter. The disc was semi-transparent white and blocked out the bright rays of the sun. Commonly referred to in Medugorje as the host, the disc was revolving around within the sun; but since it was somewhat smaller than the sun, it allowed bright rays to be emitted and it made the sun appear to be spinning. The disc would stand still and then begin revolving again, slowly at first and then faster, then slower again.

The sun itself moved about in the sky within a small area. I stood there in amazement for about ten minutes. On speaking with others, I learned that many symbolic things were seen within this same host. Some saw a cross. Others saw the Holy Spirit in the form of a dove, which appeared red to some and white to others.

On Sunday, May 19, I witnessed the dance of the sun a second time. I had been behind the church praying the rosary and had gotten up to go around to the front. At the side of the church, I noticed a large group of people looking up and pointing at the sun.

As on the first occasion, my first glance revealed nothing unusual. I continued walking and went into the church where I began to pray the rosary again. It was then about six-ten.

I noticed people entering the church, going to certain individuals, and taking them outside. I decided to go out and see what was happening. I looked at the sun, and as on May 13, saw a host somewhat smaller than the sun revolving within it. However, the light emitted around the sun's perimeter seemed more intense this time. Rays of gold and red were being sent off from either side of the top of the sun. These rays came from either side of the sun's top perimeter at opposite angles, the gold rays on the right and the red ones on the left. There were what appeared to be clouds around and behind the sun. As the colored rays flickered off these clouds, this gave them more prominence.

The relationship I now have with the Blessed Virgin because of all the events I experienced in Medugorje is something I will treasure forever. Through her intercession, I have been brought so much closer to her Son, Jesus.

New meaning has been given to my life.

Rita Schleker's Witness

(John and Rita were housed during their stay in Medugorje in the home of a family that lives at the foot of Mount Krizevac.)

For eleven days, we bathed in the loving hospitality of this family. What a joy to be submerged in Christianity! Since Our Lady came four years ago, this home has never been without a pilgrim. Sometimes these good people have housed one pilgrim and sometimes as many as twenty-five. Morning rosary and evening prayers were never omitted and happiness reigned.

In Medugorje, the priests urge one not to stand around outside the church waiting and looking for unusual signs to occur, but to go in the church and pray. That is what is important. Still, people are curious and eager to witness an unnatural phenomenon such as the sun dancing or pulsating, or the cement cross on the mountain spinning and rocking. Many people speak of such events.

On May 13, at six-ten, I was alone walking along the little

road to Saint James church when a young girl walking toward me asked, "Did you see the sun?" "No," I answered. "Well," she said, "look at it." I looked with no discomfort directly at the sun which was high in the sky. The girl standing at my side took off her sun glasses and lowered her head, saying, "I can't stand it."

I was enthralled and exclaimed, "Do you see those golden rays rising from the top left quarter of the sun? They are making an arc over the sun. Do you see the pinkish-red rays rising from the right quarter of the sun, making an arc away from the sun? Look! Do you see the bluish-green rays rising from the top of the sun and filling in between the golden and pinkish-red rays?"

The sun looked like a flat, gold disc. It came toward me and when it was halfway down, a host appeared in the middle of it. It kept coming closer to me until it looked to be about five feet above the electric wires. I knelt down at the roadside in awe.

The host was whiter than white and there was a cross marked on it. The host did not cover the sun completely for there was a rim of gold edging the host. It was obvious that the host moved within the sun or that the sun moved in back of the host, because the brilliant gold rim grew wider and then narrower.

I praised God and thanked him for his goodness, hoping that the host would come nearer. Then, I saw a heavy, thick white cloud sailing along the sky and coming right in the path of the sun, which had become a monstrance for the host. I begged Jesus not to let the cloud block out this beautiful sight. The cloud sailed right along in back of the sun and as it passed behind it, I could see the brilliance of the sunshine on the cloud.

A little Croatian lady, hurrying to the seven o'clock Mass, literally pulled me off my knees, saying, "Church, church!" As I got up, I looked at my watch. It was six-forty. For a half-hour, I had been engrossed in prayer, never taking my eyes off the sun and the host.

I linked arms with that sweet lady and we practically ran the rest of the way to the church. I regretted leaving my post and, as we went along, I tried to get a glimpse of the sun, but the tall poplar trees hid it from view. By the time we reached the church it was about six-fifty and the sun was high in the heavens and bright enough to blind me when I dared look at it.

Many people were standing outside the church, looking at the sun.

In Medugorje the deep reverence for Jesus in the Eucharist was touching. Religious and laity all genuflected devoutly. Priests at the consecration of the Mass genuflected reverently and raised the Host and the chalice slowly and with dignity.

The people never tired of answering the full fifteen decades of the rosary nor of participating in the prayers in honor of the Seven Sorrows of Our Lady. They remained after the Mass for adoration of the cross.

"I feel the urgency of spreading the message of Mary brought to us at Medugorje, which is the gospel message of her Son, Jesus. The people of Medugorje are living this gospel message, as we are asked to do." These words of John Franklin recall those with which John Craig ended his witness: "Our group agreed that what it saw in Medugorje was the living expression of what the Church has wanted to create in parishes since the Second Vatican Council." Both quotations say essentially the same thing. What God is doing through Mary in Medugorje is giving the world an example of how the Church should be lived, of what it means in the concrete to live the gospel message.

This helps one to understand why Our lady has been appearing for so long in this humble Yugoslavian village. The living of the gospel message has reached an extremely low ebb in the current era, and this throughout the entire world. The length of time of the apparitions has made it possible for literally millions of people *(the latest estimate is between four and five million)* from all over the world, even the remotest places, to come to Medugorje and witness what is going on there. The people who come do not witness the apparitions, but they witness the almost unbelievable spiritual renewal that these happenings have helped to bring about. All this would not have occurred if the apparitions had lasted but a few weeks or a few months. Our loving and merciful God has given the world an extraordinary grace at Medugorje.

Something that was said previously bears repeating here: the world is living in a time of grace during which God is calling people to repent and turn back to him. This is a time of visitation, a time of choice. At Medugorje, Our Lady has been repeating in her own words what Isaiah said to Israel in his day: "Seek the Lord while he may be found, call him while he is near" (55:6).

Appendix 3
Events In The Lives Of The Seers: 1985-88

The following information updates the book. Several important topics are involved.

Mirjana Sees Our Lady on her Twentieth Birthday

As stated earlier, on December 23, 1982, Our Lady told Mirjana, "she would be with her for the last time on Christmas." On Christmas day, 1982, Our Lady informed Mirjana that she would appear to her on each of her birthdays as long as she lives and that she would also appear to her "when something very difficult happened to her," when something "hurt her bad."

In April 1985, Mirjana wrote a report about the coming of Our Lady to her on her twentieth birthday. Surprisingly, Our Lady appeared to her on two consecutive days: on her birthday, March 18, and on the following day, March 19. Mirjana was not alone; others shared the apparition with her on both occasions:

> *(On March 18, her birthday.)* There were a number of people there. We started waiting for her at four o'clock in the afternoon. We prayed fifteen minutes. Then she *(came and)* spent fifteen minutes with us.
>
> She greeted me as always, "Praised be Jesus," and I responded.
>
> She congratulated me on my birthday and then we started our conversation.
>
> First, she complained because of unbelievers. She said:

"They are my children and I am suffering because of them, because they do not know what is awaiting them if they do not convert themselves. Therefore, Mirjana, pray for them!"

Then, we all prayed together. She started two Our Fathers and two Glory Be's.

Then she complained about the greed in the world and in Medugorje as well. She said, "Woe to those who would take everything from those who are coming *(to Medugorje)*, and blessed are those from whom they are taking everything." Then we said two Our Fathers and two Glory Be's for that intention.

I asked her that we all say the Hail Mary for her and she smiled at that.

Then we talked about the secrets. I told her that I had many questions *(about thirty)* to ask her. She smiled and told me not to worry about them, because when she comes to answer them, I will know all the answers and she will give me that grace *(sic)*. Otherwise, that would take too much time.

Then I asked her about Ivan. She said that the priests should stay with us to help us, for she has placed a heavy burden on us and the suspicions of the priests *(the distrust of us the priests have?)* hurt her.

Then I said the Hail Holy Queen.

I forgot something. When she was blessing all the holy objects and I put them next to me, she asked me to give her the rosary. She took it and started praying on it and said, "This is the way to pray on it. Tell that to everyone." She said that the rosary is not supposed to be a decoration, as it is for many.

(On March 19.) She appeared also on this day. The vision lasted seven minutes. There were four of us. We talked about the secrets and we prayed.

Nothing else important happened. She blessed us on both days.

Mirjana's Locutions

Mirjana has had six locutions between June 1, 1985, and August 27, 1985. This is a somewhat different happening than the once-a-year birthday visit which she had been told at Christmas, 1982, would be her lot from that date on. In these instances, Mirjana heard Our Lady rather than saw her.

Mary was giving her support because of a heavy burden

that she carried. That had been another promise that Our Lady made her when she discontinued her regular daily appearances: namely, to come to Mirjana when "something difficult happens to her." That something difficult was an attempt at entrapment. A girl who had been sent to befriend Mirjana at the University of Sarajevo slipped a drug into her beverage, unnoticed, as they were dining together. Our Lady spoke to Mirjana within her heart, warning her not to touch the beverage.

During a locution on August 15, Mirjana received the following message:

> My angel, pray for unbelievers. They will tear their hair. Brother will plead with brother. They will curse their past godless lives and repent. But it will be too late. Now is the time to do what I have been calling all to do these past four years. Pray for them.

Mirjana And The Secrets

Since June 1, Mirjana has chosen a priest to whom she will transmit the secrets ten days before they will occur. She has announced that the priest is Father Petar Ljubicic. He will make known each event to the public three days before its occurrence.

Another unscheduled appearance of Our Lady to Mirjana took place October, 25, 1985, at 1:50 p.m. and lasted eight minutes. Father Petar was present and Our Lady prayed twice in Latin over him and prayed with Mirjana for unbelievers, the sick, and poor people who live alone. Then the first secret was shown to the young woman like a film running before her eyes. She became very sad and tears filled her eyes. She asked, "Must it be this way?" and Our Lady answered, "Yes."

Mirjana had been told that Our Lady would come to her in a special apparition on February 15, 1986, at 2:00 p.m. Father Petar, informed of this promise, was present at its fulfillment and Mirjana said that Our Lady blessed him again. Later, on June 4, 1986, Mirjana had another apparition in which she reports that Our Lady gave her the final indications on the first secret to be fulfilled.

On January 28, 1987, Mirjana was favored with a special

apparition lasting about 10 minutes which took place in Sarajevo. The Blessed Mother gave the following message to the world:

My dear children, I came to you to lead you to purity of heart and thus to God. How have you welcomed me? At the beginning, doubtfully — in fear and distrust of the children I have chosen. Afterwards, the majority accepted me in their hearts and started to carry out my motherly requests but unfortunately that didn't last long. Wherever I appear, my Son is with me — but Satan also follows. You have unwittingly allowed him to take charge of you and rule over you. Sometimes you understand that some of your deeds are not allowed by God but you soon suppress those thoughts. Do not give in, dear children. Wipe away from my face the tears which I shed as I watch what you do. Look around you. Take the time to come to God in the church. Come into your Father's house. Take the time to meet for family prayer and to ask for God's grace. Remember your deceased; make them happy by offering Mass. Do not look down your nose at the poor man who is begging for a crust of bread. Do not send him away from your rich table. Help him and God will help you. It could very well happen that the blessing the beggar gives you will come to pass. God may listen to him. You have forgotten all this my children. Satan has influenced you. Do not give in! Pray with me! Do not fool yourself into thinking: I am good, but my brother who lives next to me is not good. You will be mistaken. It is because I am your mother that I love you and that I warn you. There are secrets my children. That is what is not known — and when it will be known it will be too late . Return to prayer. Nothing is more necessary. I would like it if Our Lord allowed me to explain the secrets to you a little, but He is already giving you enough graces as it is. Reflect on what you give Him. When was the last time you gave up something for the Lord? I will not blame you further, but once again I want to call you to prayer, fasting, and penance. If it is through fasting that you seek the Lord's grace, then let no one know that you are fasting. If it is through giving alms that you wish to obtain His grace, then let no one know but yourself and the Lord. Listen to me my children; in prayer reflect upon my messages.

On Mirjana's twenty-second birthday, March 18, 1987, Our Lady appeared to her and spoke of the secrets, of prayer, and of sacrifice during her visit of seven or eight minutes. Witnesses present included two priests, Fathers Pero and Rupcic, and a young layman studying at the University of Sarajevo, Marko Barbaric. He and Mirjana are studying economics and commerce. There are rumors of an impending marriage.

Vicka

Vicka has some serious ailment for which the doctors say they can do nothing. Sometimes she experiences excruciating pain which completely drains her physically. At these times, she has not been able to go to the church or the rectory, but Our Lady has appeared to her in her home. When she is not in pain, she is her old lively and sociable self.

Early rumors held that Vicka had a pathological condition, supposedly an inoperable cyst or benign tumor at the base of the brain. After many tests, this was disproved and then tests concentrated on the hypothesis of psychological disorders. A team of psychiatrists has since ruled this out. The prevailing opinion presently is that she suffers from a mystical malady.

For quite some time, she has been receiving details of Mary's life. During a twenty-five minute apparition in her home in early April 1985, she received the final details. She is said to have kept a written account of what Our Lady has told her.

Beside the physical suffering she was experiencing, no doubt in reparation for the sins of the world, Vicka was asked by Our Lady whether she were willing to accept three additional sacrifices, and she agreed. During the apparition on January 6, 1986, she was told that the first of these sacrifices was to begin that very day. For the next fifty days she would not see Our Lady; not until February 25. As promised, Our Lady did appear to her on February 25 and she thanked Vicka for the fifty-day sacrifice.

Then on April 24, 1986, Vicka received the ninth secret during an apparition which took place in her room. But it appeared that the second sacrifice was due and so for forty days she had to forego seeing Our Lady. The next apparition did occur on June 4, 1986. Not too long after this apparition she had to be hospitalized, but the surgery she underwent was not related to the pains in her head, but to a gallbladder ailment. Since then she has experienced the third sacrifice: a fifty-seven day period without seeing her beloved Lady; from August 25, 1986 to October 20.

Since then Vicka's life has alternated between periods of intense pain during which she is privileged to see Our Lady in company with others of the six seers and periods of twenty-five to fifty days when she does not see Our Lady but her sufferings are held in abeyance. On June 17, 1988, the *ABC 20/20 News* used almost half of its hour-long broadcast to show scenes of Medugorje and interviews with Vicka and Ivan and several priests. The television crew traveled with a group of pilgrims sponsored by *Caritas of Birmingham* and showed their reactions to what they heard and saw. Vicka was seen to be her usual smiling self, the demeanor which she displays regardless of whether she is in a period of suffering or not. Recently cooking-oil caught fire at the family stove and the flames burned her face somewhat.

Ivan

This young man had his twenty-first birthday on May 25, 1986. Facing the prospect of twelve months of active duty in some branch of the military, he had delayed reporting for military service until the latest possible date. Our Lady had told him she would not appear to him in the barracks, but only when he was on leave or visiting friends. He was assigned to a tank regiment stationed near Ljublijana in Slovenia, near Zagreb and the Austro-Italian border. He has friends in the area who have facilitated the visits of Our Lady. Besides appearing to him at times when he is off the military base, she also favors him with inner locutions while he is on the base.

His military service has come to an end and he is home once again, confident in the future and responsive to the guidance of Our Lady. Since the end of February 1988, Ivan has often been alone to receive her daily visit. He described a special apparition on Mt. Podbrdo on June 6, 1988, by saying that Our Lady appeared joyful and prayed for a rather long period over all present. She gave the following message:

"Dear children! The day is coming when it will be seven years since I have been appearing to you, and your Mother is inviting all of you to start tonight to repeat those messages. Those messages are first of all Peace, Prayer, Conversion, and Penance, and dear children, we should all do Penance.

All the messages that I have given you, dear children, are derived from those four little messages that I have just told you, and you should live the other messages also in order to understand what I want of you.

Thank you, dear children, for responding to my call. Your Mother is going to pray also with you in Heaven. Open your hearts to me."

After the people prayed the Our Father and the Glory Be, Our Lady prayed over them for a time and then left with the parting words: "Believe in Jesus, my children . . . the Peace of God, my children."

Ivanka

Just as happened to Mirjana on December 25, 1982, when she received the tenth secret and was told by Our Lady that she would not see her on a regular basis, so Ivanka has received the tenth secret and no longer sees Our Lady every day. Some of the events leading up to this development are examined here.

Since April 2, 1985, the daily apparitions have ceased taking place in the Church and Our Lady has been coming to the seers in a room in the rectory. She appears there at the usual time that she had been appearing in the Church. When the apparition begins in the rectory, the people in the church are notified and are asked to pray in silence for a few minutes.

On May 6, 1985, Jakov, Ivan, Ivanka, and Marija came to the rectory without Vicka who was ill all that day. Our Lady appeared to the four around six p.m. After two minutes Jakov, Ivan, and Marija came out of ecstasy, but noticing that Ivanka was still communicating with Our Lady, they remained kneeling for another six minutes until Ivanka's Vision had ended. Our Lady had just then entrusted the tenth secret to the young woman and had completed the information she had been giving her about the future of the world. She had also told Ivanka not to come to the rectory on the following day but to remain home and wait alone for her there.

On May 7 Ivanka saw Our Lady in her home for about an hour. She gave the following written report of this event to Father Slavko Barbaric:

As on every other day, Our Lady came with the greeting, "Praised be Jesus." I responded, "May Jesus and Mary always be praised."

I never saw Mary so beautiful as on this evening. She was so gentle and beautiful. On this day she wore the most beautiful gown I have ever seen in my life. Her gown and also her veil and crown had gold and silver sequins of light.

There were two angels with her. They had the same clothes. Our Lady and the angels were equally beautiful. I don't have words to describe this. One can only experience it.

Our Lady asked me if I had some wish. I told her I would like to see my earthly mother. She smiled, nodded her head, and my mother immediately appeared. She was smiling. Our Lady told me to stand up. I did and my mother embraced and kissed me and said, "My child, I am so proud of you." Then she kissed me and disappeared.

After that, Our Lady said to me: "My child, this is our last meeting. Do not be sad because I will come to you on every anniversary (June 25) with the exception of this year.

"Dear child, do not think you have done something wrong and that is the reason I will not be coming to you anymore. No, you did not. With all your heart, you have accepted the plans which my Son and I had and you have done nothing wrong.

"No one on earth has received the grace which you and your brothers and sisters have.

"Be happy because I am your mother who loves you with her whole heart.

"Ivanka, thank you for your response to the call of my Son and for persevering and always remaining with him as long as he asked you to.

"Dear child, tell all your friends that my Son and I are always with them when they call us and ask something of us.

"What I have communicated to you about the secrets during these years, reveal to no one until I tell you to."

After this, I asked Our Lady if I could kiss her. She nodded her head and I kissed her.

Then I asked her to bless me. She blessed me, smiled, and

said, "Go in God's peace." After this, she departed slowly with
the two angels.

Ivanka had been the only one who, in the early stages of the
apparitions at Medugorje, had declared that marriage was
her vocational goal in life. On December 28, 1986, she married a young man from the village, Rajko Elez. Father Petar
was the Church's witness, while all the other seers, including
Ivan who was home on leave, were present. This priest is the
one to whom Mirjana will confide the secrets about ten days
before the event associated with each secret will take place.
He will after praying and fasting announce each event to the
public three days before it takes place.

Ivanka helps her husband at his family's small restaurant in
Medugorje. On November 30, 1987, she gave birth to a healthy
baby girl who has been baptized Kristina. Because she sees Our
Lady only once a year on the anniversary of the apparitions and
for that reason has dropped out of the focus of attention, one
must not think that the influence of Mary on her life is fading.
A report that during Lent she fasted every day except Sunday
on bread and water points to an influence that is really deepening. It is fascinating to see the variety of situations in life and
goals of these six young people as they mature into adults and
the diversity of ways in which their lives are influenced.

Marija

Ever since she joined the group of six visionaries on June 25,
1981, the second day that the Virgin came to Mt. Podbrdo,
Marija has been a central figure and the most assiduous at
the daily meetings between Mary and the seers. Not only is
she recognized as the most spiritual of the group, but she is
also a humble and most willing and giving person. The demands on her time have been exhausting; she does not spare
herself from interviews with pilgrims who are numerous and
insatiable in their desire to converse with the seers. Among
the pilgrims in the fall of 1987 was the U.S. ambassador to
one of the central European countries, Alfred H. Kingon.
He had come to pray for his son. He suggested to Marija
that she write a letter to President Reagan which he would
deliver to the White House upon his return to the U.S.

Marija wrote the following:[2]

Dear President Reagan,

The Mother of God is appearing to us everyday in this little village of Medugorje in Yugoslavia. She gives a message of peace. We know you are working for world peace and we pray for you everyday. We would like you to know that you can count on our prayers and our sacrifices. This is the way we want to help you in your heavy task. Our Holy Mother said that with prayer and with fasting we can even stop wars. May this message help you to understand that those everyday apparitions of Our Lady are a sign that God loves His people united in prayer in the Heart of Jesus and the Heart of Mary. We send you our love and we are saying "Hello" through the Queen of Peace.

This letter written by Marija was translated by Kathleen, an American girl living with Marija. It was delivered to the President just before his meeting with General Secretary Mikhail Gorbachev in which both signed an agreement for the destruction of medium range missiles. On December 8, 1987, the ambassador called from the White House around 8 p.m. and said that President Reagan wanted to speak to Marija directly but could not at that moment because the meeting was going on. He had given the letter to the President who expressed his pleasure at reading it. Kathleen interpreted for Marija. Later in the evening the White House called three times and each time the call was disconnected before conversation could take place. On December 14, the ambassador wrote to Marija and asked her to write to Secretary Gorbachev to let him know what was taking place in Medugorje. He would transmit the letter to the U.S. ambassador in Moscow, Jack Matlock, for delivery to Mr. Gorbachev.

After Christmas Marija received a photograph of President Reagan with a short handwritten sentence:

"To Maria Pavlovic, with my heart-filled thanks and every good wish. God Bless You. Sincerely, Ronald Reagan."

On February 26, after receiving Mary's monthly message the evening before, Marija left Medugorje with a group of young women and men, part of the prayer group of which she had been a member since its beginning in May 1983. They have gone to a secluded farmhouse in Italy. They are making a retreat under the direction of Father Tomislav Vlasic, O.F.M., the original director of the prayer group, a retreat so extended that the group is not due to return until shortly before the closing of the Marian Year. There are some reports (speculations?) that this retreat is a preparation for a new form of religious life consecrated to God and in community, but the well-guarded isolation of the group does not permit one to verify whether the members of the prayer group will be involved in this new community or whether it is only a prelude to Father Vlasic's entry into contemplative life or the founding of his own order. For Marija, it is a respite from her crushing workload: as much a recuperative flight into the "desert" as an opportunity to develop the prayer "from the heart" that Our Lady constantly urges people to do. It is significant that the Franciscans have erected a building to serve as a prayer center on the grounds of St. James church. What will be Marija's role in its activities? Will Father Vlasic assume any responsibility for its functioning?

Jakov

For several years Jakov has been attending a technical school in Citluk, the equivalent of a U.S. trade school or vocational school. During the school year he cannot return from Citluk in time for the evening apparition, but on weekends he does join the other visionaries in the choir loft. He spends the summer vacation in Sarajevo and Our Lady appears to him there.

Appendix 4
Events In The Parish, The Church, And The World 1985-88

Sister Janja Boras has been appointed Vice Provincial of her order and has moved to Mostar. She does come back to Medugorje frequently to help the parish staff at times of special celebrations.

In December 1985, Father Janko Bubalo received the Vatican's coveted Sapienza Award for the best book of 1985. Written in Croatian, the book is based on an interview with Vicka, the oldest visionary.

Father Ivan Dugandzic, O.F.M., has been appointed spiritual director of the visionaries in replacement of Father Slavko Barbaric who was assigned to another parish. He is a Biblical scholar and an assistant at St. James. Since 1984 he has been a member of the expanded Bishop's Commission which met five times and interviewed the seers twice.

The Bishop's Commission met for the last time in Mostar on May 2, 1986, and submitted secret ballots to the Bishop. They indicated that they had completed their study and had no reason to meet again.

The findings of this commission have been sent to Cardinal Joseph Ratzinger, Cardinal Prefect of the Sacred Congregation for the Doctrine of the Faith. Since then, a new Yugoslavia-wide commission was created in October 1986 to investigate further. Each bishop in Yugoslavia has been asked to appoint one member to the new commission.

Besides these church investigations, scientific investigations have been conducted by two teams of medical men and/or specialists; an Italian medical team headed by Dr.

Luigi Frigerio from the Mangiagalli Clinic of Milan, and a team of French specialists under the direction of Professor Henri Joyeux of Montpellier University.

The Yugoslav national television presented a two-hour documentary about Medugorje on October 17, 1985. Not to be outdone, the television networks of other countries have sent their own crews or hired production units to film the site, the visionaries, and the parish staff and to try to catch some of the physical, atmospheric phenomena on their cameras. Germany was among the early ones. The BBC aired in February 1987 a program in the production of which it collaborated. In the United States, the work of several local station camera crews have been aired and when their productions caught the attention of the large networks, CBS's Dan Rather concluded an April newscast with a 1-minute spot about Medugorje.

A development that has captured the attention of the television reporters is the business acumen of the communist authorities who are now requiring families that take in pilgrims to charge prescribed prices for food and lodging. They regulate the charges and also the percentage that is to be remitted to the state.

The year 1987 has abounded in statements concerning Medugorje which have been carried in many newspapers, and which misinterpreted official directives or reports to the alarm of the readers. One report issued by the Yugoslav hierarchy on January 29 and commented on in *L'Osservatore Romano* on February 23 was regarded as a prohibition of private pilgrimages to Medugorje. The fact of the matter is that they are not prohibited as long as these pilgrimages are undertaken in a spirit of willingness to accept whatever decision the Church finally makes about Medugorje's happenings. Indeed on the very same day the West German episcopal conference issued an official endorsement of the faithful's right to go as private pilgrims to Medugorje; that is, provided they do not presume, still less proclaim, the Church's definitive acceptance of its supernatural character. In a telephone interview with a Croatian journalist in London on March 15, 1987, Cardinal Franjo Kuharic, Archbishop of Zagreb and President of the Bishop's Conference of Yugo-slavia, affirmed the right of people to make a pilgrimage to Medugorje according to the promptings of devotion and conscience. He stated that to stop all such private pilgrimages would be as foolish and reprehensible as hewing down a tree that produces good fruit in great abundance.

The second flurry of negative newspaper reporting occurred after the Bishop of Mostar's statements at Mass in St. James church on July 25. He was quoted as prohibiting pilgrim priests from saying Mass there. However the ban is only applicable to priests who overstep their status as private pilgrims by presumptuously speaking and acting as though the Church had already given its official acceptance.

Fears were laid to rest when Msgr. Dr. Frane Franic, Archbishop of Split, issued a directive for the faithful of his archdiocese on September 23, 1987. It is such a well-balanced analysis of the issues of private versus official pilgrimages and of the role of priests and bishops that it is reproduced in its entirety:

The session of the Croatian-speaking section of the Bishop's Conference of Yugoslavia (BCY) discussed the subject of Medugorje in Zagreb for three hours on September 16, 1987. From that discussion the following conclusions may be drawn:

1. In Medugorje distinction must be made between the alleged apparitions of Our Lady, the comprehension and dissemination of Our Lady's messages and the pilgrimages themselves, which have become a world-wide phenomenon because pilgrims are coming from all five continents in ever-increasing numbers.

2. Such numerous pilgrimages can be ignored no longer and the faithful left on their own; rather, it is necessary that priests assist the pilgrims spiritually and be at their service for confessions, preaching of the Word of God and Holy Mass in their own languages.

3. Regarding the scientific investigations of various domestic and foreign experts, especially the official New Commission named by the Bishop's Conference of Yugoslavia according to the directive of the Holy See, we must be patient and allow the investigations full freedom.

So long as the New Commission, responsible to the BCY,

has not brought forth its own official opinion about the supernatural character through the formula: *Constat de supernaturalitate* (the supernatural character is established) or *Constat de non-supernaturalitate* (the non-supernatural character is established) of the aforementioned apparitions and messages, NO INDIVIDUAL BISHOP of the BCY can pass his own official sentence about those events, because that judgment would have neither official nor binding validity.

Only when the New Commission passes its sentence and that judgment is affirmed by the BCY and by the Holy See, and only then, will that judgment, whether positive or negative, have official validity and obligate each Catholic in his (her) conscience.

4. I repeat my own interpretation that the BCY, at its proper time, forbade only "official" pilgrimages, and not private or privately organized pilgrimages.

5. In the meantime, I think it cannot be said that one "believes" by an act of faith in those events until the Church has expressed its own final judgment about the events at Medugorje, and therefore, all we who go to Medugorje must go there with the firm decision that we shall be obedient to the final judgment of the Church. Up to that point, we may have our own "opinion" of, but not "belief" in, those events.

Therefore, it is not proper to speak in favor of the validity of the messages of Medugorje from the altar, nor is it proper to attack these events, in the name of God and of the Church, as mendacious and diabolical.

6. Accordingly, I maintain that the faithful may freely make pilgrimage to Medugorje individually or in privately organized pilgrimages, meaning, thereby, in pilgrimages which are not officially organized by the Church, i.e. by bishops, pastors, monasteries or similar official Church institutions.

7. Priests may take pilgrimages to Medugorje if they go there not as organizers of pilgrimages, but rather for the sake of spiritual assistance to the faithful, again with the firm decision that they shall obey the final judgment of the Church.

If anyone should ask a priest if he believes in the supernatural character of the Medugorje events, he may freely say "I cannot believe" in those events until the Church has officially made a declaration about them.

8. It is not possible to "believe" either in the truths contained in Sacred Scripture or Divine Tradition, until the Church guarantees me that those truths are revealed by God.

That (guarantee) is also given for private revelations. The distinction is that the truths contained in public revelation obligate every Christian in conscience to accept them if he wishes to be saved, whereas, even after the final judgment of the Church, no one is obligated to accept private revelations, because they are not necessary for salvation. Only prudence can counsel us to at least accept them if the Church declares that they are in accordance with public revelation.

9. I ordain that all this is valid as a directive for my faithful, for my priests, religious men and religious women.

Archbishop:
Msgr. Dr. Frane Franic/Split
September 23, 1987

Notes

1

DO NOT FEAR, I AM SENDING YOU MY MOTHER

1. This information was gathered from a taped talk given by Father Tomislav Vlasic on August 15, 1983.

2

ON A ROCKY MOUNTAIN SIDE

1. The description of these two June 24 apparitions is based on three sources. First, there is the book *Gospina Ukazana U Medugorje* (Tisak: "A.G. Matos, Samobor, 1983) written by the Croatian scripture scholar, Dr. Ljudevit Rupcic, O.F.M. He asked many questions of all six seers. These questions with their answers are quoted word for word (pp. 35-54). He finished writing the book at the end of 1982, which means that he interrogated the seers quite soon after the events in question had taken place. The material found in the seers' answers have been worked into the present book because it came from the seers while it was still relatively fresh in their memories. The author is indebted to Mrs. Dorothy Glojek for the English translation of these questions and answers.

The other two sources are an interview between Vicka and Father Tomislav Vlasic, O.F.M., that took place on March 15, 1982, and an interview between Ivanka and Father Svetozar Kraljevic, O.F.M., held in February 1983. Both of these interviews are in Father Kraljevic's book *The Apparitions of Our Lady of Medjugorje* (Chicago: Franciscan Herald Press, 1984), pp. 7-9.

Father Svet, as he is called, told the author in October 1983, that he had found it very difficult to gather the facts concerning the first eight days of the apparitions, even though he was then living in Humac which is but a few miles from Medugorje.

2. These last two quotations and almost all the facts of this second day are taken from the interview Vicka had with Father Tomislav Vlasic on March 15, 1982. *The Apparitions,* pp. 11-14.

3. *Gospina Ukazana,* pp. 37-38.

4. This strange incident was also related by Vicka to Father Tomislav Vlasic in her March 15, 1982, interview.

5. See the French edition of Father Svetozar Kraljevic's book which was published under the title of *Les Apparitions de Medugorje* (France: Fayard, 1984), p.25. The French "adaptation" was published in the first part of 1984, considerably in advance of the English edition.

4
GOVERNMENT AUTHORITIES STEP IN

1. Most of the information concerning June 27, 1981, comes from two interviews, one that Father Svetozar had with Marinko and Dragica Ivankovic on February 27, 1983, and another which Father Tomislav had with Father Viktor Kosir on January 26, 1982. *The Apparitions,* pp. 151-157 and 111-115.

5
BELIEVING WITHOUT SEEING

1. Taken from the January 26, 1982, interview between Fathers Viktor Kosir and Tomislav Vlasic. *The Apparitions,* pp. 111-115.

2. The author received a copy of these questions and answers directly from Father Svetozar Kraljevic in October 1983. *The Apparitions, pp. 25-26.*

6
MORE GOVERNMENT QUESTIONING

1. *The Apparitions,* p. 33.

2. *Gospina,* p. 40.

3. This whole incident is taken from *Sister Lucy's Fourth Memoir.*

7

APPARITION AT CERNO

1. There is an interesting detail concerning the words Our Lady used in giving this reply. The above information about this seventh day is taken from the report of the conversation that took place between Father Jozo Zovko and the seers immediately after their return to Medugorje from the site of the apparition at Cerno. In reporting Our Lady's answer, Mirjana simply states, "She said that she will not mind," but Jakov added that the wording of her reply had been, "I will not, my angels." *The Apparitions,* p. 36.

8

EXTRAORDINARY ANSWER TO THE PASTOR'S PRAYERS

1. The facts for this day and the quotations are from an interview that Father Svetozar had with Father Jozo on August 11, 1983. *The Apparitions,* pp. 41-43.

2. Rene Laurentin - Louis Rupcic, *La Vierge Apparait-Elle a Medjugorje?* (Paris: Editions O.E.I.L., 1984), p. 83.

10

THE IMPORTANT ROLE OF THE PARISH STAFF

1. It is about 17 miles from Medugorje.

2. This is taken from a report on the apparitions written by Father Tom Forrest, C.SS.R.

11

DIVERSITY IN THE APPARITIONS

1. The eleven o'clock apparition at Mount Podbrdo, the apparition in the field, and the one in Marija's room were all related to Father Svetozar by Marinko during the interview that took place on February 27, 1983. The interview can be found in *The Apparitions,* pp. 151-157.

2. *Gospina,* p. 44.

3. *Gospina,* pp. 44-45.

4. *La Vierge Apparait-Elle,* p. 67.

5. *Gospina,* pp. 45-46.

6. *Gospina,* p. 38.

12

FROM THE FIELDS AND HOMES INTO THE CHURCH

1. It is apparently this fusion which the Bishop of Mostar sought to eliminate when on April 2, 1985, he requested the Franciscans to stop the children from using the room in the church.

2. *La Vierge Apparait-Elle,* p. 109.

13

SIGNS AND WONDERS

1. This is described at length in the author's book *The Sun Danced at Fatima.* The updated and enlarged edition was published in 1983 by Doubleday and Co., Inc., Garden City, N.Y. See pages 123-130. An earlier edition appeared in 1952.

2. Mount Podbrdo is a part of Mount Crnica.

3. All the above facts concerning the sign witnessed by Father Loncar can be found in *The Apparitions.* pp. 163-165.

4. *The Apparitions,* p. 60.

5. *La Vierge Apparait-Elle,* p. 165.

6. *The Apparitions,* p. 60.

7. *La Vierge Apparait-Elle,* p. 165.

8. The facts and quotations in the accounts of Fathers Janko Bubalo and Stanko Vasilj are taken from *La Vierge Apparait-Elle,* pp. 166-167.

9. From the August 15, 1983, interview. The information concerning the stars is from the same interview, with the exception of what is said about the American priest.

10. All of the information about the great sign and the warnings comes from Father Tomislav Vlasic. Some of it is from the August 15, 1983, interview and some from a report he sent to the Pope and to the Bishop of Mostar on December 2, 1983.

14

HEALINGS AND CONVERSIONS

1. All the facts come from this interview. *The Apparitions,* pp. 181-185.

2. *Gospina,* p. 108.

3. Father Tomislav adds this interesting bit: "Every evening the Mass we celebrate is for all of you *(he gave this information in a sermon to Italian pilgrims on August 15, 1983)* who have come to this church and for all the positive peace movements of the world. We

pray for this every night. Many groups throughout the world have begun to pray together with us at the same time we do, in the evening between six and seven. There are many groups in the United States. Even at Fatima prayers are said at the same time."

15
MIRJANA NO LONGER SEES OUR LADY EACH DAY

1. Her birthday is March 18. Our Lady appeared to her on that day in 1983 and 1984.

2. This statement seems to imply that Our Lady will be present at Medugorje on the day the great permanent sign appears.

3. Here are Mirjana's exact words as found in the English translation of her interview with Father Tomislav that the author received from Father Svetozar.

> "When I pray, then something comes to me in prayer. I really immerse myself into prayer and then it comes to me like I am speaking with somebody. Then, I express myself what should be. All this is in me talking with God. Then I continue praying again. Then again like that."

16
NEW APPARITIONS AND NEW SEERS

1. She was born on May 14, 1972.

2. Jelena said that she usually knew the answers to the questions asked and for that reason the teacher frequently did not call on her.

3. Born on October 5, 1972, she is six months younger than Jelena.

4. In both the sermon and the interview Father Tomislav was speaking specifically of Jelena, but Marijana is receiving the same kind of apparitions. The sermon was to a group of Italian pilgrims and the interview was with Dr. Julian Smyth and Dr. Diana Smyth of England.

5. This description was given in Father Tomislav's August 15 sermon. In the August 15 interview he said: "The apparitions *(to these two children)* are of another type. *(They)* do not see tridimensionally, but see it in *(their)* heart like a movie." In talking of the six seers, Father Tomislav frequently says that Our Lady appears tridimensionally to them, that is, they can see, hear and touch her.

6. *The Life of Teresa of Jesus* Translated and Edited by E. Allison Peers (New York: Doubleday & Company, Inc., Image Book Edition, 1960), pp. 99-100.

7. The comments in brackets were from an English- speaking friend of Jelena who knows her very well and was present at the interview.

17

OUR LADY'S TWO THOUSANDTH BIRTHDAY

1. Sister Janja, in a talk to pilgrims on August 4, 1984, said the message was received by Ivan on May 22 or 23. It has been said that Jelena was also told about August 5 by Our Lady.

2. In a talk to Italian pilgrims on June 3, 1984, Father Tomislav Vlasic said that Our Lady also imparted additional messages "about the day of her birthday," but that he could not tell them what it was because "the Bishop said we have to wait for the confirmation of the Pope, so as not to start privately a special feast of the Blessed Mother." According to the Church's liturgical calendar, Mary's birthday is celebrated on September 8.

3. A young lady from the United States gave the author the following written account of this same event:

> We were sitting outside the church around noontime on August 5. Sister *(the Karminskis' friend from Potoci)* who speaks both English and Croatian, had joined our group. As we were talking, a girl about seventeen or eighteen years old came over to Sister. Her face was beaming as she described how the Blessed Virgin had appeared on the mountain early that morning and all those camping around the church had seen her. She recounted how they had seen what she described as "strange lights" on Podbrdo and Krizevac late at night. They had spent almost the whole night praying and singing hymns. Then the apparition came at about seven a.m . . .

4. This information comes from a report written by the American lad.

5. These pictures form part of a video documentary which can be obtained from Stanley Karminski, 340 Prussian Lane, Wayne, PA 19087.

18

RENEWED APPARITIONS ON MOUNT PODBRDO AND MOUNT KRIZEVAC

1. This chapter, omitted by Father Pelletier from the first edition because it related activities forbidden by local authorities, appeared in the second edition in an appendix when danger of reprisals had disappeared. The editor is grateful to the Karminskis, Drew Mason, and Aggie Kuhn for the accounts quoted.

19

A MOST DISTINGUISHED VISITOR

1. *La Vierge Apparait-Elle*, p. 145.

2. Known as "the case of Herzegovina" which according to the Bishop emerges from the opposition of some of the Franciscan Fathers to orders of the Bishop and of the Holy See concerning the new distribution of the local clergy which is in effect meant to take the parishes from the hands of the Franciscans and give them to his diocesan priests.

20

RENEWAL IN THE HOLY SPIRIT AT MEDUGORJE

1. See the August 15, 1983, interview.

2. The expression "baptism in the Holy Spirit" comes from Scripture. After his resurrection, Jesus told the apostles: "...Within a few days you will be baptized with the Holy Spirit" (Acts 1:5). The baptism in or with the Holy Spirit is not a sacrament.

3. However, praying individually over people night after night without any let-up took its toll on the praying teams, for there were times when this praying went on until midnight and when they prayed over 300 people. Praying in this way over people is a draining and exhausting experience. The parish staff would have to wait until the church had been locked before it could take its evening meal! In October 1983, I was told that the daily praying over people individually had been stopped for "over a year." During the five nights I was there, the seers prayed publicly over people only once, on a Saturday night, after the Mass and special prayers to the Sacred Heart and to Our Lady. The individual praying did not go on for very long.

4. All this information, and not only the quotations, is from the August 15, 1983, interview.

5. The words within the brackets are additions or interpretations that seem in keeping with Father Vlasic's thought.

6. Having been personally involved since 1970 in a leadership role in the charismatic renewal in the United States, I was intrigued by the reports I read about the apparitions at Medugorje and what was said about the Holy Spirit in these reports. It seemed that through Mary God was telling us something about the Holy Spirit and the charismatic renewal. I sought every bit of information I could obtain about this, particularly through people who were going to Medugorje. I asked them to obtain information based upon specific questions. It soon became apparent that the charismatic prayer group at Saint James parish was not functioning like prayer groups in the United States.

When I went to Medugorje in October 1983, through an interpreter I had quite a long interview with the pastor of the parish,
Father Tomislav Pervan. He made it clear that God was doing
something unique at Medugorje and that we had to be careful about
reading into the charismatic experience going on there what was
happening in other places. He felt so strongly about this that he said
one could not fully understand what was going on in Medugorje
without living in the locality. From some of the facts that came forth
in the interview, I can understand why he said that. The parish life in
Medugorje is so different from what it is in the United States. It is a
very intense life, centering on the church, on the prayers, and on the
liturgical life that takes place there. The priests are naturally very
much involved in all of this.

7. *La Vierge Apparait-Elle,* pp. 25-26.

8. The quotation is from a tape recording by John Finkbiner
Studio, P.O. Box 96, Pleasantville, NY 10570.

21

THE MESSAGES AND THE SECRETS

1. *The Sun Danced,* Doubleday 1983 ed., Chapters 21,
23, and 24.

2. Message for the closing of the Marian Year, February 18,
1959.

3. *Gospina.* p. 46.

4. *Gospina,* p. 46.

5. *Gospina,* p. 48.

6. *Gospina,* p. 48.

7. All six seers know when this sign will be given, "but cannot
reveal it." *Gospina,* p. 49.

8. Eleven months earlier, in her January 10, 1983, interview with
Father Tomislav Vlasic, Mirjana said that the tenth secret is
"altogther bad and cannot be mitigated at all."

9. *La Vierge Apparait-Elle,* p. 160.

22

LEADING THE SEERS TO HOLINESS

1. *Gospina,* p. 53.

2. *Gospina,* p. 50.

23

MESSAGES FOR THE PARISH

1. The text of the earlier messages in this chapter are taken from a mimeographed document entitled Messages of Life prepared by Father Svetozar Kraljevic. The author has made some slight editorial changes. The sources for later messages were various newsletters published in the U.S. by Stanley Karminski and by the Center for Peace, and a British quarterly, *Medjugorje Messenger*, published by The Medjugorje Centre, London, England.

The editor also used French-language compilations: Marie-Reine de la Paix-Espoir du Monde, by Guy Girard, s.ss.a and Armand Girard, s.ss.a., Editions Paulines, Montreal, Que., 1986.

The editor's purpose was to clarify the content of the messages which were given in Croatian to the young visionaries and come to us non-Croatians only in translation. There being as yet no definitive text, comparison of the texts in various sources reveals a fairly wide range of expression.

The editor consequently felt that all one can do is to scrutinize a number of versions for harmony in thought and content and then to make a choice based on clarity of expression.

24

CATASTROPHE AND THE CRISIS OF FAITH

1. Somewhat differently than Father Svetozar Kraljevic, to whom the author owes the version above, Father Rene Laurentin reports the words of the apparition as: "Peace, peace...nothing but peace. Men must reconcile themselves with God and between themselves. For that they must believe, pray, fast and confess themselves." Father Laurentin says that Our Lady "repeated this message several times on the following days." *La Vierge Apparait-Elle*, pp. 97-98.)

2. *La Vierge Apparait-Elle*, pp. 160-161.

3. *La Vierge Apparait-Elle*, p. 160.

4. Taken from a pamphlet of his entitled *What Time is It? Servant Books (Ann Arbor, Michigan: 1984), pp. 23-24.*

25

OUR LADY QUEEN OF PEACE

1. This statement is taken from Father Tomislave Vlasic's August 15, 1983, interview.

2. While the author was in Medugorje in mid-October, 1983, Our Lady said: "People must take my messages seriously."

3. August 15, 1983, interview.

26

MONTHLY CONFESSION AND THE TRIDUUM OF RECONCILIATION

1. The wording of this important and frequently quoted statement comes from Father Tomislav Vlasic's August 15, 1983, interview.

27

PRAYER AND THE SACRAMENTS

1. Our Lady did not join the seers in the recitation of the Hail Mary at Medugorje.

2. The Bishop alluded to is the Most Reverend Pavao Zanic, Ordinary of Mostar. His diocese includes Medugorje. He established a Commission of Investigation that originally comprised four members and was later increased to fourteen. The enlarged Commission held its first meeting on March 23, 1984.

3. This was taken from Father Svetozar Kraljevic's August 6, 1984, talk to Americans. He speaks of the same apparition elesewhere in his talk and according to what he says there this apparition took place "on the hill of the first apparition."

4. This comes from a report on the apparitions by Father Tom Forrest, C.SS.R., which was written after he had visited Medugorje in the fall of 1982.

5. *Gospina,* pp. 54-55.

29

MISCELLANEOUS MESSAGES

1. *Gospina,* p. 47.

2. *Gospina,* p. 47.

3. *La Vierge Apparait-Elle,* p. 99.

4. For what remains to be done before that conversion can take place, see *The Sun Danced,* Doubleday 1983 ed., pp. 166-193.

Epilogue

MARY OUR MOTHER

1. The first statement was made in a reply to a question by Father Rupcic. The second one comes from Mirjana's interview with Father Tomislav Vlasic on January 10, 1983.

2. He also wrote a smaller tract on the same subject entitled The Secret of Mary. Both works can be obtained through the Montfort Fathers, Bay Shore, NY 11706.

3. Pope John Paul II consecrated the world to the Immaculate Heart of Mary at Fatima on May 13, 1982. At the Mass which he celebrated there on that day, he delivered a remarkable homily of considerable theological significance, an important part of which has to do with consecration to the Immaculate Heart of Mary. He read the act of consecration of the world to the Immaculate Heart at the conclusion of the Mass. The entire act of consecration and most of the homily can be found in *The Sun Danced,* Doubleday 1983 ed., pp. 184-187 and 199-208.

4. For the details of this rather involved issue see *The Sun Danced,* Doubleday 1983 ed., pp. 165-193.

Appendix 3

1. *Medugorje Messenger,* London, #11 July-September 1988, p. 8.
2. *Caritas of Birmingham,* March 1988, p. 3.

Appendix 4

1. *Medugorje Newsletter* 87-88, Center for Peace, p. 4.

Stanley Karminski
340 Prussian Lane
Wayne, PA 19087

Video Tapes Available
in VHS and BETA

Send Check For $9.95
Plus $1.75 Postage
To The Above Address

(specify type of tape desired)

Center for Peace
P.O. Box 1269
Concord, MA 01742

Obtainable Through the Center
- General Information on Medugorje
- Video Tapes
- Books
- Low Cost Pilgrimages

Medugorje Information Center
913-642-3400
8917 Cedar Lane
Prairie Village, KS 66207-2217

Tom Henshaw, Sponsor

- VCR Tapes
- Audio Cassettes
- Books on Medugorje (30 different)